T0333150

NAPOLEON'S BRITONS
and the
ST HELENA DECISION

NAPOLEON'S BRITONS
and the
ST HELENA DECISION

Paul F. Brunyee

For my father
Norman Harry Brunyee
1926–2008

First published 2009

The History Press
The Mill, Brimscombe Port
Stroud, Gloucestershire, GL5 2QG
www.thehistorypress.co.uk

© Paul F Brunyee, 2009

The right of Paul Brunyee to be identified as the Author of this work
has been asserted in accordance with the Copyrights, Designs and
Patents Act 1988.

All rights reserved. No part of this book may be reprinted or reproduced
or utilised in any form or by any electronic, mechanical or other
means, now known or hereafter invented, including photocopying and
recording, or in any information storage or retrieval system, without the
permission in writing from the Publishers.

British Library Cataloguing in Publication Data.
A catalogue record for this book is available from the British Library.

ISBN 978 0 7504 5147 3

Printed in Great Britain by Athenaeum Press Limited.

Contents

Maps and Plans

Preface

This is not a history of the feud between Napoleon and the maligned governor of St Helena, Sir Hudson Lowe. That issue has been amply covered already. Rather it is the story of Napoleon as seen through the eyes of the other Britons around him. The Royal Navy to whom, despite his protestations to the contrary, he surrendered; the people of Brixham and the surrounding district who came to gaze in awe at the man – 'their Boney' – who raised his hat in acknowledgement of the cheering that greeted him when he appeared on the deck of the *Bellerophon*. Then there were the British radicals led by Lord Holland, who, despite their misgivings about Napoleon the dictator, recalled what he had done to curb the French Revolution and promote some liberal principles across Europe, and wished to see him given greater comforts.

Opposed to them was the government of Lord Liverpool grappling with the economic aftermath of the greatest war the world had known – the World War as some called it. Then there were the soldiers, sailors and civilians who served and lived on the island of St Helena itself. It is much today as it was then – using Barnes's map of 1811 you can find your way anywhere. A little walking or a trip in a boat brings you to the lines and battery positions refurbished or built at the time. You can walk where the Emperor walked, indeed where all of the characters walked, British, French or 'Saint' (the modern nickname for local people).

To reach the island today you must travel there by one of the last remaining Royal Mail steamers; the RMS *St Helena*. It is a splendid way to travel – along the route of the East India Company merchantmen and by the warships of the Cape Squadron. On arrival the ship anchors off Jamestown – just as Napoleon and every other character in this story did, to gaze out at the town and the battery positions that still dominate the view.

Acknowledgements

Many people have kindly assisted me in my research over the last few years both in Britain and abroad. I would particularly like to thank Bryn Hughes, the General Manager of the HMS *Trincomalee* Trust at Hartlepool. *Trincomalee* is, apart from *Unicorn* and *Victory*, the last of our complete Napoleonic warships. She was built in 1817 in India and has the distinction of having anchored off St Helena during the imprisonment. She is a living link to that time. I am also grateful to the members of the 68th D.L.I. Re-enactment Society for permission to use an image of them as they drilled in front of *Trincomalee*.

I must thank the courteous staff at the archive of the University of Hull, in the library of the National Maritime Museum at Greenwich, at the National Archive at Kew, the Wellcome Library in Paddington and also the staff at the South African Archive in Cape Town. The staff at the National Army Museum in Chelsea, London were most helpful in producing what little is known about the St Helena regiments themselves. The staff of the Museum of the Royal Regiment of Fusiliers (Lancashire Fusiliers) in Bury were very helpful, as were the staff at the Shropshire Regimental Museum and the Museum of the The Rifles (Berkshire and Wiltshire) in Salisbury. I must also thank the staff at Dalmeny House in Scotland, the home of the Earl and Countess of Rosebery for granting me access to their superb collection of Napoleonica. The Lowe Papers in the British Library in Paddington have provided many fascinating days of reading and although many people have examined parts of them there is much left to be analysed and commented upon.

On St Helena itself the staff at the archive in the Castle in Jamestown were most accommodating. The Honorary French Consul on the island Michel Dancoisne-Martineau gave generously of his knowledge both whilst I was on the island and since. I must also thank my location manager – my wife, who having worked on the island prior to us going there in 2004 was consequently able to map out our joint week there with great efficiency.

I should particularly like to thank Naomi and the staff at the Malton branch of the North Yorkshire Library Service for their unflagging aid in obtaining for me the unusual and at times rare reference material with great enthusiasm. The inter-library loan service is a national treasure.

My late good friends Pat and Gerry Law were very supportive of this project and their interest and friendship was a great boost. There were many other people who helped, particularly Mick Crumplin that great authority on matters medical, who gave freely of his expertise and time and Jamie Wilson who supported the original idea for this book. Finally I must mention my wife, Lynne, again, who was and is as great a support at home as she was on the island itself.

Any errors within the text are of course attributable to me alone.

Paul F. Brunyee

Paul Brunyee is a historian, teacher and educational consultant to English Heritage. He lectures on the Napoleonic Wars to historical groups across England.

A former Territorial Army infantry officer, he is Membership Secretary for the Association of Friends of the Waterloo Committee and a member of the education sub-committee of the Waterloo 200 group. When visiting St Helena during his researches for this book he gained access to unseen documents in the island archive. Paul lives in Malton, Yorkshire, England.

Chapter One

Chaining the Ogre – What Shall we do with Boney?

The misfortune to us at this moment is, that Buonaparte remains in existence. Saddled as the world must be with this fallen despot, it is of the utmost moment to place him where he never can disturb its repose again. If he could escape into France, or get possession of Italy, which would rather live under his sole dominion than be parcelled out as it is likely to be; if he could carry French soldiers and followers into either country; if his large pension is paid him, and if the other dangers to which I have alluded above are to be apprehended – it might be well to consider, before the act is irretrievable, whether a far less dangerous retreat might not be found.

Sir Charles Stewart, as Napoleon began his reign on Elba.[1]

Others would also have told him about the murmurings within the French Army where some officers wished to depose the Bourbons but not invite Napoleon back. Then there were the visitors who brought gossip by word of mouth to Napoleon and newspapers which contained gossip about the political turmoil in France.

Lord Holland writing to his Whig friend the politician and wit, Thomas Creevey in October 1814 remarked perceptively that the current peace 'satisfies no one class of people'. Within her borders the French people felt humiliated and beyond there were many who thought that she had not been sufficiently emasculated and was still dangerous. Creevey was then living in Brussels. Whilst dining at Lady Charlotte Greville's, he spoke with the Duke of Wellington, with many of the other guests listening in. Was Wellington 'playing to his audience' when he said that a

… republick was about to be got up in Paris by Carnot, Lucien Buonaparte, &C.,&C.,&C. I asked if it was with the consent of the Manager Buonaparte, and what the nature of the piece was to be. He said he had no doubt it would be tragedy by Buonaparte, and that they would be at him by stiletto or otherwise in a very few weeks. I, on the contrary, thought the odds were in favour of the old performer against the new ones, but my Lord would have it B. was to be done up out of hand at Paris: so *nous verrons*.[2]

Creevey confided in his diary that he thought on several occasions during the evening that the Duke 'must be drunk' to speak as he did 'but drunk or sober, he has not the least appearance of being a clever man' in conversation. Creevey did concede however that their 'conversation was mightily amicable and good,' considering that they had clashed vigorously in the Commons over the behaviour of Wellington's brother Lord Mornington, in India.

Then events began to accelerate. Writing in the early hours of Friday morning as the Duchess of Richmond's ball broke up he recorded that a battle had just taken place between Buonaparte and the Prussians. All that was known was that the French had won. In Brussels, as he wrote, the Allied troops were moving off. The Duke, he noted, had been at the ball 'as composed as ever'.

After Waterloo, Lord Ossulston, a Whig friend of Creevey, wrote from England at the end of July that the feeling in England was that Napoleon 'ought to be placed out of the reach of again interfering in the concerns of the world'. Ossulston's wistful afterthought was that it was 'difficult not to feel for a man' who had made such an impact upon the world, if he were destined to end his days in 'such a place as St. Helena'.[3]

Three years later, in the autumn of 1818 Creevey met the Duke in Brussels. In answer to the comment that Sir Hudson Lowe was 'a very unnecessarily harsh gaoler of Buonaparte' Wellington had replied:

> By God! … I don't know. Buonaparte is so damned intractable a fellow there is no knowing how to deal with him. To be sure, as to the means employed to keep him there, never was anything so damned absurd.

Wellington then described the three or four places from which he thought a prisoner could escape. He then commented that with a little work they were capable of being made quite inaccessible when defended by 'a mere handful of men'. With regard to Sir Hudson Lowe, whom Creevey had met in 1815, Wellington said:

> As for Lowe, he is a damned fool. When I came to Brussels from Vienna in 1815, I found him Quarter-Master-General of the army here, and I presently found the damned fellow would instruct me in the equipment of the army, always producing the Prussians to me as models; so I was obliged to tell him that I had commanded a much larger army in the field than any Prussian general, and that I was not to learn from their service how to equip an army. I thought this would have stopped him, but shortly afterwards the damned fellow was at me again about the equipment, &.c, of the Prussians; so I was obliged to write home and complain of him, and the Government were kind enough to take him away from me.[4]

On 21 June 1815 an ordinary post carriage rattled into the courtyard of the Elysée Palace. Sentries snapped to attention as the Emperor stumbled out and hurried into the palace. The great gamble had failed.

Only an Austerlitz or Marengo victory could have bought him the popular support he needed at home. And even that would not have pacified the Allies who wished to see him stripped of all political and military power. Before Waterloo he had declared that, 'Emperor, soldier, consul, I hold everything from the people,' whilst privately despising those who, when enraged, became the mob. After Waterloo, that popular support largely evaporated. Elements of both the old and new aristocracies, the professional classes and those who had lost most in thirty years of war, their sons and husbands, now waited, aghast, for the Allies to march on Paris – again.

With the army broken and in disarray, the lower classes stunned, Napoleon had no significant group of supporters left in Paris. His cause was lost and he, as a man, was also lost. Hurriedly gathering his Council of Ministers he told them that he could amass an army by early July and meet the Allies behind the Somme. Paris would be defended. The Fédères and the National Guards would be mobilised. A series of earthworks would be flung around eastern Paris.

Fouché spoke for many members of the government when he declared: 'This devil of a man! I thought he was going to start all over again. Fortunately, we are not going to start all over again!'⁵

In the French Parliament, the hero of the Revolution, Lafayette, at the prompting of Fouché, spoke of the need for the government to act. He proposed that they, the Chamber of Representatives, should now declare themselves to be a provisional government. Further, that they declare themselves to be in permanent session and that any attempt to disband them would be taken as an act of high treason. It also crucially, gave itself powers to deal directly with the advancing Allies. This particular power had previously belonged exclusively to the Emperor. Wisely, it also appointed its own security force from the National Guard. There was to be no repeat of Napoleon's seizing of power as on the 18 Brumaire.

Lafayette also spoke passionately of the principles of the Revolution and urged Frenchmen to rally to the nation. But it was not to be. Twenty-six years had elapsed since 1789. Almost a million and a half Frenchmen had died, 'from the sands of Egypt to the snows of Russia,' as Lafayette described it. This was the answer which most of France had for the Emperor. There had been too much war, too many deaths.

On 22 June Fouché, Jacobin, regicide, and with as much revolutionary blood on his hands as anyone, was appointed president of the governing cabinet of ten. Fouché was one of the great networkers of the age. Those important persons over whom he had no direct influence he was usually able to direct through someone else. As General Grenier wearily said of Fouché, casting his deciding vote over who should be the head of the new government, 'He is necessary.'⁶ A few Bonapartists in the Chamber of Peers protested but they were too late. The commission installed itself in the Tuileries palace.

Throughout the campaign Fouché had played his double game with incredible skill. He had assessed the political situation when he learnt of the Emperor's landing and waited briefly before deciding to appease both sides. Prior to their departure from Paris he had assured the Bourbons that he would save the monarchy, 'if they would save the king'.

He worked for the survival of France as a leading European power and that survival was also his survival. Both men had a lust for power but unlike Napoleon, Fouché placed pragmatism above his ego. Unlike Napoleon, he was a good listener. That quality alone made him an excellent choice as Napoleon's Police Minister. He well exemplified President Roosevelt's maxim, that one should 'Speak softly and carry a big stick'. He knew that most of the country was proud of the achievements of the Empire and yet wearied by the demands of the Emperor.

Throughout the spring of 1815, as Napoleon had worked to prepare for war with the Allies, Fouché was in contact with Louis XVIII at Ghent as well as Metternich and Talleyrand in Vienna.

Now with the Empire falling apart Fouché controlled the government. Louis XVIII was about to re-enter Paris in the 'baggage train' of the Allies. They had already occupied France in the last year. They had left political negotiations in Vienna to carry out a war focussed specifically against Napoleon, not the French state. Napoleon had been declared to be 'an outlaw' having broken the terms of the treaty which had made him King of Elba. Napoleon could only conquer with an army at his back. That army had to be emasculated. Senior and middle ranking officers who were loyal to Napoleon were to be removed and the army was to be turned back to its earlier oath of loyalty to the Bourbons.

Prussia would demand the same kind of massive war indemnities that Napoleon had demanded of it several years ago – unless the government could obtain better terms. Everyone in the French administration knew that Blücher or 'the old Devil' as he was referred to in France, was going to stamp all over Paris if he was not placated.

If the Emperor could be removed from Paris itself, that might deflate the anger of sections of the army and of the people. The one was still smouldering over Waterloo and the other feared the return of the Royalists – particularly those ultra-Royalists who would demand retribution against those who had supported the 'outlaw' in his diabolic adventure.

Although Blücher and many Prussians wanted Bonaparte hanged, Fouché knew that this might lead to civil war. Fouché's aim was for as smooth a transfer of power as possible – with himself at the helm. Far better that the Emperor was removed, quickly and quietly from Paris. Even better, that neither British nor Prussian hands were laid upon him in France. If he was to be humiliated, brought to trial and subsequently punished, then let it be done elsewhere – out of sight of the French Army and the people. John Croker saw Fouché at a dinner a fortnight later and described him thus:

> The wonder was to find ourselves at table with Fouché, who, to be sure, looks very like what one would naturally suppose him to be – a sly old rogue; but I think he seems to feel a passion of which I did not think him capable; I mean

same, for he looks conscious and embarrassed. He is a man about 5ft. 7in. high, very thin, with a grey head, cropped and powdered, and a very acute expression of countenance.[7]

Meanwhile, the city was in a brittle mood. Every day, elements of the *Armée du Nord* were gathering around Paris. Many of the poor still thronged the Avenue de Marigny outside of the Elysée to try and glimpse the Emperor.

The provisional government expected the Prussians and the English would soon be in Paris. Paris had already experienced the surrender and abdication of 1814. Desperate times required desperate measures. He had to go, or the Allies would demand his head. The Emperor was subject to the declaration of the Congress of Vienna, which made him an international outlaw. He had been the sovereign of Elba who had then invaded France, and removed both the legitimate ruler and his government.

Paris was largely undefended. The great earthworks which Napoleon had ordered be constructed around Paris were not complete. The gunners, artillery pieces and infantry to man them did not exist. And all the time the Prussians raced ahead of Wellington's army eager to get to Paris. Blücher wrote to his wife from Compiègne, nine days after Waterloo on 27th June. 'It is possible and highly probable that Bonaparte will be handed over to me and Lord Wellington. I could not do better than to have him shot. It would be rendering a service to humanity,'[8]

The same driving energy that Blucher had displayed throughout the Waterloo Campaign remained and Napoleon was well aware of this.

On 22nd June the commission had informed Napoleon that if he did not abdicate for the second time, he would be deposed. His immediate reaction, after Davout, the Minister for War, had delivered the ultimatum at the Elysée was short and predictable: 'I'll never abdicate to that bunch of Jacobin hotheads, that liberal canaille!'[9]

He threatened the use of his Guard, the fédères and the National Guards, though, it is likely that the largely middle class National Guards would have remained loyal to the government. After all, some of them were already providing security for the very government that Napoleon threatened to tear down.

Turning on Davout, he pointed to the window, beyond which the crowds could be heard cheering for the Emperor:

If I wanted to put myself at the head of those good people, who have the instincts of the *patrie's* true needs, then I would soon be done with those who have no courage against me except when I am without defence.[10]

But it was not to be. He feared the power of the mob. This was the outburst of a man who had risked everything – his throne, his health, and his life. He was suffering from the effects of his massive workload and intermittently from piles and cystitis. Waterloo had taken place only four days before.

There are strong indications that he knew how slim his chances of success were whilst he had toiled to prepare the army and the nation for war in the spring. He had worked furiously in the build up to the Waterloo Campaign, but not, 'tirelessly'. Those days had gone. Physically, he was significantly overweight, and middle aged. He no longer possessed that elastic ability of youth to bounce back as he had done before. Without it that mysterious, magical factor that had made men tremble before him, had lost some of its power. As a young man he had declared that a man such as he 'had only so many years for war'. Those years had now gone. More importantly he had misjudged the mood of the nation. They had wanted the Empire back but without the egotism of the Emperor.

The further he had delved into the French bureaucracy the more he realised how things had changed since his abdication in 1814. As he had prepared for the Waterloo Campaign he discovered a war-weary attitude amongst many of his government officials. Targets that he set for the provision of arms, the manufacture of uniforms, the training of recruits, were not met.

Not surprisingly, after Waterloo people close to him commented on his depressed state. He was clearly being outmanoeuvred by Fouché and he knew it. In one of his furious flashes of insight he declared that his greatest mistake on his return had been in not having Fouché either exiled or shot.

He realised early on in his return that having taken the nation to war, when only the army and elements of the poor desired it, he would lose everything if he did not win a devastating victory against Wellington and Blücher. He had not only lost — he and his army had been crushed.

He might in his rages hint at turning to the mob for support, as he had with the Minister of War but this threatened civil war and on that he looked with horror.

This second abdication followed by his physical removal from his seat of power in Paris would be offered to the Allies as a peace offering, in exchange for the Allies sparing the city. That same day, just forestalling his overthrow, he abdicated once more, in favour of his son. The chamber accepted his demand for the accession of Napoleon II and then, once Napoleon had left Paris, ignored it.

Amidst all the shocks and worries that still haunted him, Napoleon probably feared public humiliation through either assassination or capture above all else. On the battlefield he had faced death on countless occasions and suffered sleepless nights and physical privation amongst his soldiers but never humiliation. He could not face the shame associated with capture, trial and subsequent execution or imprisonment within France.

On 24th June a little known deputy stood in the Chamber of Deputies and proposed that Napoleon be invited to quit Paris, for the good of the nation. Prior to this statement supporters of Fouché had spread the real concern that the Emperor's person was in danger if he remained in Paris. The spectre of Blücher was raised. They pointed out that a coup could still erupt if the Emperor remained in Paris. A motion was voted upon and so Marshal Davout, Minister of War, found himself delivering the message to his Emperor. The Emperor agreed. He would leave and move to Malmaison with Queen Hortense, his stepdaughter.

That same day Fouché had the Royalist Baron de Vitrolles quietly released from prison. Interviewing him face to face, Fouché assured him that his goal was the restoration of the King. Another message was despatched to Talleyrand in Ghent inquiring whether the Royalist party favoured the appointment of the Duc d'Orléans. The reply was favourable – to Fouché anyway. There was no appetite for d'Orléans but there was probably a place for Fouché, or the Duc d'Otrante, in King Louis's government.

Fouché also arranged for Lafayette and a delegation to leave Paris in order to find and negotiate with the Allies – but its real purpose was to ensure that Lafayette did not become a popular rival for power.

Napoleon's stepdaughter, Hortense, discussed where he should seek asylum. He declared that he would not ask for asylum from the Emperor Alexander of Russia, as he was 'not to be trusted' and as for his father-in-law, the Emperor Francis, he complained that he could not accept assistance from a man who had kept his wife and child from him.

It was then that the idea of retiring to that new nation, the United States of America, was raised. He was observed at Malmaison 'absently' turning over the pages of the early volumes of Alexander von Humboldt's great book on the Americas. There he could buy an estate, and as one supporter put it, should the Bourbons falter, 'still make his enemies tremble'. Napoleon also said that he would consider the English but Hortense declared this to be impossible. They would lock him up in the Tower of London, she declared. The United States was settled on. A message was despatched to the provisional government requesting passports and the use of two frigates to take him and his entourage to the United States. The lack of passports and the command and control of the frigates would be hurdles that Napoleon would not be allowed to overcome. At this moment, his moods swinging between a desire for action and despair, he did not know this.

He requested that Mme Walewska might come and bid farewell. She did and brought with her Alexandre, his five-year-old son. Also in the palace was Charles Leon, his thirteen-year-old son by Eléonore Denuelle and seven-year-old Louis Napoleon, Hortense's son – the future Napoleon III.

Marshal Bertrand, on behalf of the Emperor, visited Decrés, the Minister of Marine. Bertrand enquired about the state of the two frigates at Rochefort. Decrés immediately wrote to the naval prefect at Rochefort, M. de Bonnefoux, urging him to ensure that all was ready to enable a French minister to embark for the Unites States along with a suite of twenty persons. He was to be treated with all the courtesy appropriate to his position but above all the arrangements were to be undertaken 'with the utmost secrecy'.

On 25 June, just after noon, the Emperor's carriages drove out along the rue du Faubourg-Saint-Honoré, taking General Gourgard and General Montholon and Count Las Cases as well as a number of aides out to Malmaison. The first carriage had a military escort. People on the streets believed that they had seen the Emperor.

Meanwhile, accompanied by General Bertrand, Napoleon moved discreetly through a garden gate from the Elysée onto the Champs Elysée. Outside he quietly climbed into a plain carriage without a coat of arms on the doors. His valet, Noverraz sat on the box. Quietly the carriage moved away from Paris. Outside of the city gates they met the other convoy of vehicles and Napoleon transferred to his imperial carriage. He was leaving Paris for the last time.

The same day, his brother Lucien was at Boulogne, hoping to cross to England and obtain passports for himself and for his relations. He was not allowed to cross to England and he returned to Paris.

Marchand wandered through the emperor's apartments, 'so full of eager courtiers a few days before, and today so empty'. Assisted by his wardrobe boy he collected together some 'small portable furnishings' including small portraits and busts along with the silver washstand made by the silversmith Biennais. These items he felt would be of use to the Emperor 'where [ever] he would go'.

At Malmaison Napoleon was received by his loyal stepdaughter Hortense. He would be protected by an officer and 25 men of the Imperial Guard. Whilst others around him worried about the approach of the enemy, Napoleon appeared unconcerned.

Marchand arrived at Malmaison later that evening with his coach 'full to breaking' with the Emperor's personal effects. Later, as the Emperor was retiring for the night he informed him that he had called upon both Mme. Pellapra and Mme. Walewska. They would both visit tomorrow to say their farewells. So they did and Napoleon would see his Polish son for the last time.

That evening, General Becker arrived to take charge of the Emperor's security. With him came several hundred soldiers. Nominally assigned to be Napoleon's personal escort, they were there to ensure that the Emperor did as he was told. Becker offered his letter of authority to the Emperor, signed by Davout. Napoleon saw the letter for what it was, yet with typical foresight he also put Becker's mind at rest. Becker, Napoleon said, was held in high esteem and furthermore he was satisfied that he had an honourable man in charge of his security.

As the days wore on more and more visitors came to see the Emperor. Aides came with more intelligence about the movements of the English and Prussian armies. On 27th June Bertrand wrote from Paris that the government were offering two frigates, *Saale* and *Méduse* to the Emperor. These were based at Rochefort on the Atlantic coast. Relay posts were being arranged along the route so that a swift journey could be made to the coast. There was, however, one significant problem; the frigate captains had orders not to sail until the passports had arrived.

Fouché had set in motion the exit strategy for both the Emperor and the Provisional Government. Napoleon was being urged to leave for the coast on a daily basis. However, he had not received the passports he required. What he did receive via General Becker was a passport which entitled Becker, his personal servant and his secretary to travel to Rochefort. The idea being that the Emperor would travel incognito as Becker's secretary. Once there however, he would be a virtual prisoner, awaiting the arrival of the passports to America. Not surprisingly,

Napoleon refused to move from Malmaison even though the Allies were fast approaching Paris.

On 27th June Fouché had also verbally authorised Bertrand to arrange to collect porcelain and table linen for the Emperor's party from the Tuileries, books from the Rambouillet library, maps and monies for travel expenses. Flight was not far away.[12]

Next day, Becker received orders that should the enemy attempt to seize the Emperor at Malmaison he was to destroy the local bridges at Chatou and Bezons over the Seine. Later that night Marchand quietly brought Decrés and Meurthe into his bedroom. They informed the Emperor that the army feared for his safety now that the enemy were about to attack Paris.

They had other news. The Provisional Government had removed the regulation that he must await passports being delivered to Rochefort before he could sail. They had brought with them passports for all those who would leave with him. Events were pushing him to act – to move away from Paris and the Prussians and on to the coast where he only faced the ocean and the Royal Navy.

There were other Britons close at hand, Wellington's army, but their leader wanted nothing to do with the arrest and possible execution of Bonaparte. Fouché had already approached Wellington and found the answer to be a stern, 'no'. If Bonaparte was to be arrested and prosecuted then it ought to be done by the agents of the legitimate government of France, and not the British Army.

Wellington had already made it clear that it was neither his nor Blücher's business to arrest, hang or shoot Bonaparte. When his much trusted Prussian liaison officer, General Baron Muffling raised the matter with him, Wellington's answer was succinct:

> The Duke stared at me in astonishment, and in the first place disputed the correctness of this interpretation of the Viennese declaration of outlawry, which was never meant to incite to the assassination of Napoleon. He therefore did not think that they could acquire from this act any right to order Napoleon to be shot, should they succeed in making him a prisoner of war. But be this as it may, as far as his own position and that of the Field Marshal [Blücher] with respect to Napoleon were concerned, it appeared to him that, since the battle they had won, they were become much too conspicuous personages to justify such a transaction in the eyes of Europe.[13]

All the while the Prussian Army had come closer and closer to Paris – urged on by Blücher – and was now within grasping distance of Bonaparte. It had now but to get over the Seine and he was theirs!

As he waited at Malmaison Napoleon was overwhelmed by great mood swings. He fantasised about what might be done with him leading the army simply in the role of a general officer. With the parting of the Anglo-Dutch and Prussian armies the Emperor saw a gap and an opportunity to attack. The government had only to appoint him as a 'general' to lead the army and he would gain them a better bargaining position, before handing over his command and leaving for the United States.

It was not to be. The government returned his offer without a direct answer reminding him that he could best serve France by leaving as quickly as possible, preferably in the guise of General Becker's secretary. His response was to subside into inactivity.

Napoleon may have appeared resigned most of the time but he did make certain preparations. Marchand was summoned. The Emperor handed him a tiny vial which contained a red liquid which was to be attached to some part of his clothing at all times. Their eyes met and for a moment there was silence. They were then both distracted from the shocking moment by an announcement that a visitor had arrived. That evening Napoleon asked Marchand what he had done. The tiny bottle was now protected by a leather pouch with an eyelet from which was attached a cord. The pouch could be affixed to his left suspender and easily found by his right hand. Napoleon silently took the leather sheath, lifted out the vial, replaced it and said, 'That's fine.'

Marchand was deeply affected at this point and the Emperor pressed his hand to his cheek and told him to make sure that everything was ready, as they would probably leave the next day.[13]

Marchand arranged with M. Colin, comptroller of the Emperor's household, that two carriages would be loaded immediately with the Emperor's silver, table linen and crockery and stand ready to leave at a moment's notice. With some delight Marchand says that Colin had taken silver, far in excess of that proposed by Fouché, from both the Elysée and the Tuileries. They stood in the dark stables, loaded with the Emperor's household goods, only requiring the horses to be harnessed.

Meanwhile in London his ultimate fate was being decided. Castlereagh was informed:

> If you should succeed in getting possession of his person, and the King of France does not feel sufficiently strong to bring him to justice as a rebel, we are ready to take upon ourselves the custody of his person, on the part of the Allied Powers.[14]

Liverpool also stressed that this should be done without any Allied commissioners being appointed. As to the place of detention he mused on Britain, Malta, St Helena, the Cape of Good Hope or 'any colony we might think most secure'. The government's favoured places were St Helena or the Cape, being 'at a distance from Europe'. Castlereagh in reply informed Liverpool that the Russians supported the idea of sending 'a strong note' to the Americans, 'calling upon them to arrest and surrender Buonaparte' should he yet manage to escape there.[15]

Castlereagh had also come to the same conclusion as Napoleon when he said that he was convinced:

> … that there is not a class in France, not excepting even the army, that will venture to adhere to him at the hazard of again being overrun by the armies of Europe, with the certainty of being dismembered, and loaded with contributions.

Notes

1 Alison, Sir Archibald, *Lives of Lord Castlereagh and Sir Charles Stewart*, William Blackwood & Sons, Edinburgh & London, 1861. Page 460 Vol 2, quoted in Stewart to Bathurst, *Castlereagh Correspondence*, ix. 450, 451

2 Maxwell, (Ed) Sir H., *The Creevey Papers:*Volume I, John Murray, 1903, page 215

3 Ibid., page 244.

4 Ibid., pages 288–289.

5 Dallas, G., 1815 *The Roads to Waterloo*, Pimlico, 2001, page '383.

6 Ibid., page 422.

7 Marchand, L-J., *In Napoleon's Shadow*, Proctor Jones, 1998, page 258.

8 Briefen, p. 154, quoted in Aubry, Octave, *St Helena*, (trans.), Livingston, Arthur, London: Gollancz, 1937, page 43.

9 Englund, Steven, *Napoleon: a political life*, Harvard University Press, 2004, page 444.

10 Ibid., page 444.

11 Marchand, L-J., op cit, page 267.

12 Ibid., page 264.

13 Ibid., page 267.

14 Webster, C. K., Liverpool to Castlereagh, June 15th· *British Diplomacy 1813–1815*, G. ell & Sons, 1921, pages 334–5.

15 Ibid., page 348.

Chapter Two

The Flight from Malmaison

As the escape of Buonaparte to America may yet be effectuated, it is worth every collateral aid that can be derived towards the accomplishment of this object. The first that occurs, and it is one to which the Russian Minister inclines, is to address a strong note on the part of the Allied Powers to the American government, calling upon them to arrest and surrender Buonaparte to them. Such an appeal could do no harm; at the same time I should expect little good to come from it. I do not see how the President could of his own authority take such a step. [1]
Castlereagh writing from Paris to Lord Liverpool in July, 1815.

On 29 June a little after five in the afternoon, Napoleon began the last phase of his journey out of France. The passports for America had still not arrived but he could delay no longer. Napoleon, kissing his mother's hand, took his leave of her. As he spoke with loyal Hortense she gave him diamonds which she had stitched into a belt. To another loyal woman, his mistress, Mme Walewska, he could give nothing as he sadly declined her request to accompany him into exile.

Parting from them all, he left Malmaison, not by the main courtyard entrance, which was crowded with soldiers ready to salute him, but by a rear exit. Silently he picked up his hat and walked into the vestibule. Hortense and a few others quietly followed him. He had issued instructions that those who were not accompanying him could not go beyond the hallway. He paused here, amongst the statues and paintings that had been brought back from the wars in Italy and then passed out into the garden, walking on to the iron gate on the south side of the park with Becker, Savary, and Bertrand.

Beyond the gate stood a large yellow coach drawn by four horses. It stood silent, waiting on the Celle Saint-Cloud road. Having reached the coach, he turned, looked through the garden at Malmaison itself then

… with a sudden motion flung himself inside. His three companions climbed in after him. Aly, the Mameluke, mounted the driver's box. The horses started off through the woods forthwith at a rapid trot, taking the direction of Rambouillet. [2]

A lone rider scouted ahead checking the road for 'suspicious characters' and to order the preparation of the next set of post horses. Unfortunately for Napoleon, this same outrider would not be seen again, as he, like so many other servants quietly slipped out of Imperial service. Later that same day, the main convoy of carriages with Napoleon's staff and servants left Malmaison by a slightly different route.

In Paris, meanwhile, the government declared the city to be in a state of siege. The regular troops were to be sent out of the city to defend the main approach roads. The National Guard troops were to police Paris and the unstable Fédères were to act in support of the regular troops outside of the city limits. Fouché's aim was to remove Napoleon's supporters from the city by supporting their request to 'defend the motherland' and to calm the middle classes within it, who feared mob rule.

That night the Imperial convoy rested at Rambouillet. The next day Napoleon set off again with the main convoy of carriages several hours behind. The following day he travelled through Tours on the road to Poitiers. That second night he sent a messenger on to the naval commander at Rochefort announcing his imminent arrival. On 2 July, Wellington's army took up positions facing St Denis whilst Blücher swept south and clashed with elements of the French Army. A French request for a ceasefire was refused by Blücher.

At three in the morning on 2 July, the Emperor's party reached Niort. Here Napoleon received intelligence that although the two French frigates were available Rochefort was now blockaded by a line-of-battle ship of the Royal Navy. Meanwhile, the officers of the 2nd Hussars had visited Napoleon imploring him to march on Paris, at the head of the army. Napoleon wisely refused. Later that same day he held a planning conference about how he might avoid the blockade by going out from Rochefort on board a small boat to join either a French or American sea going vessel that could take him to America.

The next day he came to the end of his final journey on French soil when he stepped out of his carriage in Rochefort. On 4 July Napoleon's baggage was placed on board the two frigates but at this point any notion of an enthusiastic and concerted effort by the two captains to support the Emperor evaporated when Captain Philibert refused to support Captain Ponée's plan. The latter had offered to engage the overwhelmingly powerful Bellerophon as a means of enabling the Emperor to escape out to sea in the smaller *Saale*. It was a gallant, if foolhardy offer.

On 7th July newspapers arrived from Paris announcing the entrance of the Allies into the capital. Next day Gourgard was sent to consult both the frigate captains to determine how the Emperor might leave France. Their conclusion was that there was little hope of them getting out to sea. They were trapped in their own anchorage. The Emperor however was decided. He would embark at Fouras, for the *Saale*. And so it was that at ten past five that afternoon, the Emperor, Becker, Bertrand, Gourgard, Lallemand and Savary were rowed from mainland France and towards the *Saale*, where he was greeted formally but without a salute being fired.

On 9 July, Napoleon went ashore on the Ile d'Aix and inspected the batteries and the fortifications. The inhabitants of the island followed him, crying out '*Vive l'Empereur!*' Then he came back on board. At nine o'clock the Maritime Prefect arrived with further depressing news from Paris. The Provisional Government insisted that the Emperor leave France within 24 hours, either in a despatch boat, or with the two frigates, or under a flag of truce.

Opinions as to what the Emperor should do next were divided. Some wanted him to go on board the *Bayadère* which lay off Bordeaux, or in an adaptation of Ponée's plan to embark at once on an American ship at anchor in the river, whilst both the frigates engaged the *Bellerophon*. Others advised that he leave aboard one of the local small boats. Some thought he had better make a stand on the Isle d'Aix, or return to the mainland and join Clausel at Bordeaux.

That evening it was decided to send Las Cases and Savary to the British, to ask if the passports had arrived, and if so, whether they would be allowed to depart freely. Las Cases was to listen carefully to what was said on board whilst giving the impression that he did not fully understand spoken English in order that he might gain some intelligence of what the British intended. The next day, Las Cases went on board the *Bellerophon* and after he had returned to the *Saale* the *Bellerophon* was seen to move further up the passage, confirming what Las Cases had heard – that the British believed that Napoleon was now on board the *Saale*.

The noose continued to tighten. On 11 July newspapers arrived confirming that Louis XVIII had entered Paris. Napoleon now sent General Lallemand to speak about the possibility of leaving for America in the Danish vessel, *Bayadère*, commanded by a Frenchman, which lay at anchor in the Gironde.

On 12 July preparations were made to land Napoleon's baggage on the Ile d'Aix. There was to be no return to the mainland. A few hours later he was rowed out to the island. On the island, according to Gourgard he was met with enthusiasm as he made his way ashore. This was not so surprising given the large amounts of money which Napoleon had invested in defensive works over the previous years. In a remarkable coincidence, the *Bellerophon* was heard firing a salute shortly afterwards – probably in honour of Louis XVIII or to celebrate the entry of the Allies into Paris. Meanwhile, in Paris Croker strolled about the city, seeing the Prussians and 'the old Life Guards patrolling the Boulevard, as they used to do Charing Cross during the Corn Riots'.[3]

The following evening at Rochefort the sound of gunfire was heard and it became clear that there were now smaller British warships blocking the other channels that a smaller craft might navigate. Savary returned. His news was also bleak. The officers who were to crew the boat now thought it highly unlikely that they could slip past the British. Hours later Lallemand returned from Bordeaux. There was talk of Napoleon going to sea in the Danish vessel whose captain had been an officer in the Marines of the Imperial Guard. The ship had a cargo of brandy to load and one of those barrels could contain the Emperor. It was not to be. The Emperor could not contemplate leaving his France like a skulking thief. If he was to leave then it was to be with his imperial dignity intact.

He had spoken earlier to Gourgard, musing on the benefits of going to America rather than England. Napoleon, at that moment perceived that America, the young nation state, would be regarded by history to have been a better place for him to retire to and live as a private gentleman. Whereas, were he to live in England, he saw a great humiliation in having given himself up to the English.

The next morning Gourgard saw Las Cases and Lallemand rowed out to the *Bellerophon*, with a tricolour flying on their boat. After they had returned Napoleon invited them and Gourgard into his room and asked them for their opinions of what had occurred on the British warship. All of them urged him to go on board the British ship.

Having dismissed the others Napoleon showed Gourgard the rough copy of the now famous 'Themistocles' letter. Gourgard read it and had tears in his eyes when he had finished. It was to be his task to carry it to the Prince Regent. He was, on reaching England to

> … hire a country house, not to enter London in the daytime, and not to accept any
> of his going to the colonies. Then he dictated to me a letter that Bertrand was to
> write to the English commodore, when he should send me with Las Cases on board
> his ship, as quartermaster to prepare his quarters.[4]

Taking the rough copy of the letter as his own, he left carrying another for the Prince Regent. Meeting General Becker outside he asked him on his return to Paris to inform his mother how and where he was. He did not however tell Becker of his mission to England. Collecting an usher, a page and a footman, he met Las Cases and together the small party went out to the *Bellerophon*.

They were well received. Maitland invited them both to breakfast. He had already arranged for the two sloop commanders, Gambier and Sartorius, to be present as witnesses. Las Cases still pretended that he knew no English.

In conversation with the three British officers Gourgard was convinced that what was said was that he would receive a favourable welcome in England; that he would be able to go on to London in order to deliver his message. The conversation was awkward. The British spoke only a little French and the two French officers continued to hide Las Cases's fluency in English. The British officers, Gourgard claims, were very impressed by the letter. Las Cases urged Gourgard to write to the Emperor, certain that he would be 'well received in England'. Maitland had no authority to promise anything. On the other hand he was the only diplomat to hand. His aim was to ensure the smooth transference of Napoleon from shore to ship.

All the references to Maitland suggest that he was indeed a gentleman. He may have exceeded his orders but as the senior commander man present it was for him to act as he saw fit. In essence Maitland assured the French negotiators that Napoleon's rank and position in society would be respected in Britain.

Captain Maitland RN, whose diplomacy and courtesy so pleased Napoleon.

Later Admiral Hotham would comment favourably on Maitland's actions in dealing with Napoleon – that he felt sure the government would approve of what Maitland, had done to secure Napoleon.

Napoleon and Las Cases must have realised that they were dealing with a naval captain and not a senior admiral. He was clearly not the squadron commander and said so. If they did not then it was their foolish mistake and one thing Napoleon was not, was foolish.

Maitland may well have agreed to the suggestion that Gourgard could be allowed to travel to London, which was a mistake, as he had not been granted any powers to negotiate with Napoleon or his party. Napoleon either surrendered to Maitland or risked a humiliating capture. There was no alternative. Napoleon was indeed, between the devil and the deep blue sea.

Maitland did what he could to draw Napoleon into surrendering. Some writers have described his actions as duplicitous, which he was not. Maitland never promised Napoleon anything. He only reassured him that his person would be respected. Napoleon, on leaving the *Bellerophon*, was to thank Maitland twice for his courtesy and conduct and to offer him a gift as a token of this esteem which Maitland tactfully refused – though he did accept the minor gift of an engraved tumbler from a travelling case that had once belonged to Josephine. Throughout the whole episode Maitland believed that he had acted in the best interests of the Service and of Britain.

It is likely that he assured Las Cases (who *was* duplicitous, in pretending he did not understand English) that Napoleon would be received in England with all the honours due to his rank and station. As the old saying has it, possession being nine-tenths of the law, once Napoleon jumped into Britain's arms he became whatever she decided he should be.

That evening, Captain Sartorius escorted Gourgard, accompanied by only his servant François, to the *Slaney*, a corvette of four guns and eight carronades. On 15 July 1815 the *Slaney* fell in with the flagship *Superb*:

> Our captain went aboard her but soon returned. At nine o'clock we had tea, at four dinner; at six they signalled an English frigate which had overhauled a Danish vessel. The wind being north west, we tacked. An English sailor was flogged.[5]

On the 15th they saw the schooner *Telegraph*. He dined in the wardroom with the officers, who were 'excessively polite to me'. His other entry that day being that 'they do not play cards, nor even chess, on Sundays'. Steadily they sailed for England.

By 19 July they were to the south of the Ile de Sein and were passing through some rough water. The next day they were off Ushant though the wind was against them. Later in the day they saw the *Chatham* and a corvette. Signals were exchanged and finally the wind veered and they moved on.

At six in the morning on 22 July they finally sighted England and in the evening they reached Plymouth. At nine o'clock that night Captain Sartorius was rowed across to speak with the Commander in chief, Admiral Lord Keith. On his return Gourgard asked to be taken to speak with Keith but was refused. He then asked permission to go up to London with the Emperor's letter in order that he might present it to the Prince Regent. This was refused. Gourgard declared that he had been 'duped', whilst Sartorius had his trunk and portmanteau taken on

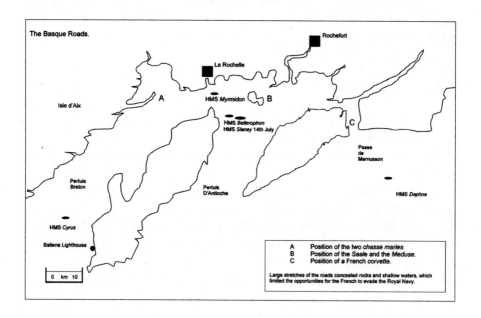

The Basque Roads.

A	Position of the two *chasse maries*
B	Position of the *Saale* and the *Meduse*.
C	Position of a French *corvette*.

Large stretches of the roads concealed rocks and shallow waters, which limited the opportunities for the French to evade the Royal Navy.

shore before posting up to London himself. The Emperor's plans were unravelling. Gourgard realised that he was no longer an emissary but a prisoner. The boat that had taken Sartorius on shore returned at midnight with orders for the First Lieutenant: he was to weigh anchor and to sail into Torbay.

Gourgard objected once more. He repeated his request for permission to go ashore and this was refused again. He asked for a refusal in writing, which was not given. The ship then hoisted a quarantine signal, a sign of isolation which served only to confirm his position as a captive. Guards were posted to prevent any communication with the *Slaney*. One exception was made when a boat brought a newspaper.

Two days later on 24 July the *Bellerophon* came in sight and anchored close by. Gourgard was granted permission to go on board her in order to inform the Emperor of the situation. Over the next 24 hours their status as prisoners became even more obvious. Both vessels remained at anchor. Guard boats patrolled the waters around the warships and kept the increasingly eager water-borne crowds at bay. Newspapers arrived from Exeter but these were not shared with the French. Madame Bertrand, on discovering this refusal to share the newspapers became angry and fell out with Captain Gambier.

In the early hours of 25 July Sartorius returned from London and by three o'clock they were putting out to sea heading for Plymouth. Later that day Gourgard saw Maitland who had been on shore to speak with Admiral Lord Keith, Commander of the Channel Squadron, which also included all of the vessels along the west coast of France. He came back looking 'much embarrassed' with no positive news for the French. Las Cases (who was now wearing the Legion of Honour, much to Gourgard's irritation) maintained that the Emperor would be received and that Napoleon II would be proclaimed in France. Lallemand completely disagreed with Las Cases and the sense of unease deepened. During the night another warship arrived, the *Eurotas* under Captain Lillicrap, which also put out row boats to guard. They were surrounded.

Notes

1 Webster, C. K., Letter from Castlereagh to Liverpool, 17 July 1815, *British Diplomacy 1813–1815*, G. Bell & Sons, 1921, page 348.

2 Aubry, Octave, C. K., *St Helena*, trans., Livingston, Arthur, London: Gollancz, 1937, page 48.

3 Letter to his wife dated Paris, 12 July 1815 in Jennings L. J., Ed., *The Croker Papers*, London: John Murray, 1884.

4 Latimer (trans.) Gourgard, *Talks with Napoleon*, London: Grant Richards, 1904, page 19.

5 Ibid.

Chapter Three

Between the Devil and the Deep Blue Sea

It may appear surprising, that a possibility could exist of a British officer being prejudiced in favour of one who had caused so many calamities to his country; but to such an extent did he possess the power of pleasing, that there are few people who could have sat at the same table with him for nearly a month, as I did, without feeling a sensation of pity, allied perhaps to regret, that a man possessed of so many fascinating qualities, and who had held so high a station in life, should be reduced to the situation in which I saw him.[1]

Captain Maitland

The man tasked with securing the French coastline in 1815 was Lord Keith. Between 1812 and 1814 he had held the prestigious post of commander of the Channel Fleet. The tentacles of this command reached out to the Low Countries and down the Atlantic coast of France. Although he had never commanded the Royal Navy during a great fleet action, he had achieved a great deal. It should always be borne in mind that with men such as Keith, it was not for want of trying. After all, there were only six such actions across the entire sweep of the French Wars.

At sea from the age of thirteen he had served in the American War of Independence, captured the Cape of Good Hope from the Dutch, served in the Mediterranean during the French invasion of Egypt, commanded the North Sea fleet which had opposed Napoleon's invasion fleet and latterly coordinated the huge maritime effort to support Wellington's army in Spain and Portugal. This had involved the supply of stores and material, and participation in combined operations. It had also involved the suppression of the French Navy in the Bay of Biscay. This latter experience was to aid him significantly in his later search for Napoleon.

In 1814, after Napoleon's abdication, Keith coordinated the repatriation of Wellington's Portuguese troops and the relocation of British troops to either North America or Britain.[2] Less than a year later, although now aged 69, and in poor health, such was his standing with the government and the Prince Regent as an administrator of large fleets, that he was re-appointed to the command.

Remarkably, although the government had been quite rightly keen to retrench on its naval spending after Napoleon's abdication they were still very concerned about the American threat. The French wars had stretched from the early 1790s until 1814. On their ending a rapid reduction of the Army and Navy seemed both logical and financially necessary. However, Britain was still at war with the United States. Only two years previously the Royal Navy had suffered a series of spectacular defeats at the hands of the tiny yet pugnacious American Navy. The American government had prosecuted a war against Canada, which had only ended with the Peace of Ghent, signed in December 1814.[3] Consequently Keith probably had more ships at his disposal in 1815 than he might have expected.

In those earlier years his principal objectives had been to blockade the French ports to prevent men and materiel reaching Napoleon and to cooperate with Wellington in the Peninsula as his campaign took him ever further north, across Spain. Reappointed on 28 April, he found matters were not as straightforward as they had been the year before. The Congress of Vienna had declared war against Napoleon and his followers, not against the French nation. The British government did not wish to inflame the minds of war-weary Bonapartists, who had grudgingly accepted the Bourbons. Such Frenchmen might feel obliged to rally once more to Napoleon's colours if they saw the entire nation threatened by a war at sea. Initially, the decision not to interfere with merchant shipping going about its lawful business was made known only to naval officers and otherwise kept secret.[4]

This policy was reinforced with a later secret letter, directly from the Admiralty Office dated 28 April, reminding Admiral Hotham that in operations along the coast to support French Royalists he was to 'desist from all acts of hostility' unless directly asked for assistance by the officers of King Louis. Britain was to maintain a policy of being at war only with Napoleon and his adherents, not with the French people at large. When news arrived of the shattering defeat of Napoleon at Waterloo Keith saw that his mission must change, and anticipating the orders he would receive from government, immediately blockaded the coast to prevent Napoleon escaping across the Atlantic.

The man who commanded the squadron blockading the Gironde and the coast covering Rochefort was Rear Admiral Sir Henry Hotham. He too had enjoyed a successful and varied naval career. He had served in the Mediterranean, on the North American station and most importantly on three separate occasions in the Bay of Biscay. He was an active commander who had already won praise from Lord Keith especially for his seamanship in the Bay of Biscay. Hotham was both a good seaman and an aggressive leader.

The other man in the triumvirate was Maitland, captain of the *Bellerophon*. Maitland came from an aristocratic Scots family. He had entered the Navy at an early age and his intelligence, leadership and personal courage marked him out as an excellent naval officer. He had served in the Mediterranean, on the North America station and along the western coast of France. In 1809 he served under Lord Gambier during the attack on the Basque Roads, near Rochefort, a most useful experience for what he was to undertake in July. In early 1815 he had been appointed to the *Boyne* which was ordered to take a convoy to North America. However, bad weather had prevented his convoy from sailing and instead he was appointed to the *Bellerophon* (74 guns) popularly known as the 'Billy Ruffian', under the command of Admiral Sir Henry Hotham. Both officers had an extensive knowledge of the coastal waters of western France. In the Bay of Biscay, they would be the right men in the right place at the right time.

On 2 June 1815, Captain Senhouse, captain of Admiral Hotham's flagship *Superb*, received orders to organise the landing of artillery, arms and ammunition for a group of Royalists in the Vendée, providing it could be done without it falling into the hands of Bonaparte's troops. Again this activity was to be carried out as an operation strictly in support of legitimate Royalists. It was made very clear that no Britons were to go ashore and fight alongside them. Further, though Royalists who were in danger from attack by Napoleon's troops could be taken off by the boats, the English were to avoid contact with or aggressive action against, any of Bonaparte's troops save in their own defence.[5] At the same time efforts were to be made to reconnoitre both the Isle Dieu and Belle Isle with a view to subverting the Imperial troops garrisoned there or supporting the local Royalist groups.

On 24 May *Bellerophon* had sailed from Cawsand Bay under Captain Maitland. His secret orders, issued by his squadron commander, Admiral Hotham, were to 'send into port, all [French] armed vessels' and to reconnoitre the shipping in the Rochefort road stead. It was feared that a corvette might leave France carrying proposals from Bonaparte for the West Indies 'to declare in his favour'.[5]

There was also some speculation that an American vessel was currently loading with Napoleon's personal property somewhere along the west coast – as a precaution against his great adventure failing. In reality, the only noteworthy occurrence was on 9 June when the French corvette *Vésuve* came into the roads from the north, making good use of the wind which had pushed Maitland's ships off station. With a flourish as she passed the Chasseron lighthouse, she immediately raised the tricolour.

On 18 June, the day of the battle of Waterloo, Maitland detained a French store-ship, the *Aeneas*, loaded with ship-timber for the arsenal at Rochefort. However, Admiral Hotham released her and her crew, deciding she did not come within the description of 'national ships' given in the secret orders. Three days later, the 220 men of the French 9th Regiment of Light Infantry en route from Martinique were not so fortunate.[6]

On 27 June the *Cephalus* brought news that war had been officially declared against France. From then on, a succession of smaller coasting craft were intercepted and either sent off or burnt.[7] It was one of these vessels which passed on the startling news that Napoleon had been defeated at Waterloo. Two days later, on 30 June, a boat came off from Bordeaux. With it came a letter, written on very thin paper, tightly rolled up and hidden in a quill, stating:

With great degree of certainty, being informed that Buonaparte might have come last night through this city from Paris with the Mayor of Bordeaux, with a view to flight, by the mouth of this river, or La Teste.[8]

At the same time an order arrived from Keith to celebrate the victory with an official salute, to be fired by all the Royal Navy ships along the coast.[9] The writer then went on to outline the 'Grand Army being totally defeated and destroyed', the abdication of Napoleon and the march on Paris by the Allies. He urged the Admiral to keep a sharp eye on all American vessels and particularly named Captain Caleb Cushing of Philadelphia as the man who was to carry General Bertrand across the ocean.[10]

On 6 July the tempo was raised when the *Ferret* brought Hotham news that Bonaparte had indeed abdicated. At least one source suggested that he intended to come to England but Lord Keith dismissed this, believing that he would try and get to America instead. He ordered Hotham to

send out everything you can to such places as you may think best for this purpose, I do not think he will try Brest, the Road is not open to him but he may try Nantes, or Rochefort, both places are in his interest and the country near them.

Keith also thought that the Gironde, south of Rochefort might be an option for him. Keith had already been informed by Croker at the Admiralty that the Provisional French Government had applied for a passport for Napoleon so that he might travel to the United States in safety. This application, approved of by Fouché, had of course been rejected and its purpose had been to alert the British to the likely whereabouts of Napoleon.[11]

Croker informed Keith that once Napoleon was on board with his family, he was to be taken to England as quickly as possible. On arriving off the coast of England, he was to be kept in isolation from the shore and the whole matter of his presence regarded as 'a profound secret' until further orders were received from the Admiralty.

Maitland was convinced that Napoleon would attempt a flight from Rochefort rather than from Bordeaux, so he decided to send only the *Myrmidon* there and the *Cephalus* to blockade Arcasson. This left him with the battle ship *Bellerophon* to stand guard over the port of Rochefort and the three roads out of it. His decision was a sound one. The two French warships anchored off the Isle d'Aix were frigates, no match for a well handled line of battle ship, even an old one like the *Bellerophon*. They each possessed only half of the guns that she carried and these were of a smaller calibre. In any 'pounding match' her heavier guns would destroy the thinner walled frigates.

In any sea battle of the period the convention was that a battleship would only fire on a frigate if the latter opened fire first. If she did then the results were invariably one sided and catastrophic. At the battle of the Nile in 1798 the French frigate *Sérieuse* had bravely engaged the British battleship *Orion*. In moments one broadside from the *Orion* had dismasted the frigate and destroyed her ability to fight or manoeuvre. She had then drifted into the shoals of Aboukir Bay, badly holed.

On 6 July Admiral Hotham was able to confidently write to Keith:

I consider every part of the coast under my control from hence to the Basin of Arcasson inclusive well guarded, and a tolerably good outside line of ships too; but two more frigates could be well bestowed, if your Lordship could send them to me, one to join the *Bellerophon* and another for the Loire, where I have only two brigs, one close off and the other outside.[12]

Off Rochefort, Captain Philibert commanded the *Saale* and the squadron. He had distinguished himself by retaking the *Algésiras* at Trafalgar, been awarded the Legion of Honour and had commanded a battle ship under the king. He was, however, no great enthusiast for Napoleon. Captain Ponée, on the other hand, was. He commanded the *Méduse*, a frigate recently arrived from Martinique. He also had a distinguished service record.[13]

Both men were under the orders of the provisional government. They would have to return to France once they had delivered Napoleon to his chosen destination. It was an unenviable position. The messages that came through the naval telegraph spoke of the need for haste to remove the Emperor from France, hinting that soon Louis would be restored.

Some time on 4 July – the day after he arrived in Rochefort – Napoleon chaired a meeting of the Admiralty Council, which had been summoned by the port commander, Bonnefoux. Bonnefoux was himself a royalist and seems to have floundered during the meeting, seeing the need to support the provisional government, and proposing little that was positive for Napoleon. He concluded that the channels out of the roads had already been well sealed by the Royal Navy.

In a more constructive manner, the retired Admiral Martin proposed that if the frigates could not break out into the ocean then the Emperor should consider a very different plan. He should move south to the little town of Royan on the Gironde. From there he could board one of the two warships lying there. Bonnefoux decided to ask the commander of the corvettes for his opinion of the proposal. The next day Captain Baudin, who commanded the corvettes, declared that if the Emperor boarded one of the very fast sailing American privateers, the *Ludlow* or *Pike*, lying close to the corvettes, then he, Baudin could hold up any British attempt to interfere with the Emperor's escape until the privateer was well out to sea and on the way to the United States. The Emperor approved of the plan and yet would not commit himself. He wanted his horses and carriages to arrive so that he might leave the country in the style of at least an ex-Emperor.[14]

This prevarication probably lost Napoleon the best opportunity he had of escaping into the open sea. He had three channels to choose an escape route from, two frigates at his disposal and only one, admittedly powerful, battleship against him.

On 1 July Maitland had spoken with the master of a ship from Rochefort, who assured him that the frigates had taken in powder, 'and were in all respects ready to put to sea'. He was also informed that some 'gentlemen in plain clothes, and some ladies supposed to form part of Buonaparte's suite, had arrived at the Isle d'Aix'. Maitland had moved the *Bellerophon* as close to the island and the frigates as the onshore batteries would allow and began training his crew for the possible interception of the frigates. He selected 100 of 'the stoutest men' who, after the *Bellerophon's* gunnery had silenced one of the frigates, would board and secure her. He would then leave the scene of the engagement and pursue the other vessel, containing Buonaparte.[15]

The same day he received new orders from Admiral Hotham, who spoke of the need to plan for any and all of the rumoured destinations of Buonaparte. Hotham urged Maitland to keep any frigate that came into his area of responsibility under his command, as the *Bellerophon* alone could not cover the three exits from the island. Maitland was able to reply in a very positive manner. The *Endymion* (50 guns) had joined him and along with the *Myrmidon* his squadron 'should prove quite strong enough for the squadron in the Basque Roads'.[16] He was right. Napoleon had missed that window of opportunity to set sail and escape.

Since his last letter to Hotham, one of the corvettes had been able to take advantage of a land breeze to work out of the Mamusson Passage whilst *Myrmidon* was in the offing and move into the Gironde and on to the nominally Bonapartist port of Royan. A storeship or corvette had come up from Rochefort and lay all night on 1 July off the Isle D'Aix. She was on 6 July in the Mamusson passage with two brigs, waiting to make for the Gironde or the sea. The balance of fire-power was clearly still with Maitland.

The *Méduse* meanwhile had hoisted a broad pendant. The frigates had, for the first time since Maitland had been on station, crossed their main top yards. Even so, he said 'I cannot however believe they will have the temerity to attempt to force their way past this ship, and as I generally anchor in Basque roads when the wind serves to bring them out, they cannot well give us the slip.'[17]

He was also able to inform Hotham that two days previously he had boarded a merchantman out of Rochefort who told him that three carriages had arrived prior to the arrival of the British vessels, whereupon the frigates had taken powder in board and prepared for sea. Further, that the following day a party of people, including Bonaparte, had come out to the Isle D'Aix and that 'they were imme-diately to embark in both the frigates'.

Maitland like every other British commander along the coast did not dis-count such information and stood in to see for himself. There were no signs of 'the bustle of ships about to proceed to sea with numerous passengers'. He did consider it feasible that if they were preparing for sea then they might be provi-sioning the ships under cover of darkness. He had already taken steps to prevent any movement at night by having boats row across each potential escape channel. The information Maitland had received became less convincing when the master of the merchant ship assured Maitland that two galliots were to arrive and join the frigates prior to sailing. No such vessels had been seen either near Rochefort, nor creeping up or down the coast. As far as Maitland could tell nothing seemed to be happening. He continued to look out 'most anxiously for the White flag to appear on the steeples hereabouts but the three colours are still displayed every-where'.[18]

Maitland was rightly concerned about his mission but he had prepared a set of tactical plans for every likely eventuality, whether it was an attempt to break out during the day; an attempt to force one of the channels at night in small craft; or to leave Rochefort in a small merchant vessel. This was all in painful contrast to events in Rochefort. The inertia which had enveloped Napoleon since Waterloo remained. He would not leave without the passports. To do so would risk the humiliation of being discovered in a merchant vessel whilst hiding like a fugitive. If he was to leave then it would be with some style, accompanied by his attend-ants, servants and his household effects.

On 6 July Maitland received further information from the Admiral: 'It is believed that Napoleon Buonaparte has taken his road from Paris to Rochefort, to embark from thence for the United States of America.' Maitland then lost the *Endymion*. Suddenly he had no other major vessel to watch the other channels but was told he could keep the *Slaney* of 20 guns, for ten days, to watch one of the other channels.

In Rochefort General Bertrand was told to investigate the idea of the Emperor being smuggled out on the *Madeleine*, a small merchant vessel, which was about to set sail for the United States with a cargo of brandy. Money was advanced to the captain, a former French naval officer, Besson, to enable him to prepare a hiding place in a specially modified barrel. Gourgard was sent to the Gironde to assess the feasibility of the Royan scheme. On 6 July, the port telegraph brought news that Louis was on his way to Paris and that the Emperor's departure must be expedited. On 7 July, it said that the Prussians had begun to enter Paris and that Davout and the army had left Paris. Members of the government were already jockeying for positions in the new Royalist administration.

On 8 July the pressure was again increased in a letter from Hotham. Admiral Lord Keith had sent word that the French Provisional Government had applied to the British for a passport and safe conduct for Bonaparte to travel to America. The request had been rejected. Hotham's considered opinion was that he was on the road to Rochefort intending to board one of the two frigates there. But it was only his opinion. If he was right, then the same problem remained. There were three possible escape routes off Rochefort and Maitland now only had the *Slaney* and the *Bellerophon*. He could not watch the other. Other ships of the squadron blockaded Bordeaux, to the south and Quiberon Bay and Ushant to the north.

Meanwhile Hotham had received orders from Lord Bathurst to finally take positive action to support the Royalists, as Bonaparte had abdicated and there was currently no 'acknowledged government' in Paris. Any efforts against the Isle Dieu were to be ended. Belle Isle, however, could now be taken providing that only the white Bourbon flag were hoisted.[19]

In Paris the provisional government met for the last time. The Allies had agreed to restore Louis to the throne. At three o'clock in the afternoon the tricolour flags on the pubic buildings came down to be replaced with the white flag of the Bourbons. King Louis then made his entry into the city proceeded by those marshals who had remained loyal.

Hotham, echoing both his and Keith's thoughts, ordered Maitland to bolster his forces by keeping any warship that might appear off the Aix Roads with him to watch over the three potential escape routes. Hotham's conclusion – which was entirely correct, was that Bonaparte was most likely still awaiting confirmation of his request for passports and that he would either leave in a naval vessel or secretly in a merchant vessel.

In Rochefort, Napoleon had taken lunch and then said farewell to Bonnefoux, giving him a gold box which had a monogrammed 'N' outlined in diamonds on it. As he walked to his carriage he waved briefly to those around him, turned and climbed into the carriage. Quietly leaving the town, he joined the column of carriages that had left earlier and they made their way to the seashore at Fouras. Here they met the boats from the *Méduse* and *Saale,* which were to take them out to the Isle d'Aix. As the boats could not come in close a local man know as Père Beau carried the Emperor on his back to the *Saale's* longboat. After rowing out into some choppy waters they were out in the channel close to the island and the anchored frigates. The Emperor understood that the weather was favourable – he would go on board the frigate right away, in case they might begin their voyage. Coming up the side he was received in the Imperial style but without the firing of any cannon. The enemy was too close for that. The crew waited during the night but the wind fell.[20] It was clear there would no breakout that day. At daylight on 9 July they were able to take on board the rest of the Imperial baggage and distribute the other members of his retinue amongst the two frigates.

The Emperor decided to visit the tiny island. Landing on a rocky beach he walked on to see the 14th Marines drawn up ready for church parade. He inspected them as the drums beat the general salute. He then ordered that some drill movements be carried out, with which he declared himself satisfied. Still the people who had gathered called out, 'Long live the Emperor!'[21]

He then inspected the fortifications on the island, accompanied by the local artillery and engineer officers. He walked along walls which he had in part planned. As he looked out into the main channel, there, just beyond the range of the island guns, lay the *Bellerophon*, waiting.

On his return to the *Saale*, Bonnefoux had a letter for the Emperor from the Minister of Marine, Decrès. The Emperor was yet again urged to leave France as soon as possible. It was of the greatest importance for the safety of both France and himself that he did so. If the frigates could not leave then a despatch boat sailing without the knowledge of the English could be the answer. The alternative was that he might prefer to go onboard one of the vessels of the English squadron. It was emphasised that once at sea, he must not set foot on French soil again.

On 9 July Captain Brine of the *Sheldrake* (16 guns) relayed information to the *Cyrus* that Napoleon was at Nantes. The previous day a gentleman had informed Brine that Napoleon Bonaparte with his brother and nine officers of distinction were at Nantes at the House of General Le Marque. Further, that they were shortly to board an American vessel which would move down to 'St Nazaire on Friday or Saturday so as to start the first favourable moment that offered'.

Captain Brine, was rightly concerned. If this were true, his vessel was no match for the superior French force. This apparently consisted of eight guns boats, a French brig and the 'large American ship'. He looked in to St Nazaire at the end of the day on the 8th and must have been most relieved to discover only a brig and an armed lugger lay in the river.[22]

Meanwhile, Maitland maintained his position and waited. For two nights his boats continued to row guard across the channel. Then at daylight on 10 July a small schooner was seen coming out from the Isle d'Aix. Maitland, not sure whether this was an attempt to reconnoitre, prior to a breakout, ordered the ship to be readied to sail should it prove to be so. She in turn hoisted a flag of truce and came alongside. That same day Lord Keith was writing orders to Hotham urging him to closely reconnoitre the ports of Rochelle and Rochefort.[23]

Up the side of *Bellerophon* came General Savary and Count Las Cases. They brought with them a letter from General Bertrand addressed to the admiral who commanded the vessels before Rochefort. During the interview Las Cases remained almost mute, shielding the fact that he both spoke and understood English very well. It was a useless bargaining point for as the Frenchmen were shown into Maitland's great cabin, the *Falmouth* arrived alongside with orders and 'four late and very interesting French papers' from Hotham. With the arrival of these documents Maitland was provided with all the background information he required. The newspapers explained in detail the arrangements that had been made to provide 'for Buonaparte's escape from France'. It revealed how he had left Paris at four o'clock on 29 June and had taken the road to Rochefort. Maitland and Hotham now knew far more about Buonaparte's potential predicament than his emissaries wished to reveal. A weak position had just been irreparably damaged with those newspapers. The Emperor Napoleon was no longer a man who commanded the politicians and monarchs across Europe – he was a man in flight.

The letter handed over by Savary and Las Cases confirmed what he now knew for certain that Napoleon was at that very moment, on board one of the two frigates lying off the Isle d'Aix

9th July, 1815

Admiral,

The Emperor Napoleon having abdicated the throne, and chosen the United States of America as a retreat, is, with his suite, at present, embarked on board the two frigates which are in this port, for the purpose of proceeding to his destination. He expects a passport from the British Government, which has been promised to him, and which induces me to send the present flag of truce, to demand of you, Sir, if you have any knowledge of the above-mentioned passport, or if you think it is the intention of the British Government to throw any impediment in the way of our voyage to the United States. I shall feel much obliged by your giving me any information you may posses on the subject.

I have directed the bearers of this letter to present to you my thanks, and to apologise for the trouble it may cause.

I have the honour to be,

Your Excellency's most obedient, &c. &c

Grand Marshal Count BERTRAND [24]

This letter was not as open as it appeared to be. No member of the British Government had 'promised' passports for The Emperor Napoleon and of course Maitland already knew this. In the cabin both sides discussed the issue for some time. Maitland made it clear that his orders were that '[he] could not permit the frigates to pass with him on board'. Equally he could not allow any vessel, 'under whatever flag she may be, to pass with a personage of such consequence'.

After two or three hours Las Cases and Savary left the ship and returned to the Emperor. Captain Knight sailed to rejoin Admiral Hotham taking despatches from Maitland and his own impressions of the discussion. Hotham would therefore receive two versions of what had passed in the great cabin. That night the boats of the *Bellerophon* continued to row across the channel ready to raise the alarm if an escape were attempted.

The next day, 11 July, at noon, a small boat rowed by four men brought two 'respectable-looking countrymen' from the Ile d'Oléron to see the captain. They requested to speak privately with Maitland and were shown into his cabin where they revealed that a messenger had arrived on their island that morning offering a large sum of money to the one pilot who had previously taken a frigate through the Mamusson passage. They understood that the escape would involve either a corvette or a Danish brig that was close at hand. [25]

Maitland reacted immediately, beating out of the Pertuis d'Antioche. He sent the *Myrmidon* off the Mamusson, whilst he remained under weigh between the lighthouses. Later that evening the *Slaney* rejoined him. On the 12th he signalled the *Cyrus* (20 guns), to close in with the Baleine lighthouse and to examine every vessel that came her way as Bonaparte was 'on the spot, endeavouring to escape to America'. He was also able to use the *Daphne* (22 guns), which had arrived that day to patrol the southernmost channel, the Passe de Mamusson.

That evening Maitland saw a heartening sight – the Bourbon flag appeared above Rochelle. As an encouragement to those who had raised it, Maitland sailed close by and also raised the Bourbon flag himself, firing a royal salute as he did so – a salute that was clearly heard by the Imperial party across the channel. However, later that same evening, it was removed and replaced with the tricolour. The removal of the white flag cannot have disheartened Maitland a great deal. The fact that it had been raised earlier in the day showed how unstable were the sympathies of the people on shore. His trap was set. He need do nothing; Napoleon however, had to do something, in order to maintain his dignity.

The next day the Bourbon flag rose again and this time stayed up. In the distance boats were plying to and from the shore bringing food to the frigates. They were clearly making ready for sea. Some of the crew were in the rigging apparently making ready to leave. Maitland was also ready. The ships under his command had 'slip buoys on their cables' – floating markers so that they might let go of their anchors in a moment and set off in pursuit, without having to spend half an hour or more in weighing them. Again, the frigates did not move. That night the boats were out equipped with a system of signals to inform the *Bellerophon* what might be happening in the darkness. Nothing happened.

At daybreak on 14 July, the signs were even more auspicious for the British. The Bourbon flag appeared again and according to Lieutenant Bowerbank of the *Bellerophon*, 'in all the neighbouring towns'.[26] The officer of the watch informed Maitland that the *Mouche* was approaching, bearing a flag of truce. Count Las Cases and General Count Lallemand came on board. Maitland invited them to breakfast and signalled to the *Slaney* for Captain Sartorius to join them. They came to ask whether the passports the Emperor had demanded had arrived with Captain Maitland. He assured them that he had absolutely no knowledge of any such passports. They then discussed the possibility of the Emperor being allowed to travel to America, either with the French squadron (Bowerbank gives this as the two frigates, two corvettes and a brig.) or a single French or British man-o'-war. Maitland refused, pointing out that none of these options were available to him as the senior officer blockading Rochefort. Bowerbank was convinced that Maitland 'explicitly declared that that as he had been vested with no authority to grant any promise. Buonaparte's coming on board must be perfectly unconditional'.[27]

Maitland did point out that if Napoleon came on board his ship, he would be able to transport him to England. Maitland also said

> … if however he adopts that plan, I cannot enter into any promise as to the reception he may meet with, as, even in the case I have mentioned, I shall be acting on my own responsibility and cannot be sure that it would meet the approbation of the British Government.[28]

Not surprisingly, 'there was a great deal of conversation' on this subject. Lucien Bonaparte's experiences of living for four years in England were cited.[29] Maitland emphasised that he could not give any assurances whatsoever as to what might happen once they were in England. Las Cases paused as he was about to leave the ship, looked at Maitland and said: 'Under all circumstances, I have little doubt that you will see the Emperor on board the *Bellerophon*.'[30]

They left but then returned late in the afternoon. They had with them a letter from General Bertrand. It heralded the end of the blockade:

> Captain,
> Count Las Cases has reported to the Emperor the conversation which he had with you this morning. His Majesty will proceed on board your ship with the ebb tide to-morrow morning, between four and five o'clock.

I send the Count Las Cases, Counsellor of State, doing the duty of Maréchal de Logis, with the list of persons composing his Majesty's suite.

If the Admiral, in consequence of the despatch you forwarded to him, should send the passport for the United States therein demanded, His Majesty will be happy to repair to America; but should the passport be withheld, he will willingly proceed to England, as a private individual, there to enjoy the protection of the laws of your country.

His Majesty has despatched Major General Baron Gourgard to the Prince Regent with a letter, a copy of which I have the honour to enclose, requesting that you will forward it to such one of the ministers as you may think it necessary to send that general officer, that he may have the honour of delivering the letter with which he is charged to the Prince Regent.

I have the honour to be,

Sir

Your very humble servant,

COUNT BERTRAND

L'Isle D'Aix

14 July 1815[31]

The letter also included a list of the persons of Napoleon's suite. There was also a copy of another letter – the one that that General Gourgard was to take to the Prince Regent. This is the most famous letter of that unfortunate period. In this short and rhetorical piece, Napoleon declared that his political career was at an end and like the hero of antiquity, Themistocles, he had come, as a defeated warrior to 'throw himself' upon the hospitality of the British people. He also claimed the protection of British law from the most 'generous' of his enemies. It made for an excellent newspaper report: grand images, a reference to the heroic past, an acknowledgement of the noble nature of the British people and his submission before the law. In essence, he had lost, the chivalrous British had won and from them he now asked for sanctuary:

Rochefort, July 13th, 1815.

Your Royal Highness,

A victim to the factions which distract my country, and to the enmity of the greatest powers of Europe, I have terminated my political career, and I come, like Themistocles, to throw myself upon the hospitality of the British people. I put myself under the protection of their laws; which I claim from your Royal Highness, as the most powerful, the most constant, and the most generous of my enemies.

NAPOLEON[32]

A sharp piece of writing and a clever piece of propaganda, short, just seventy words in translation and succinct. It was perfect for discussion at all levels of society; in government, in the homes of the influential, in the newspapers, in the taverns and the street. Everyone could take the central message from this letter. Here was a victim seeking a Good Samaritan.

The very second word is 'victim'. Napoleon has been thrown out of his land by the 'factions' within it. By implication he has been a man above 'faction' as he has been thrown away, discarded. He has been further victimised, bullied, by the 'enmity' of the great European powers. Beaten down, he has finished with them. He compares himself with the noble and tragic figure of Themistocles, the brilliant Athenian general who saved Athens from Persian invasion but was forced out by political manoeuvring and gained sanctuary with the Persian King Artaxerxes I. (It would probably not have escaped Napoleon's notice that Themistocles' reputation in his homeland was entirely rehabilitated after his death.) Napoleon has turned to the noble British for charity, for they are a great and chivalrous people living in harmony under their laws.

There is no direct mention of why it was that the recently appointed King of Elba had fled from France, trusting to the Royal Navy to deliver him from his enemies. There is no mention of why it was that that some of those 'factions' within France had demanded that he abdicate the throne for a second time. There is no mention of the fact that those very cruel European powers were Britain's allies. He is here, at the gates of Britain having been driven to them, most cruelly, by peoples and events beyond the shores of Britain. He justifies nothing, admits no wrongdoing and accepts no responsibility.

For some Britons this was very flattering. For others their constancy over more than twenty years of war was not seen as a mark of honour, but rather at the very least an inconvenience visited upon them by the Emperor and at worst, as a time of terrible loss. The Waterloo lists of killed and wounded had only recently reached some rural outposts, such as Torbay. And unlike Napoleon, we shall hear what some of those people had to say when he reaches that place.

Maitland assured Las Cases that he would receive Bonaparte on board and arrange for General Gourgard to sail by the *Slaney* to England. He also made it clear that Gourgard would not be allowed to land until permission was received from the Government in London.

Las Cases then called for paper that he might write a letter to Bertrand telling him of the arrangements that had been agreed on board the *Bellerophon*. Meanwhile, Gourgard prepared to accompany Captain Sartorius in the *Slaney*. They would also take Maitland's despatches informing the Admiralty of the impending arrival of Napoleon Bonaparte in Torbay, where he would 'await such directions as the Admiralty may think proper to give'.

Maitland also informed the Admiralty that General Gourgard had 'further particulars, which he is anxious to communicate to his Royal Highness'. Las Cases, having completed his letter, gave it to his aide, a French naval officer who departed in the barge. Maitland and he then discussed the matter of the accommodation for Napoleon and his suite. Maitland proposed dividing the after cabin into two, thus allowing the ladies to have a private drawing room. On this Las Cases said it would be better to give the Emperor the entire cabin as he could then take exercise privately.

There were still nervous moments to be endured, unsurprisingly, these were momentous events. At ten o'clock a boat requested for permission to come alongside. On one of the crew coming on board, Maitland was told that Bonaparte, dressed in a sailor's great coat, had passed Rochelle that morning in a chasse marée. Along with another vessel, they were preparing to make for the sea by the Pertuis de Breton. Maitland was doubtless shaken by this report, as his despatches announcing the imminent surrender of Bonaparte were now at sea. He had already declared officially to his superiors that 'Boney [was] in the bag.' He decided to quiz Las Cases to find out whether he was the dupe in some clever ruse to enable Bonaparte to escape at the last moment. Las Cases assured Maitland on his word of honour that he had left the Emperor at five-thirty that afternoon. So the claim of the informer, that he had seen him on board at ten in the morning seemed false – particularly as the informer freely admitted that he had never seen the Emperor before. Maitland was roused again at three in the morning with the same story, when another boat asked to come alongside with the same information.

In a footnote, Maitland partially substantiates the sailor's claims. He learned later that two chasse marées had actually been prepared for flight. Though whether, given their small size and lack of accommodation they would ever have carried Napoleon and maybe one or two followers across the Atlantic is unlikely.[33]

Saturday the 15th July was another fine summer's day. The *Bellerophon* was at anchor off the Basque Roads, perhaps four miles from the French frigates. Early in the morning before six o'clock the brig, *l'Epervier* was seen under sail working her way out to the *Bellerophon*.[34] At the same time, coming down from Quiberon Bay, the *Superb* with Admiral Hotham could be seen. It looked as though *l'Epervier* would come alongside just before the *Superb* came up. Then the weather and the tide upset Maitland's plans. The ebb-tide failed and the wind moved to blow onshore. *L'Epervier* seemed to stand still. She was perhaps a mile distant from the *Bellerophon*, whereas the *Superb* seemed to double her efforts as the wind shifted and the tide brought her in towards the *Bellerophon*. Maitland, not wanting his prize to go elsewhere, ordered Lt. Mott to take the barge and bring Napoleon on board. Mott said later that most of the crew of the *l'Epervier* had tears in their eyes as Napoleon transferred to the barge. As they pulled away the Frenchmen cheered, until they could be heard no more.

At around six o'clock, with the marines drawn up by the poop and Captain Maitland ready to receive him, General Bertrand came up the side and announced to Maitland: 'The Emperor is in the boat.' Napoleon then came up and stepped onto the deck in his 'olive-coloured great coat' over his green uniform and military boots. He raised his hat and declared to Maitland, in a firm voice: 'Sir, I am come to throw myself on the protection of your Prince and of your laws.' He then bowed to the officers and was led by Maitland into the great cabin. Napoleon remarked upon its fine qualities. On seeing a picture of Mrs Maitland he commented on how young and pretty she was. He asked after Maitland's family, wanting to know how many children he had, where he was born and so on. He asked to see all of the officers and of each one he 'asked several questions'. He then asked to see around the ship but as the lower decks were being cleaned he was asked to wait until the work had been completed.[35] The new war had begun.

A quarter of an hour later he again asked to be shown around the ship, accepting that the sailors would still be cleaning around them as they visited each deck. Maitland outlined the conversation they had as they progressed. Napoleon praised the cleanliness of the vessel, the neatness of the seamen – which appeared so superior to the French service. Throughout the tour Napoleon evidently asked leading questions about the admirable qualities of the Royal Navy enabling Maitland to praise his crew and officers and their training in gunnery.

They then retired to take breakfast together, though as this was 'in the English style, consisting of tea, coffee, cold meat, &c,' he ate little. On discovering later that he invariably had a hot meal for then, Maitland immediately gave orders that Napoleon's cook was to be given every assistance in order that Napoleon might have his usual dishes for breakfast. During the meal Napoleon asked many questions about life in England, declaring: 'I must now learn to conform myself to them, as I shall probably pass the remainder of my life in England.'[36] Neither Napoleon nor Maitland could know that the decision about his final destination had already been made in London. It would not be relayed to Napoleon until he had been at anchor off the coast of England for several days.

As the day continued the ship's boats moved to and fro bringing the rest of his suite and his baggage on board. According to Bowerbank, the officers of the *Bellerophon* were shifted out of their cabins and these were given over to the ladies and Napoleon's senior officers.[37]

The *Superb* having come up, Maitland went on board to report to Admiral Hotham, who congratulated him heartily: 'Getting hold of him on any terms would have been of the greatest consequence; but as you have entered into no conditions whatever, there cannot be a doubt that you will obtain the approbation of his Majesty's Government.'[38]

Napoleon wished to meet the Admiral and a visit to the *Bellerophon* was arranged that afternoon after Bertrand had formally called upon the Admiral. It appears to have been a very convivial meeting. Admiral Hotham, along with Captain Senhouse and the admiral's secretary, Mr Irving, met Napoleon in the after cabin. Captain Senhouse described his first sight of Napoleon.

His figure is bad: he is short with a large head, his hands and legs v small, and his body so corpulent as to project very considerably: his coat made very plain as you see it in most prints and from being very short in the back it gives his figure a more ridiculous appearance than it has naturally. Naturally his profile is good and is exactly what his prints and portraits represent him but his full face is bad. His eyes are a light blue, heavy and totally contrary to what I had expected, his teeth are bad, but the expression of his Countenance is versatile and [expresses] beyond measure the quick and varying expressions of the mind. His face at the moment bears the stamp of good humour. And again immediately changes to a dark penetrating thoughtful scowl, denoting the character of the thought that excites it. He speaks quick and turns from the subject to another with great rapidity. His knowledge is extensive and very various, and he surprised me much by his remembrance of men of every character in England. He spoke much of America and asked many questions concerning Spanish and British America, and also of the United States.[39]

Napoleon showed them his portable library in its small travelling cases. Hotham and he then talked about the management of the Royal Navy and finally Napoleon invited them all to stay for dinner. This was served on Napoleon's dinner service. Maitland freely admitted that at dinner

Buonaparte, viewing himself as a Royal personage, which he continued to do while on board the *Bellerophon*, and which, under the circumstances, I considered it would have been both ungracious and uncalled for in me to have disputed, led the way into the dining room. He seated himself in the centre at one side of the table, requesting Sir Henry Hotham to sit at his right hand side, and Madame Bertrand on his left. For that day I sat as usual at the head of the table, but on the following day, and every other, whilst Buonaparte remained on board, I sat by his request at his right hand, and General Bertrand took the top. Two of the ward-room officers dined daily at the table, by invitation from Buonaparte, conveyed through Count Bertrand ... He conversed a great deal, and showed no depression of spirits.[40]

The whole event replicated any splendid dinner described by Jane Austen, replete with undercurrents. People put themselves out to be convivial, the principal guest took charge and flattered them all, putting himself at the centre of the dining table and directing where the others should sit. It was still less than a month since Waterloo, he had left France for the last time that very morning and now he had a diplomatic war to win. Captain Senhouse was present:

Dinner was served entirely in the French style by Napoleon's Domestics. Without any Ceremony he commenced eating. No notice was taken of any Individual and we had all only to eat and drink as fast as the Servants plied the plates and glasses with food and wine.[41]

After taking coffee, he stood and invited the Admiral and the others to join him in the after cabin – which had of course been given over to him in its entirety. After some conversation, he announced in a cheerful manner that he would show everyone his campaign bed. Marchand was sent for, told to bring the bed and he returned with two leather cases. One contained the folded iron parts of the bed and the other the green silk curtains that surrounded it and the mattress. In three minutes the whole had been erected. Senhouse was amazed to see that the bed had a golden ball, which could not be fitted due to the lack of height in the cabin. Napoleon then left the cabin, took the air on the quarterdeck for some time and then retired to his cabin some time after seven-thirty. Shortly afterwards, the Admiral, wishing to take his leave, was told that he was undressed and going to bed. The party broke up but as an arrangement had been made earlier to meet for breakfast on board the *Superb* the gaiety would continue.

Next morning Maitland saw that the *Superb* had made preparations to salute the honoured guest. The tompions (stoppers in the mouths of the cannon to keep them waterproof) were out of the guns, indicating that a salute might be fired on his approach and the man ropes on the yards were loose to enable the sailors to 'man the yards' (standing on them as if on parade). Maitland sent the officer of the watch to the Admiral to ask if he should do the same on Bonaparte leaving his ship. The Admiral told him not to do so but that he could 'man the yards' on his return. Maitland admits he had decided to offer no honours on his approach the day before as it was before eight o'clock, the hour at which the colours are hoisted and the day's business begins. Further that no instructions had been issued as to Napoleon's status once he had been taken into a ship, 'I made the early hour an excuse for withholding them upon this occasion.'

Guest, prisoner, imperial or royal prisoner? Legally he was no longer the Emperor of France, as he had abdicated, again. Technically he was possibly still the King of Elba, and he was also an outlaw. Senhouse had noted in his letter that 'he plays the Emperor in everything, and has taken possession of Maitland's after cabin.' He had indeed taken possession of Maitland's cabin – but only after Maitland had offered it in conversation with Las Cases two days previously. Less than 48 hours ago Maitland had taken the greatest prize of all, the person of Napoleon Bonaparte. Admiral Hotham had already congratulated Maitland without reservation – he had got him on board the *Bellerophon* without any con-ditions. Napoleon might indeed 'play the Emperor in everything' but Napoleon presently only ruled over his own image. He was the man of the age but he had no control over his immediate future. He had surrendered his future into the hands of the British government. Unfortunately for the government, quite which laws he was subject to would be a source of some confusion once the *Bellerophon* reached England.

At ten o'clock in the morning, a captain's guard of Royal Marines was on parade and the barge was manned. Napoleon saw the marines, of whom Maitland was evidently very proud, and with his usual eye for seizing the moment, inspected them, commenting on what fine soldiers they were. With Maitland as his inter-preter, he asked to speak to the longest serving soldier present and then asked for the marines to be put through some exercises with the musket and bayonet. He made some civil comments and then moved to the side of the ship and down into the barge.

Looking around at the barge's crew he praised their turnout. In a moment of good humour, he looked at Las Cases who was wearing for the first time in Napoleon's service the uniform of a French naval officer. Napoleon teased him, looking amazed.[42] It was a sunny day and the good humour continued as they were rowed cross to the *Superb*. Napoleon asked Maitland questions about the ship, her service and armament and the men on the yards. On coming alongside, Bertrand went up the side first, announcing to Admiral Hotham as he came onto the deck, 'The Emperor is in the boat.' Again a guard of Royal Marines was drawn up. He was shown into the cabin where he asked to see the officers of the ship. In turn they were presented to him and he asked the same questions about service and age that he had put to the *Bellerophon's* officers the day before. He then asked to be shown around the ship, which was done in the company of some of his suite, the Admiral, Captain Senhouse and Maitland. In anticipation of this the men were drawn up in their divisions and 'everything was in the nicest order'. Again he endeavoured to seduce his audience, praising the superior construction of the British warships compared to the French; whereupon General Savary, evidently unable to contain himself, commented that all the new French ships that had been built at Antwerp had been constructed along these very same lines.

Senhouse, as captain of the *Superb,* was his immediate escort and saw how Napoleon had deteriorated physically:

> We went through the whole of the Ship even the store rooms etc but [he] seemed to look with painful sensations as if he were afflicted with gout. I was obliged to assist him up and down the ladders with the Count de Montholon, and his weight was rather more than Convenient. What a lesson Napoleon's state affords us? Showing so forcefully the instability of all human greatness!![43]

On returning to the quarterdeck he questioned both the Admiral and Maitland 'very minutely' about the feeding and clothing of seamen. On hearing that it was entirely in the hands of the purser, he shared a joke with them alone, declaring that the purser in either service could be 'a little rascal'. After this he asked to speak to the chaplain, who of course was an Anglican, and quizzed him about the number of Catholics and foreigners who were in the crew and how many of them spoke the French language. After this interview he was led into the cabin where breakfast had been prepared. He talked at length but ate little – again the meal was a cold one. Not everyone was as apparently relaxed as Napoleon. Maitland noticed Colonel Planat sitting at the table with tears 'running down his cheeks,' much distressed by the situation his master was in; and not only him. As the voyage progressed, Maitland came to see that all of his followers, 'without exception' were devoted to him.

After breakfast, the party moved into the after cabin, where Napoleon's conversation centred on the movement of his horses and carriages from Rochefort to England. Maitland had already agreed to take on board the *Bellerophon* two carriages and five or six horses. As these had not arrived, the Admiral gave orders that a passport be issued to enable all of them to be transported. Maitland believes that this was sent into the Isle d'Aix but neither the horses nor carriages arrived in England. At the end of the visit Senhouse confessed that they had all been charmed by the great man, 'leaving a very favourable impression on our minds', his face being a picture of 'good humour' throughout the visit.

The party returned to the *Bellerophon* where the anchor was weighed. Admiral Hotham's orders to Maitland were that he should take *Myrmidon* under his command, and place on her

> ... such persons composing a part of the suite of Napoleon Buonaparte as cannot be conveyed in the *Bellerophon*, you are to put to sea in H.M.S. under your command, in company with the *Myrmidon*, and, make the best of your way with Napoleon Buonaparte and his suite to Torbay, and there landing the officer of the ship bearing my flag, whom I have charged with a despatch addressed to the Secretary of the Admiralty, as well as an officer of the ship you command, for the purpose of proceeding express to Plymouth with the despatch you will herewith receive, addressed to Admiral Lord Keith, and a copy of these instructions (which you will transmit to his Lordship,) await orders from the Lords Commissioners of the Admiralty, or his Lordship, for your further proceedings.[44]

Some days later, Melville on learning of the 'royal respect' and deference accorded to Napoleon during his visit to the *Superb* wrote a short letter to Keith, outlining his worries. If he were to continue to be so treated then there was a real danger that 'the same follies in this respect are likely to be committed as were exhibited last year by some officers in the Mediterranean'.[45]

On the island of Elba there had been only one unofficial commissioner, Sir Neil Campbell – labelled afterwards as 'the man who let Boney go,' and only one warship on patrol, the sloop *Partridge* under Captain Adye. Campbell, convinced that all was well, took himself to the Italian mainland thus allowing Napoleon to begin his gamble. Captain Adye looked into the main harbour briefly whilst the loading process was underway, saw nothing to alarm him and sailed away. All of this had taken place five months ago, in February, with barely a battalion of infantry and a handful of dismounted cavalrymen. With them at his back Napoleon had conquered all of France 'walking with his hands in his pockets'. Melville was understandably worried that he was about to charm, dazzle and outmanoeuvre those around him again. Was he still capable of attempting something similar?

The same letter told Keith that St Helena had been decided upon as his residence and that Admiral Cockburn's appointment as Commander-in-Chief at the Cape, which had been suspended upon the cessation of hostilities in 1814, would be reactivated. The Cape Station included St Helena in its area of supervision. A second letter, written by Melville in a more agitated state took both Admiral Hotham and Captain Maitland to task. Melville had interviewed the officer sent with the despatches from Rochefort. From him he had learnt of the respectful manner in which Napoleon had been treated whilst on board the *Bellerophon*. Melville was quite clear in his instructions to Keith: Bonaparte was to be regarded both as a prisoner of war and a general officer. Consequently he was only to be accorded those privileges due to that rank alone. At the same time Melville was equally clear:

No British officer would treat his prisoner with inhumanity, and the recollection of the station which Bonaparte has so long held in Europe would naturally, and almost involuntarily, lead an officer to abstain from any line of conduct that could be construed into insult, and therefore to go beyond [rather] than to fall short of due respect; but such indulgent feelings must be restrained within proper bounds, and I would be obliged to your Lordship to give such hint on this subject as may appear to you necessary.[46]

Perhaps it was as well that those six carriages and horses were not to be transported to England. His last home would not require many horses.

The last direct link with France disappeared with the *Mouche*, which had brought four sheep and fresh provisions, a gift for the Emperor. As she returned to Rochefort, *Bellerophon* and the exiles were on their way, temporarily, to England.

Over the next few days Napoleon seems to have been frequently on deck until dinner, asking questions of Maitland about the sea, the routine of the ship and about the occasional vessel they saw in the distance. They only saw one warship, the sloop *Bacchus* (18 guns), and Napoleon speculated whether, had his party got past Maitland's blockade, they might have made it to America.[47] Maitland assured him that the rest of the squadron would have caught him but discovered some time later that he may indeed have escaped:

The *Endymion* had gone into the Gironde; the *Liffey* had sprung her bowsprit and sailed back to England for repair and the others, from various causes, having quitted the station so that, had he passed the squadron off Rochefort, there can be little doubt he would have made his voyage in safety to America.[48]

The guest remained gracious and interested in the workings of the ship but there were moments that revealed the tensions within him. On Tuesday 18 July, whilst at dinner, a French servant pouring coffee slipped with the pot and coffee was poured over the Emperor's lap. Bowerbank, who was a guest, saw a look given to the servant that seemed to 'annihilate the man', who promptly left off serving and retired from the cabin. Bowerbank also noted other moments once the voyage to England was underway when Napoleon finally showed a reaction to the monumental reverses he had experienced: looking out to find the French coastline, or ignoring the company around him and seeming to be entirely wrapped up in his own thoughts.

Napoleon's spirits were restored by the time he attended a play, *The Poor Gentlemen*, performed principally by the midshipmen and Assistant Surgeon Graebke. According to Graebke, Napoleon found it very amusing, particularly the female roles played by the midshipmen. Madame Bertrand sat by him and translated. He remained until the third act, when he retired to his cabin.[49]

Early on the 20th they met the *Swiftsure*, sailing south, to join the blockade of Rochefort. As Captain Webley came aboard, Maitland said

'Well, I have got him.'

'Got him! Got whom?'

'Why, Buonaparte; the man that has been keeping all Europe in a ferment these last twenty years.'

'Is it possible?' said he; 'well you are a lucky fellow.'

As Napoleon was still in his cabin, Captain Webley was unable to meet the great man, and so the ships parted. Meals continued to be full of conversation as Napoleon was still very keen to learn more about English life, 'asking many questions about the manners, customs, and laws of the English'.

On Sunday 23rd July they were off Ushant and Napoleon spent a great part of the day on deck staring at the French coastline and saying little. When he spoke it was to Maitland, asking questions about the particular part of the English coast that they were making for.

That evening at eight o'clock, the high land of Dartmoor was seen. Maitland went to inform Napoleon in his cabin and found him in a flannel dressing gown, almost undressed and preparing for sleep. He immediately put his greatcoat over the top and came on deck, to stare across the sea towards the land, asking about the time of their arrival in Torbay.

At daybreak on the 24th July they were close to Dartmouth. Bertrand informed Napoleon who came on deck at four-thirty, remaining on deck until the ship anchored. Again he spoke admiringly of the scenery, of how it reminded him of Porto Farrago in Elba. As they came to Tor Bay, a mile or so from the Town of Brixham, Lieutenant Mott was preparing to go ashore with letters for Admiral Keith whilst Lieutenant Fletcher of the *Superb* was to carry the news to the Admiralty in London. Close by, the *Slaney* was at anchor. This sight must have initially given some cheer to the French party. Its presence suggested that Gourgard was in London arguing the case for Napoleon's detention somewhere in England.

A naval officer was already coming out to the *Bellerophon* from the *Slaney*. The officer had orders from Admiral Lord Keith for Captain Maitland. Meanwhile, over at the Brixham quayside local boats were putting off from the shore. Soon local traders would be alongside, offering to sell fresh food and other goods to the sailors. One of the last to leave the shore was a local baker with some very inquisitive boys in his boat.

These new orders stated that Admiral Keith had received his despatch carried by Captain Sartorius late on 22nd July. He had immediately despatched Sartorius to the Admiralty in London, so that they might know first-hand what had occurred during the negotiations which had resulted in Bonaparte coming on board the *Bellerophon*. Maitland was now ordered

> … to prevent every person whatever from coming on board the ship you command, except the officers and men who compose her crew; nor is any person whatsoever, whether in His Majesty's service or not, who does not belong to the ship, to be suffered to come on board, either for the purpose of visiting the officers, or on any

pretence whatever, without express permission either from the Lord Commissioners of the Admiralty, or from me. As, I understand from Captain Sartorius, that General Gourgard refused to deliver that with which he was charged for the Prince Regent, to any person except his Royal Highness, you are to take him out of the *Slaney*, into the ship you command, until you receive directions from the Admiralty on the subject.[50]

Keith had also enclosed a private letter to Maitland. In it he re-emphasised the need to keep everyone out of the *Bellerophon*, whether they were government officials or even very senior naval officers. Keith urged Maitland to make sure that '[he] and his want for nothing' and if Brixham could not provide it then Maitland was to ask Keith and he in turn would have it sent by a small vessel. Keith also asked Maitland to convey his personal thanks for the attention his nephew Captain Elphinstone had received after being twice wounded and captured in the withdrawal to Waterloo on 17 June. Napoleon had apparently noticed the young hussar officer and ordered that he be attended by his surgeon. Keith was very obliged for his nephew, 'must have died, if he had not ordered a surgeon to dress him immediately, and sent him to a hut'.[51]

On the quayside the baker was putting his sack of bread into his rowing boat. It was John Smart's birthday on 24 July, and he was on holiday from school. Schools had given an extra weeks off to celebrate the victory at Waterloo. John met with his friends, Charlie Puddicombe and his younger brother Dick, on the quay. They were about to discuss how they should spend the day and what they might do with John's two birthday half crowns, when they saw the two warships sailing into the bay,

> … the first a large man–of–war, and the other a three masted sloop. The ships were coming in quickly with wind and tide, but we heard faintly the sound of the boatswain's whistle, and in a moment the sailors were scrambling up the rigging and out on the yards to take in sail.[52]

Then the anchors were let go and they came to swinging round on the flood tide, perhaps a mile from Brixham Quay, with *Bellerophon* being the nearer to the shore. The younger boy, Dick, was told to run up to Mrs Hawkins, the baker's wife and tell her that there were King's ships off the quay who would want fresh bread. Already some local men were untying their boats at the quay, but as they did so a boat had set off from the *Bellerophon* for the shore. The older boys moved to the pier steps to see the gig rowed in. There were eight men at the oars and three officers sitting in the stern sheets. It came neatly alongside and two of the officers jumped out. The older was about 35 and he had a cloak over his arm and a portmanteau carried ashore. The younger officer turned to the midshipman who now commanded the gig and said he would be gone for ten minutes, turned to go, paused and reminded the midshipman that there was to be no talking whilst they waited off the quayside.

The senior officer then asked the man who had picked up his portmanteau where they might find a post chaise. They were led to the London Inn and minutes later the boy witnessed a horse being put into the old yellow post chaise. The officers then reappeared from the inn, whilst the landlord came after pouring out two glasses of wine. The older man mounted the chaise and then spoke: 'Goodbye Dick; here's to our next meeting!' 'Here's to your safe arrival in London!' said the younger one, 'and goodbye.'

With that the post-boy mounted and the chaise made its way up narrow Fore Street towards the main London Road. John Smart had seen Lieutenant Fletcher of the *Superb* set off for the Admiralty in London. The younger officer now made his way smartly back to the quay and signalling to the gig, had her return to the pier. Before the boys could ask anything of the sailors he had sat down and called out for the crew to move away from the quay.

Shortly afterwards the flour-covered baker, Michelmore, arrived with his apprentice and a sack of bread. Saying, 'Come boys, let's be off to the ship,' the Puddicombe brothers took one oar, the apprentice baker the other, whilst John sat in the bow and Michelmore took the tiller. As they steered for the *Bellerophon* John saw that the others local traders had gathered in a group some way from her. One man was standing apparently arguing with someone on the deck of the warship. On coming up to the other traders Michelmore asked why they were standing away from the ship. The answer was that no one was allowed to trade with her.

Michelmore evidently thought this could not apply to him as he had fresh bread for sale and so he allowed his boat to drift to the stern of the warship. Here was a marine sentry with a musket and an officer standing with him. The latter leaned over and called out:

'Come, sheer off; no boats are allowed here.' 'But,' said Michelmore, as he made a grab at a lower deck port sill with his boat hook, 'I've brought you some bread.' 'If we want bread,' replied the officer, 'we'll come ashore and fetch it, and if you don't let go I'll sink you.' The tide had drifted us right under the gallery, and what was my horror to see the sentry drop his musket and seize a large cannon-ball, which he held exactly over my head. 'Let go you old fool, or by the Lord I'll sink you!' said the sentry; and to my great relief Michelmore let go, and we were soon out of harm's way.'[53]

As they pulled away from the ship they noticed that the lower ports were open, and the decks crowded with men. But they could not stay and talk with the sailors, as a boat had just been lowered into the water with a crew of at least a dozen sailors and an officer. The sailors were armed and the officer told the baker to move away from the warship. Defeated, for the moment, they rowed back to the cluster of Brixham boats and heard that it was the same round the sloop. There was an armed guard rowing around her as well. Slowly and separately the Brixham boats departed for the shore, apart from Michelmore the baker. Once more, with the encouragement of the boys, Michelmore steered the boat back towards the *Bellerophon*, this time keeping a proper distance from the ship. Luckily, as they passed under the bows the tide took them closer than they would have rowed and they saw a sailor at one of the lower gun ports. He nodded to them in an agitated manner and stood back from the gun port as if frightened of being caught out. He caught John's eyes and placed his fingers on his lips with a warning gesture:

> We were past him in another moment, but I was greatly excited, and wanted to turn back to see him again. However, Michelmore decided it would be safer to complete our turn; and accordingly we did so, but regulated our pace with the guard boat, so that it was at the ship's stern when we again approached the bows. This time the man was still standing back, and even less visible than before; but his hand was just visible on the port sill, and as we passed he let something drop from his fingers into the water. We dare not approach, but we kept it in view as it drifted along. I had my hand dragging as if carelessly in the water, and when we were a good hundred yards clear of the ship, Michelmore steered so as to bring the object into my hand. It proved to be a small black bottle.

Frightened and yet longing to see the message inside, they steered for the shore. John was shielded from any inquisitive eyes on board the *Bellerophon* with being in the bow and he uncorked a 'foreign-looking' bottle whose oily perfumed smell he could recall years later. Inside there was a small piece of paper, and written on it, 'We have got Bonaparte on board.' Within five minutes of reaching the shore: 'there was not a soul in Brixham, except babies, ignorant of the news'.

Anyone who owned a boat was busy that day as the news spread and more and more people gathered with a view to going out to catch a glimpse of 'Boney'. Every sort of boat that could either be rowed or sailed was set on the water. There was such a bustle on the quayside that the people on the *Bellerophon* must have known that their secret was out. Soon these craft were heading for the warship and then the cries were set up of 'Bonaparte! Bonaparte!' from all the boats, soon confirmed it. Then, members of the French party appeared and everyone cried out again, even though few of the visitors would have been able to recognise any of the Frenchmen – until that is Napoleon showed himself. He appeared at the stern windows and Smart remembered how small he seemed and that he was rather fat. He wore a green uniform with red facings, gold epaulettes, white waistcoat and breeches and high military boots. He took off his hat, which had a cockade on it, and bowed to the people, who in return took off their hats and shouted 'Hooray!'

It was a time of 'triumph' mixed with a 'natural satisfaction at seeing a wonderful sight'. Napoleon, thought Smart, seemed to accept all the applause as a compliment to himself, not seeing it in part as a cry of triumph at having snared him. Smart also noticed how the officers and crew were very respectful to him as they took off their hats when they spoke to him.

It was a glorious day, says Smart, for the people of a town that had once wel-comed King William of Orange to Brixham and now was able to welcome an Emperor – 'the conqueror, the tyrant, the villain – a safe prisoner in an English ship'. Here he was for all to see, high up above them. He was in the enormous battleship whilst they were down on the surface of the sea. Both parties were able to gaze at each other at a safe distance, rather like seeing the lion in the zoo, the people in their boats could leave, knowing that the beast was staying securely in his floating cage.

This feeling of separation was further enhanced as the crowds were kept back from physical contact with the ship by the guard boats. Communication between both parties was of course hampered by Napoleon's lack of English. He was a caged wonder, a beast to be admired. The visitors were having an adventure, coming out to see him in the boats. It was all rather like a grand pageant. The people slowly milled about the warship, like crowds at a fair. It was delightful to be part of this unique spectacle, to see and be seen, rather like people taking the air in Bath Spa, where examining the other visitors was part of the experience.

Smart is convinced that the officer who had gone off in the yellow post chaise 'only held his tongue till he got to Exeter', for that evening, Brixham received the first post chaise 'crowded with gentlemen'. People came in from Dartmouth, on foot, by cart, by carriage and some around the point by boat. The next day Torbay teemed with small boats.

One of those who was on the water was the Archdeacon of Totnes, the Revd. Froude. On Monday, he and friends had hired a boat for the entire day to take them out to the *Bellerophon* but they did not think that they would actually see Bonaparte. But, as they made their way to the stern of the *Bellerophon* – the 'extraordinary personage' was there at the windows. To Froude, he appeared more like a spectator, rather than as the object of curiosity. Of course he was attempting to analyse the crowd as much as they were analysing him.

An officer of the *Bellerophon,* presumably in one of the guard boats, gave Froude a copy of the Themistocles letter, which Froude transcribed whilst sitting in the boat. Clearly Napoleon's appeal to the Prince Regent was having some limited success.

Maitland saw Napoleon come on deck frequently throughout that Monday, and show himself at the gangways. If a pretty woman caught his eye he would raise his hat and bow. He also, as the Revd Froude saw, made himself visible through the stern windows on several occasions.[54] As John Smart later remarked, 'It seemed a gala day as the boats thronged round the *Bellerophon*'.

Maitland also received many requests for permission to come on board and visit. Amongst them was a lady who lived locally, who had a basket of fruit deliv-ered to the ship, with her request that a boat be sent for her on Tuesday morning. Politely, Maitland had to decline the proposal. Lord Gwydir and Lord Charles Bentinck also applied and were also politely but firmly refused.

It was probably at the end of Monday that Napoleon and his followers first had an inkling of what might happen next. He was keen to hear what the press had to say, and had Las Cases translate the newspapers which came on board. *The Times* for example was convinced that he should be delivered up to 'the justice' of King Louis. Before this took place, the paper declared that a commission of inquiry be appointed to enquire into the mysterious death of a British citizen, Captain Wright, whilst imprisoned in France and of the apparent murder, on Napoleon's orders, of a German civilian on the charge of publishing a pamphlet criticising the behaviour of the French Army in Germany.[55]

The Courier had similar harsh words. It regretted that Britain was unable to punish him as he had 'so amply and so often deserved', and demanded he should at least be politically dead. The paper had heard rumours that Dumbarton Castle on the Clyde had been selected as a spot both beautiful but 'from which it is next to impossible that anyone should escape'. Other rumours had proposed the Tower of London and Sheerness as possible places of imprisonment but now many believed that it would be the island of St Helena, where an English regiment would be stationed to watch over him.[56]

What made Napoleon particularly uneasy is that some of the calls for punishment came from those papers that he understood were either sympathetic to the government, if not actually unofficial organs for Lord Liverpool's ministers. Several of them had already announced that it was the intention of the government that he be sent to the island of St Helena. Maitland found the topic of Napoleon's proposed exile to St Helena raised with him on several occasions that day, with members of Naspoleon's entourage declaring earnestly that the government 'had no right to send him there'.

Madame Bertrand was a Dillon by birth and had received part of her education in England. She spoke English very well. She conversed with Bowerbank, declaring herself shocked by the assertions in some of the newspapers that the Emperor would be sent to the island. She confided in him that the Emperor had solemnly declared that he would not go. Bowerbank placated her as best he could, saying that all of these articles were, at the moment, only speculative. Madame Bertrand would prove to be a very theatrical woman over the next few days.

Napoleon had always objected to the independence of British newspapers. For him it was inconceivable that the press should have independence from government control. During the Empire the press had always been ultimately censored. It had always puzzled him why the English government exercised so little control over the press. He was still expecting some hint within their pages of a favourable outcome to his decision to 'throw himself upon the laws of England'.

The mood in the French party had been further chilled by the arrival of General Gourgard from the *Slaney*. The sloop had sailed before the *Bellerophon*, and Napoleon had expected some news of the interview with the Prince Regent on his arrival. The *Slaney* lay at anchor in Torbay as the Bellerophon arrived. Her commander, Captain Sartorius, had himself gone up to London and the Admiralty. Gourgard had not. He had been forbidden to land. There was to be no direct appeal from one royal personage to another – Napoleon to the Prince Regent. The idea of Napoleon gaining the ear of the Prince Regent was one that would make even the tough Admiral Keith shudder when he reflected on it.[57]

That evening at dinner, Napoleon 'conversed as usual', wanting to know about the kinds of fish that were caught in English waters. He also spoke about the fishermen who smuggled intelligence for him and assisted prisoners of war to escape. He claimed that a number of them had offered to smuggle Louis to France, presumably from Hartwell House in Buckinghamshire. As they could not guarantee that the king would be alive when he landed, he declined their offer.

The Admiral was not the only one who would shudder at the thought of Napoleon. On Tuesday John Smart was to go out in Mrs Hawkins' boat and view the *Bellerophon* and hopefully Boney as well. Mrs Hawkins had a very decided opinion of Bonaparte, 'Do they show him, then?' she asked. 'Is he loose?' She had imagined him in chains, and declared him to be 'a monster who deserved treatment as a murderer'. When they rowed out it was morning and Napoleon had not made an appearance. But they did see a French officer in a blue and silver uniform, with a lady on his arm, parade across the deck. There was already an audience of people in other boats eager to see 'the monster'.

One of the men in the guard boat offered snippets of information to the crowds who waited on the water. Some of it was a little suspect – but it was a holiday atmosphere and he was presumably playing the role of street entertainer. He pointed out that Boney had invited the Captain to dine with him, 'as if the ship belonged to the French fleet.' Napoleon had been allowed by Maitland to behave as a superior, if not a royal personage. Napoleon's followers behaved entirely as members of the Imperial court. Each side quietly accepted the arrangement. Later, a blackboard was used with messages chalked on it, such as 'He is at dinner'.

Smart admits that the town, rather like the crew of the *Bellerophon*, felt that possession of Boney somehow made him 'their' man. Others in Brixham had the same view as Mrs Hawkins. A neighbour of John Smart's, a churchwarden, promoted the idea that Napoleon should be executed immediately and for a while had a band of local supporters.

However, before local protests could be made, the *Bellerophon* received orders to sail. At three in the morning Captain Sartorius returned from London. He had orders for Maitland to proceed to Plymouth Sound along with the *Slaney* and *Myrmidon*. When they were at sea, Madame Bertrand complained that the Emperor was 'excessively offended' at not being informed of these new orders. Maitland thought, on making enquiries of Las Cases, that Madame Bertrand was exaggerating.

The fact they the ship was moving away from London, and not towards it, did trouble Napoleon's followers – though he himself said nothing. Napoleon remained on deck for most of the day as they beat up against a strong northerly wind. He spoke appreciatively of the breakwater being completed in Plymouth Sound and marvelled at the modest amount of money it had cost to build. Once they had anchored Maitland informed Napoleon that he was going to report to Admiral Lord Keith and inquired if he could forward a message from him. Napoleon was very keen to meet Keith as the naval Commander-in-Chief.

On hearing this Keith in turn said he would have been pleased to 'wait upon him' but as he had no directions as to how Napoleon was to be addressed with regard to status and rank he felt it better to delay until he had those instructions. However as he had already received the second letter of 25 July, from Melville, he already knew how the prisoner was to be addressed. Perhaps it was also a wish on Keith's part not to have to hide the fact that he knew precisely where Napoleon was going next.

Admiral Keith then gave some further orders to prevent the escape of Napoleon. The ships *Liffey* and *Eurotas* were to be anchored on either side of the *Bellerophon*. They were to provide the armed boats to row guard. Even the captains of the ships in Keith's squadron were not allowed to visit the *Bellerophon*. Anyone who did need to visit would have to get Admiral Keith's permission, in writing. Even Lady Keith, 'Queeney', came no closer than going on board the *Eurotas*.[58]

A letter of guidance to the captains of the *Liffey* and *Eurotas* stated that they were there for 'preventing the escape of Buonaparte, or any of his suite, from that ship'. During the day sentries were to be placed specifically for preventing any communication between ship and shore. There was also to be a manned and armed boat kept alongside, ready to take any appropriate action. At night sentinels were to be on duty and the armed boat was to row guard constantly, its crew being relieved every hour. No boat was to approach closer than a cable's length (200 yards) to the *Bellerophon*. When Maitland returned with his orders he found the *Liffey* and *Eurotas* in position. Napoleon declared that he was anxious to see the Admiral and would be content to see him in a private capacity until the British Government decided how he was to be treated. He also complained of the moored frigates, that it was too much. Surely, he said, he was perfectly safe in a battleship. The guard boats had also been firing off their weapons, presumably in order to frighten away sightseers. Napoleon sent a message that he found this disturbing and Maitland had it stopped.

The next morning Maitland had an interview with Keith, pointing out Napoleon's uneasiness created by the newspaper reports regarding St Helena, and mentioned Napoleon's desire to see him even in a private capacity. Keith said that he would 'wait on him to-morrow forenoon.' Several officers of Napoleon's suite were also directed to the *Liffey*. They were being prepared for the final voyage.

Maitland's strict attention to his orders is best illustrated by an incident the same day. In the afternoon, whilst at anchor, a boat carrying Sir Richard and Lady Strachan, along with Mrs Maitland, came alongside. Napoleon was on deck at the time and learning that Mrs Maitland was in the boat, went over to the gangway, doffed his hat in salute and invited her to come up and visit him. She in reply shook her head and Maitland added that his orders were so strict that he could not even allow her on board. Napoleon looked at Maitland and said: 'That is very hard.' Then turning to look at Mrs Maitland: 'Lord Keith is very severe, is he not?' Finally he turned to Maitland and said: 'I assure you her portrait is not very flattering; she is handsomer than it is.' Maitland also pointed out that Sir Richard Strachan was the second-in-command of the Channel Fleet and it would seem that even he did not have the written permission of Admiral Lord Keith to come on board.[59] As in Torbay, the boat was surrounded by sightseers, among them a number of well dressed women. Again, his charm offensive was in play as he commented favourably on them.

That evening Maitland received a letter written that very day by Admiral Keith. In it Keith mused on Napoleon's uneasiness about the matter of St Helena. He ordered Maitland to double all the sentries and take any other measures he deemed appropriate to deter an escape attempt.

Next day, as promised, Keith arrived and was shown into Napoleon's cabin. Napoleon, he said later, looked well, very much like his pictures and that for half an hour he and Napoleon talked about many subjects, such as Toulon and the East Indies. It was a polite meeting, but it did nothing at all to allay Napoleon's fears of being transported to St Helena Island. As Keith came out of his meeting he was intercepted by Madame Bertrand, who drew him aside and repeated what she had said many times to Maitland, that it would be unjust to send the Emperor to the island. If he were to be sent, then she entreated Admiral Keith to 'interfere in preventing her husband at least from going'.

Two days later, on Sunday 30 July, Keith was informed that Major General Sir Harry Bunbury was on his way to Plymouth for a formal interview with Napoleon. Maitland already knew that this would confirm the St Helena rumours, as Keith had already told Maitland. However, Maitland was not to inform Napoleon. That was to be the responsibility of Bunbury and Keith.

The seaborne crush of sightseers around *Bellerophon* was even greater that before. Maitland maintains that 'upwards of a thousand were collected round the ship, in each of which, on an average, there were not fewer than eight people'. If it were only half that number it would still mean that some 4,000 people were on the water wishing to see Boney. Maitland was very alarmed to see that in their desperation to keep the sightseers away one of the guard boats would sometimes run against the small boats, 'with such force as nearly to upset them and alarming the ladies extremely'.

Next day Keith informed Maitland of the conditions laid down in the written order. Napoleon or 'the General', was to be allowed to take three of the senior officers who had accompanied him from France and twelve servants. Savary and Lallemand were not to be permitted to accompany him. Maitland now returned to his ship to await the arrival of Bunbury and Keith. He had now been released from his oath of silence and was able to answer Napoleon's burning question of where was he being sent. Maitland says that he complained about the injustice of the decision but he did so quietly and showed little emotion. Maitland was convinced that as the principal English newspapers had all pointed to St Helena as his final place of imprisonment, it was no shock to Napoleon to have it announced. At that moment the Admiral's barge was seen approaching and Maitland prepared to formally receive both Bunbury and Keith.

After introductions were made, the government's decision, written in English, was proffered. Napoleon asked for it to be translated into French. Keith, never a good linguist, began a stumbling translation until Napoleon halted him and suggested that Bunbury translate. Napoleon, unsurprisingly, objected. He declared that he 'no longer had any power; that he could do no harm; that he would give his word of honour to hold no communication with France'. He said that he had come aboard the *Bellerophon* in good faith, believing that he would be treated as a citizen of England and not as a prisoner of war. He demanded to be treated as an English citizen, subject to the laws of England and told them both that he preferred death to going to St Helena.[60]

In his subsequent report to Melville, Keith added an enclosure. After they had both withdrawn to the quarterdeck, Napoleon had asked to see Keith again – alone. Turning to him he asked his advice. Keith pointed out that as an officer he had discharged his duty on behalf of his government and if Napoleon had anything else to say then he had better call in Sir Henry Bunbury again. At this Napoleon called out:

'Oh no, it is unnecessary.' He then said, 'Can you, after what has passed, detain me until you hear from London?' to which I answered, 'That will depend upon the arrival of the other admiral, of whose instructions I am ignorant.' He then said, 'Is there any Tribunal to which I can apply?' To which I replied: 'I am no lawyer, but I believe none. I am satisfied there is every disposition on the part of the British Government to render your situation as comfortable as is consistent with prudence.'

He immediately took up the papers from the table and said with animation, 'How so; St Helena?' To which I observed, 'Sir, it is surely preferable to being confined in a smaller space in England, or being sent to France, or perhaps to Russia.'
'Russia! Dieu garde!' was his reply.[61]

Maitland had withdrawn from the cabin before the interview began and so knew nothing of the proceedings. However, on being called in half an hour later, he found all of Napoleon's followers gathered there and all of them 'much distressed'. Maitland presented each of them in turn to Keith and Bunbury. He spotted Madame Bertrand attempting to induce Keith to intervene with the Emperor on her behalf, to prevent her husband going with Napoleon to St Helena.

Lallemand and Savary were probably the most distraught of all Napoleon's followers. The royalist French papers had already declared that they were proscribed. Now that they had been excluded from the group of senior officers who might accompany the Emperor to St Helena they both wondered if this was the first step before handing them both over to the French government. This they considered was the only explanation for being excluded. Savary:

Were I to be allowed a fair and impartial trial, I should have nothing to fear, never having accepted a situation under Louis; but at present, when faction runs so high,

I should inevitably be sacrificed to the fury of party. Lallemand's case is quite different: he held a command under the King, and, on Napoleon's return from Elba, joined him with his troops; therefore, his situation would at any time be a dangerous one: – but I lived in the country all the time Louis was in France, and did not come forward until Buonaparte's arrival in Paris, when he directed me to take command of the Gendarmerie.[62]

Savary, an accomplished soldier and diplomat, had spent fours years from 1810 to 1814 as Napoleon's chief of police, after Napoleon had dismissed Fouché. Living quietly during the first Restoration, he had later supported Napoleon during the Hundred Days. In a letter to the Prime Minister from Paris dated 24 July, Castlereagh had referred to both men as 'two very flagrant criminals'.

Devoted to Napoleon, Lallemand, like his brother the artillery officer, had become involved in the plot for Napoleon's return in 1815. At Waterloo Lallemand had commanded the famous *Chasseurs a Cheval de la Garde*. Unfortunately for him, during the first restoration he had accepted both a prestigious award, the *Chevalier de Saint Louis* from the King, as well as a military appointment. Not surprisingly, after Waterloo he had been found guilty of treason and was currently under sentence of death.

Maitland felt some responsibility for them. He had assured Lallemand whilst the *Bellerophon* was lying off Rochefort that having come on board he was immediately under the protection of the British flag. Later that day Maitland, having gained the guarded approval of Lord Keith, wrote directly to Lord Melville. He explained why it was that he felt a commitment to these two: that having given his word that they were safe once on board he felt that his honour would be compromised were they to be arrested and handed over to the government in France. Maitland's impassioned letter may well have ensured that both men were not returned to France to face imprisonment or execution.[63]

As Keith and Bunbury took their leave, Napoleon asked Keith to speak with him privately. Leaving Bunbury he returned and Napoleon asked his advice. Keith refused to give it without having Bunbury present. Napoleon pressed him again. Was there any tribunal to which he could appeal against the decision of the government? Keith assured him that there was not.

Napoleon then took up the papers from the table and gazed at them. Keith quietly reminded him that it was the intention of the British government to ensure that his confinement was as 'comfortable as is consistent with prudence' Once Keith had left the ship Napoleon sent for Maitland again and repeated his complaints. St Helena was

… a perfect horror to me … I would prefer being delivered up to the Bourbons. Among other insults, but that is a mere bagatelle, a very secondary consideration – they style me General! They can have no right to call me General; they may as well call me Archbishop, for I was head of the church, as well as of the army. If they do not acknowledge me as Emperor, they ought as First Consul; they have sent

Ambassadors to me as such; and your King, in his letters styled me brother. Had they confined me in the Tower of London, or one of the fortresses in England, (though not what I had hoped from the generosity of the English people) I should not have so much cause of complaint; but to banish me to an island within the Tropics! They might as well have signed my death warrant at once, as it is impossible a man of my habit of body can live long in such a climate.[64]

Napoleon then took the only course of action open to him. He wrote a letter to the Prince Regent. Maitland that same afternoon delivered the letter to Keith, who in turn sent it on to London. Keith had agreed to passing on the letter, even though he felt it could not influence the decision of the government. If a reply were forthcoming then it would be received before the convoy set sail as Keith estimated that it would be another week before the squadron, currently being assembled, would be ready.

The letter simply repeated the points made in the earlier one to the Prince Regent; that he had come on board voluntarily and that consequently he was not a prisoner of war but a guest. That he had an assurance, given by Captain Maitland, that he would be taken to England if he so requested it. That he would rather live within the interior of England than go to St Helena and die, or be confined in some fortress. He assured the Prince that he did not intend ever again to interfere in the affairs of France.[65]

That evening at dinner Maitland was amazed to see Napoleon conversing pleasantly, as usual: 'It was quite astonishing with what elasticity his spirits regained their usual cheerfulness, after such trials and disappointments.' But not everyone was equal to the tensions of the day. After Napoleon had retired, the French officers and their ladies usually gathered in the wardroom to socialise and to drink a glass of punch or bishop – a mixture of port, Madeira, nutmeg and other ingredients. Maitland was sitting with Montholon when Madame Bertrand came in. Maitland invited her to sit and have a drink with them but she muttered something in reply, which he did not understand, crossed the floor to her cabin and disappeared inside. Montholon, who was more aware that something was amiss, rose and followed her. On entering her cabin he found her half way out of the cabin window. Montholon grabbed hold of her:

There was instantly a shriek from the cabin, and a great uproar; and some one called out 'The Countess is overboard.' I ran upon deck, that, in the event of its being so, a boat might be lowered down, or the guard boats called to her assistance. On looking over the quarter, and seeing no splash in the water, I felt satisfied it was a false alarm.[66]

Maitland later discovered on talking with Montholon that he had found her half out of the gallery window, held back only by the protective metal bar which was placed half way across, precisely to prevent people falling into the sea. He was only able to drag her back in when someone came in to assist him.

Madame Bertrand, having been placed on her bed, was hurling abuse at the English people and the government in both French and English. Lallemand was outside her cabin, walking up and down the wardroom muttering much the same, elaborating on the theme to the effect that it was 'horrible to bring a set of people on board the ship for the purpose of butchering them'. At this, Maitland interrupted him, saying that he could accept and excuse Madame Bertrand's outburst but that he would not accept the abuse which Lallemand was heaping upon his country. Later, as Maitland sat writing his letter to Lord Melville, Lallemand, accompanied by Gourgard and Montholon, came to see him. They raised again the 'cruelty of their situation' concluding that the Emperor would never go to St Helena; that he would sooner commit suicide than go and if he wished it, that the three of them would end his life for him. So ended the Grand Guignol drama of the day.

The next day Maitland reported what had occurred to Keith and showed him the letter he had written regarding Lallemand and Savary. Although Keith did not agree that Maitland's 'honour or character' were impugned he 'saw no harm in the letter'. He also told Maitland to remind the three generals that the punishment for murder was the gallows. After this meeting he met with Bunbury and explained the content of his letter to Lord Melville. Maitland recalled that Bunbury listened without interruption and then said that he would repeat all that he had heard to Lord Melville.[67]

Madame Bertrand remained in bed for the entire day. When Maitland went to see her she abused Napoleon at length – lamenting that her husband was still determined to go with him to St Helena. On another occasion she came into the cabin that Maitland occupied and begged him to write to Lord Keith on her behalf. She implored him not to tell anyone else in the French party. She was sure that Lord Keith could prevent her husband from going to St Helena. She implored Maitland to become involved on her behalf as well, but not surprisingly he declined. Bertrand then vented some of her anger about Napoleon in front of Maitland. He, when he was able to interrupt, reminded her repeatedly that only a wall of canvas separated them from the wardroom, where there was invariably a French officer sitting. Her anger mounted and she reverted from English to French. She had just left him when Montholon arrived and begged to speak to him in his cabin on the quarterdeck. As Maitland had predicted, he had heard everything.

Montholon led him up to his cabin on the quarterdeck. There he found Gourgard and Lallemand. They all three wished to assure him that quite contrary to what she had said in Maitland's cabin, they would all willingly follow the Emperor wherever he was sent and lay down their lives for him. They begged Maitland to keep what she had said a secret. Maitland, wishing to find out if he had been spied upon, refused, unless they revealed how they knew what was being said. There had been no great subterfuge – one of them had been next door in the quarter gallery and overheard everything.

The French were not the only ones who were finding the waiting extremely wearing. Keith admitted in another letter to his daughter, dated 1st August

I am miserable with all the idle people in England coming to see this man. Here is among others my niece Anne, with 'dear friends' she never saw before, arrived from Exmouth! Sir J. Hippisley and Sir H. McLean and family– people all the way from Birmingham – not a bed in all the town … I wish him at the – or anywhere else but here.[68]

Maitland records very little for 2 August but there was clearly the beginning of a change in Napoleon. He did not appear on deck the entire day and he refused to nominate the people who would accompany him. He still hoped to hear that the Government were reconsidering the decision to send him to St Helena. However, for half an hour that day he talked to Maitland. He complained of the cruelty of the decision but also asked him many questions about the island, 'as to its extent, climate, and productions, whether it would be possible to take exercise on horse-back, if there was game of any kind upon it, &c.'[69]

Clearly Napoleon was preparing himself for his fate. Next day he stayed in his cabin. On going to see Lord Keith, Maitland met him escorting some ladies who were with Sir William Lemon.[70] Sir William enquired about the report circulating around Plymouth that Bonaparte had escaped in a boat which came under the *Bellerophon's* stern the night before. Maitland told him no, then immediately left in order to check that all was well. Lieutenant Mott told him that Napoleon had not appeared at breakfast and that the only people who had seen him were 'his own people'. Maitland, not surprisingly, was now anxious and sent across to the *Eurotas* – which watched over the stern of the *Bellerophon* – and enquired if they had seen him at the stern windows. No one had. Maitland now ordered one of his 'young gentlemen' to crawl out on the spanker boom, the boom that juts out over and beyond the stern of the ship, and to look into the stern windows. Still no sighting. Maitland now admitted to being 'extremely uneasy', and finally decided on direct action. He sent his servant into the cabin: 'to bring some paper out, who on entering found the object of my anxiety stretched out on his bed with his clothes on, and the curtains drawn close round him, with every appearance of being unwell.'[71]

This confirmed what Bertrand had said to Maitland earlier, that he had passed a bad night. Later, instead of retiring to his bed, Napoleon was heard pacing about the cabin for some two hours, probably in the company of Bertrand. Consequently, Maitland gave directions that one of the guard-boats was to remain under the stern for the entire night. Napoleon had still not nominated those persons whom he wished to accompany him to St Helena.

At three o'clock in the morning of 4 August a letter from Keith was brought to Maitland. A courier had just arrived from London, with information that the *Bellerophon* would probably be required to put to sea, 'at a moment's notice'. At daybreak Maitland had the ship readied. Maitland was aware that many of the French party seemed alarmed and 'annoyed by all the preparations'. They repeatedly questioned him as to why there was such a hurry to prepare for sea at the break of day. Maitland could not give an explanation.

Matters became clearer when Maitland reported to Keith some time before eight o'clock that morning. Keith now knew that a lawyer, Alexander Mackenrot, was in Plymouth to serve a writ of *Habeus Corpus* on Napoleon. Mackenrot was a minor West Indian lawyer, who, it seems, felt a great need to draw attention to himself. The document required the attendance of Napoleon in the court of King's Bench in November. The reason given in the writ for this bizarre legal move was that Mackenrot was involved in a civil high court case against Admiral Sir Alexander Cochrane. Cochrane was suing Mackenrot for libel after Mackenrot claimed that he had failed to attack the combined naval squadron of Williamez and Jerome Bonaparte in the West Indies in 1807.

Mackenrot wanted Napoleon to appear in court as a witness for his defence. Bonaparte, he claimed, would be able to show that in 1807, Williamez's squadron was in a poor state of repair and therefore vulnerable to attack by Cochrane. In his original application, made in early June 1815, Mackenrot had wanted to call both Admiral Willliamez and Jerome Bonaparte. It would seem that one of the great movers in the Foxite Whig circle of Bonapartists, the lawyer Capel Lofft, was linked to Mackenrot. As the one pursued Napoleon's person across Portsmouth, the other was pursuing a correspondence in the national press.

Keith was not clear in his own mind about the legal niceties of his prisoner's situation, even though his orders from government were consistently clear: the man was not to be put ashore, under any circumstances. At the same time, as a servant of the crown Keith did not wish to appear to flout the English legal system. From Keith's standpoint, not allowing the writ to be served saved a great deal of potential embarrassment. Whether he was right or wrong in this regard is almost irrelevant. The opposition in Parliament could appear morally outraged in the press, making a case (however flawed) that the Admiral was defying the laws of Britain. Maitland, in an extensive footnote in his memoirs, cites an unnamed barrister who maintained that as Napoleon was a prisoner of war, he could not be summonsed to appear as a witness in a British criminal or civil case. In Melville's opinion, Mackenrot was mentally unstable. Mackenrot had first appeared at Keith's house, on 3 August, but had found only Keith's secretary there, Mr Meek, who informed Mackenrot that Lord Keith had finished work for the day. Meek did not offer any further suggestions as to where he might have gone. As soon as Mackenrot left, Meek set off to inform Keith on board the *Tonnant* that the problem, in the form of Mackenrot, had arrived.

Keith meanwhile was busy reacting to the courier message and was already preparing to put to sea. Having stepped out from Keith's house Mackenrot then presumably asked along the quayside where Lord Keith was likely to be and discovered that Keith had been rowed out to the *Tonnant*. The next morning he hired a cutter and had himself rowed out there.

On coming on board the *Tonnant* he was met by Captain Brenton, who clearly had no time for this friend of Napoleon. Brenton declared that as Mackenrot was so keen to free Napoleon, he would only speak to Mackenrot in French. Meanwhile, in slapstick fashion, Keith was having himself rowed away from the

Tonnant in his barge. On looking about him Mackenrot saw the Admiral's barge heading away. Breaking off from his irritating conversation with Brenton he once more set off in pursuit of Keith. Unfortunately for Mackenrot the Admiral's barge could not be caught and it finally disappeared as it went round Rame Head. Here, Admiral Keith found the *Prometheus*, which he boarded. From her Keith sent a note to Maitland, presumably unaware that the latter was experiencing his own difficulties with Mackenrot:

> Received August 4th, in the afternoon.
> I have been chased all day by a lawyer with a Habeas Corpus: he is landed at Cawsand, and may come off in a sailing-boat during the night; of course, keep all sorts of boats off, as I will do the like in whatever ship I may be in.
> KEITH

At the same time, the *Bellerophon*, having received the signal to weigh anchor was slowly being towed out of Plymouth Sound. The flood tide and a light wind were against them and so Maitland had ordered the guard boats to tow her out. They had barely begun when a 'suspicious looking person in a boat' was seen approaching. It was Mackenrot. If he could not subpoena Keith to produce Napoleon, then he could deliver his subpoena to Napoleon through Maitland. Maitland was aware, from Keith, that a writ of habeas corpus was to be delivered up to him. Here was the enormous battleship, *Bellerophon*, running from a rowing boat. Maitland at once ordered one of the guard boats to stop towing and move to the stern in order to stop anyone boarding.

On Maitland's return to the ship, even Napoleon was concerned now. Why was there this sudden urgency about the ship? What did it mean? Maitland told him that it was intended that his transfer to the *Northumberland*, the ship that would take him to St Helena, should take place at sea. They were sailing to meet that ship. In reply Napoleon asked him to write to Keith saying that he would very much like to see him. Bertrand also asked Maitland for the current newspapers in order to glean some idea of what was to happen to them. Maitland wrote to Keith, who declined to attend, but who informed Napoleon that the government had not in any way altered their previous instructions for his detention on St Helena.

Keith now asked that the list of persons who were to accompany him should be prepared. This information Maitland passed onto Bertrand, who immediately went into Napoleon's cabin. On his coming out Maitland pressed him for the list. Bertrand looked at Maitland and said: 'The Emperor will not go to St Helena.' In a private letter to Lady Keith later that same day, the Admiral wrote:

> What a mercy I left the house before the constable came to it. He followed me to *Tonnant*: I left that ship and went to the *Eurotas*, he followed; I went out at the opposite side and rowed to sea. Neither of the Captains were in their ships (so much for wives!). After a time I landed at Cawsand, but my friend followed. I therefore went out to the point and got on board the *Prometheus*, and remained till dark, when I had

seen the man land at Cawsand. I should have been had up before the Justice; and Bony under my wing till November next![72]

On 5 August Napoleon, having worked in his sleeping cabin, even taking his meals there, had produced another letter of protest for the Prince Regent.[73] In it he protested again that his 'most sacred rights' had been violated, that he had been forcibly robbed of his 'liberty'. He claimed to be a 'guest of England' as the Captain of the *Bellerophon* had 'instigated' the invitation; and that Maitland had told him that he had orders from the British Government to receive him and his suite and to carry them to England. He pointed out that as he had boarded the *Bellerophon* he was under the protection of English law.

What he did not explain in the protest was that he had fled from Paris and an ambivalent population and that the flags of the Bourbons had begun to compete with the Tricolour amongst the roofs of Rochelle and Rochefort. These were pressing reasons for coming on board. When the proposals for embarking on the two French frigates and fighting their way out of Rochefort had been suggested he had found that only one of the captains was an ardent Bonapartist. The other proposal, to hide in a small merchant vessel and hope to good luck to see them past the blockade and across the Atlantic Ocean to the United States was a miserable idea. He had been appalled at the idea of the international public humiliation he would have to endure, if he had been caught.

There is no reason to suppose that Maitland did anything other than keep the trap door open. There was nowhere else for Napoleon to go. He was not pushed into the *Bellerophon* – he jumped. Had Britain 'disgraced its flag'? Captain Maitland had repeatedly asserted that he did not know what would happen to Napoleon on their arriving in England. He had correctly surmised that Napoleon would be a prisoner and not the recipient of a 'friendly hand' and had remained silent. He was not the only one to keep quiet. Las Cases had remained silent about his ability to speak and understand English. These were both political manoeuvrings as the one-sided negotiations began. Napoleon could not compete. He speaks in the letter as though he had options – ultimately, the power to say no. But he had been declared an outlaw at Vienna, had been crushed on the battlefield, lost much of his brittle popular support at home and fled to the coast. The Bourbons were in his (or their) capital. Napoleon had physically moved out of Paris to Malmaison and then on to the coast. He had then moved from Rochefort to the tiny Isle d'Aix. He could go no further – it was a case of swim or surrender.

On the morning of 6 August Maitland spoke with Napoleon who complained again about the conduct of the British Government. Napoleon told him that he could have chosen to accept the protection of the troops from Rochelle who offered to take him back to the army that still adored him. He explained his refusal – with some special pleading – as he saw

... there was no prospect of ultimate success, though I might have occasioned a great deal of trouble and bloodshed, which I did not choose should take place

Admiral Sir George Cockburn in later life. He ensured that Napoleon was treated with respect both on board ship and on the island as a senior general officer. A professional sailor, he would support the modernisation of the Navy for the steam age. Courtesy of the St Helena Archive.

on my account individually – while the empire was at stake, it was another matter.[74]

At nine o'clock, with 'fresh breezes and cloudy weather' the *Northumberland* appeared and the entire squadron moved to the west of Berry Head and anchored in twenty fathoms. Along with the *Tonnant* were the *Bellerophon*, the *Nimble* and *Eurotas*. The *Actaeon* had been left behind in order to direct the other vessels coming from Plymouth to the assembly point. At four o'clock they were joined by the *Bucephalus* and *Ceylon*. Maitland was able to tell Lord Keith that Bonaparte had finally decided to move from the *Bellerophon* to the *Northumberland*, 'without force being used' and that Count Bertrand wished to see him in order to discuss the movements of the people who would accompany Napoleon. Bertrand then met with Admiral Cockburn, on board the *Tonnant*.

At the same time on board the *Bellerophon*, the ship's surgeon, Mr O'Meara, told Maitland that he had been asked to accompany Bonaparte to St Helena as his surgeon. His French doctor, Monsieur Maingaud, had suffered badly with sea-sickness and could not face the voyage. Maitland urged him to go 'if it appealed' but reminded him that first he must gain the approval of the Admiral and of the government, and a guarantee from the government that he would be paid his salary whilst in that post. Quite unknowingly, Maitland and Keith facili-tated the inclusion of the most dangerous man in Napoleon's band of followers. With his caricatures of Sir Hudson Lowe, he would create a sensation amongst thousands of both ardent and lukewarm supporters of Napoleon across Europe. This exchange between Mr O'Meara and Maitland was the first intimation that Napoleon was thinking seriously about the people who would accompany him.

That evening on board the *Bellerophon*, Bertrand and Montholon were busy drawing up lists of what would be required for the French party to live on the island. Lord Keith brought Admiral Cockburn and introduced him to Napoleon. Once Bertrand had completed his list, and was free, Maitland told him that Napoleon would be removed to the *Northumberland* the following day. He also imparted Keith's instruction that all arms were to be removed from him and his suite – these would be returned once they had reached their destination. Maitland reported that Bertrand 'seemed much hurt'.

This seems a strangely insensitive comment from Maitland, given the thought-ful manner in which he had, up to that moment, cared for his prisoners. His male prisoners were being asked to give up one of the principal symbols of their status as both soldiers and gentlemen, their swords. Waterloo had taken place less than two months previously, they were defeated but at least they retained the trap-pings of their profession. These swords, more than their pistols, represented their once great authority. It was a small act, a petty humiliation and it clearly affected Bertrand.

Keith appeared before Napoleon with both Admiral Sir George Cockburn and Mr Meek. Again Napoleon protested, 'repeating in detail, and almost verba-tim' how he was not a prisoner, but a guest who was entitled to the protection of British law; that he was entitled to all the protection that a Habeas Corpus could afford and that this was being actively denied him; that he was only addressed as 'General' even though in other years his ambassador had represented him as First Consul. In reply, Keith reminded Napoleon, again, that both he and Sir George Cockburn could accept no plea or demand made by him as they were

> ... officers in the execution of duty prescribed to us by our superiors, we could only listen to the remarks he had made, but were not authorised to answer them. The General replied that he was perfectly aware of it; but as we were the only persons permitted to approach him, he owed it to himself and to the world to protest before us, and he did it in the most earnest manner, against the measures pursued by our Government with regard to him; adding that he trusted a faithful report would be made of all he had said.[75]

Cockburn then asked at what hour he would be ready to transfer to the *Northumberland* and it was agreed that sometime after breakfast, after ten, would be acceptable. Later that night, Maitland received an amended order from Keith. Napoleon might cross to the other vessel wearing his sword. Had Maitland told Keith of Bertrand's reaction? Perhaps. It certainly avoided providing a new bone of contention for Napoleon to gnaw on.

That same evening Napoleon sent for Maitland and asked whether he would write to Bertrand, outlining the orders he had received for his forced removal to the *Northumberland*. Napoleon wanted some evidence to show that he had objected to his removal to the Island. Before Maitland left, he condemned the government once more, stating that he had only wanted to purchase a small property in England and end his life there in peace and tranquillity, as opposed to passing the rest of his life 'on a desert island'.

The next morning there was a fresh breeze, hazy weather and light airs. At eight o'clock Las Cases delivered another letter of protest to Lord Keith on behalf of Napoleon. He explained once more that on first coming on board the *Bellerophon*, Captain Maitland had promised that Napoleon would be allowed to remain in England. In Las Cases' memoirs he claims that the Admiral became very angry at this, declaring that if Captain Maitland had given such an assurance he must have been a fool to do so.

That afternoon Maitland would receive a note from Keith, asking him to comment on these assertions. However, this interview did not disrupt the day's preparations. Napoleon would leave the *Bellerophon* for the *Northumberland*. The day was charged with tension. General Gourgard discovered that his name was not on the final list of those who would accompany the Emperor and used 'some very strong language' to General Bertrand. Finally, on the intervention of the Emperor, he replaced Colonel Planat on the list. All the while the ship's boats plied between the *Bellerophon* and *Northumberland* transferring the property of the French party.

Not surprisingly, Madame Bertrand still had not come to terms with the impending transfer and removal to St Helena. Captain Maitland had remained at the breakfast table as a matter of courtesy to Bertrand, who came to it very late after completing preparations for the transfer. He had only sat a little time when Madame Bertrand turned to him and demanded that he leave the Emperor and remain in England. Bertrand sat, 'distressed and silent'. Madame Bertrand then turned to Maitland and begged him to give an opinion on the matter. He reminded her that she had already demanded an opinion from him on these 'unpleasant dis-cussions', saying 'If your husband quits his master at such a time as the present he will forfeit the very high character he now bears in this country.'[76]

With that he rose and went out onto the deck. Madame Bertrand was not to be silenced so easily for she shortly afterwards followed him out and asked whether it were true that the Emperor was not to have the whole of the after cabin on board the *Northumberland*. On learning that this was the case she said: 'They had better treat him like a dog at once, and put him down in the hold.'[77]

At this remark, Maitland's patience finally ran out and he told her exactly what he thought of her: that she was a 'foolish woman', without respect for his government and that it would be better if she did not speak to him at all. But she did return later in the morning in a conciliatory manner to ask to shake hands with him. Much more flattering for Maitland was the final interview he had with Napoleon:

> I have sent for you to express my gratitude for your conduct to me, while I have been on board the ship you command. My reception in England has been very different from what I expected; but you throughout have behaved like a man of honour; and I request that you will accept my thanks, as well as convey then to the officers and ship's company of the *Bellerophon*.[78]

He then asked for Maitland's opinion of O'Meara, both as to his character and as a medical man. Maitland, spoke highly of him, praising him as a man of 'principle' and of 'integrity'. O'Meara was not to live up to this character reference. In July 1818 he would be dismissed from his position and expelled from the island. Napoleon also spoke affectionately about General Bertrand, alluding to the 'strong efforts' that Madame Bertrand had made to dissuade her husband from accompanying him to the island.

At nine-thirty Cockburn came on board the *Bellerophon* with the task of searching Napoleon's personal baggage. He was instructed to ensure that a member of Napoleon's suite attended the opening of the trunks. Bertrand found the whole matter so insulting to the Emperor that he refused to attend or to appoint anyone else in his place. General Savary agreed and was present along with Marchand. Maitland says that the tops of the trunks were 'merely opened' and Mr Byng, Cockburn's secretary, 'passed his hand down the side, but the things were not unpacked'. When they came to two boxes containing money, Marchand was allowed to take out monies for those servants who were not accompanying the Emperor to St Helena. The remaining monies were handed over to Maitland, who on his return to London delivered it over to the permanent governor, who in turn would hold it on behalf of Napoleon.

Maitland believed that when the after cabin door was opened and Napoleon briefly saw Mr Byng, he acknowledged 'the delicate manner in which he conducted the search' by bowing to him. Hidden money would travel to St Helena.

At about this time Montholon came to see Maitland and asked him for a second time whether he would be willing to accept, as a personal gift from the Emperor, a box studded with diamonds that bore his portrait. Maitland, again with great regret, refused the generous gesture, saying it would be highly improper. On the journey from Rochefort, Madame Montholon had broached the subject of Maitland accepting a personal gift from the Emperor, which Maitland had politely declined. However at some point Maitland did acquire a tumbler from the Emperor's travelling case, which bore Josephine's cipher upon it.[79]

At eleven, Lord Keith in his dress uniform came alongside in the *Tonnant's* barge, ready to accompany Napoleon across to the *Northumberland*. The bosun's whistle shrieked, the Royal Marines presented arms and the Admiral, accompanied by Rear-Admiral Cockburn, came up the side. General Bertrand reported to the Emperor that the Admiral had arrived – and everyone waited. Keith and Cockburn talked, Keith inspected the marines and told Captain Maitland about the slurs made against his name by Las Cases that morning. Cockburn was anxious to move Napoleon and said with some irritation in his voice that Napoleon should be reminded of who he was keeping waiting. Keith urged him to be patient, reminding Cockburn that much greater men than they had waited longer hours to see him. After more waiting, Keith was invited in to see Napoleon. After an exchange of pleasantries Napoleon returned to his protests:

'Would you go to St Helena Admiral? – Oh, no, *Plutôt la Mort*. I will not leave this ship, you must take my by force.'

'Surely you will not reduce an officer like [me] to a measure so disagreeable.'

'Oh no! But you shall order me,' and at the door of the outer cabin he said: 'Admiral I have given you my solemn protest in writing. I now repeat I will not go out of this ship but by force – you must order me.'

'My barge is ready for your reception, and if you choose to go in her, please to warn them and the ladies. It depends on you, and I order you to go.'

'Allons.'[80]

At one o'clock Napoleon emerged from his cabin with Keith. At a nod from Lord Keith, a roll appropriate for a general officer was beaten on the drums and

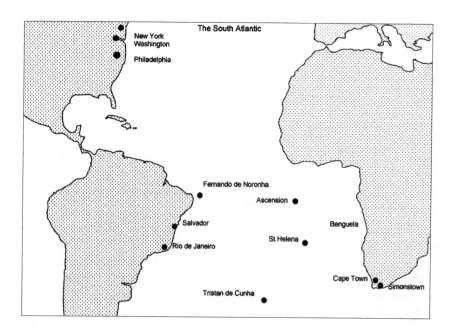

the marines presented arms. Emerging with a firm step Napoleon went up to Maitland, took off his hat and thanked him. He then turned to Maitland's assembled officers, thanked them, walked to the gangway, paused and bowed two or three times to the ship's company who were gathered in the waist and forecastle, before descending into the barge. His officers and their wives followed him and finally Lord Keith followed on. After the barge had gone thirty yards, he stood and bowed again before sitting down and engaging Lord Keith in conversation. Maitland commented on Napoleon's 'apparent composure, as if he had been only going from one ship to the other to pay a visit'.

As he sat with Keith he conversed about St Helena, laughed at the ladies complaining about feeling seasick and questioned Keith about the *Tonnant*. Was she the ship that had fought at the battle of the Nile? How old was the *Bellerophon* and why had Keith changed his name from Elphinstone to Keith? He continued with his rapid questioning as they came up into the *Northumberland*. Shortly afterwards, having formally handed him over to Admiral Cockburn, Keith took his leave, returning to the *Tonnant*.

Maitland did see Napoleon once more, later that same day when he went on board the *Northumberland* to bring generals Lallemand and Savary back to the *Bellerophon*. They were saying their final farewells to the Emperor. They were allowed some time alone with Napoleon before Maitland went into the after cabin to remind them that it was time to return to the *Bellerophon*.

> ... he embraced each of them most affectionately, after the French manner, putting his arms round them, and touching their cheeks with his. He was firm and collected; but, in turning from him, the tears were streaming from their eyes.[81]

Shortly afterwards, with the summer sun fading, Keith threw out the signal to make sail. The group of ships then parted, with *Tonnant*, *Bellerophon* and her accompanying smaller craft returning to Plymouth and the *Northumberland* and her squadron making sail for St Helena.

Notes

1 Maitland, F., *Narrative of the Surrender of Bonaparte*, Blackwood & Sons, Edinburgh & London, 1904, pages V–VI.

2 Most of the information for this sketch of Keith come from McCranie, K. D., *Admiral Lord Keith and the Naval War against Napoleon*, Uni. Press of Florida, 2006.

3 Unfortunately, news of this treaty came too late to prevent the British reverse at the Battle of New Orleans on 8 January, 1815.

4 Undated secret letter to Hotham from Rear Admiral Hallowell DDHO/7/13/7.

5 Substance of orders given to Captain Senhouse, DDHO/7/12/6.

6 Maitland, F., *Narrative of the Surrender of Bonaparte*, Henry Colburn, 1826, Second Edition, page 4.

7 There was no significant French naval threat during the Waterloo Campaign, so much so that on 19 June Keith received orders directing him to send four battleships of the Channel Fleet into port. Kerry, Earl of (Ed.) *The First Napoleon: some unpublished documents from the Bowood Papers*, Constable & Co., London 1925, page 141.

8 Maitland, F., op cit., 1826, pages 5–6.

9 Keith's journal for 22 June, in Kerry, Earl of (Ed.) op. cit., page 143.

10 Shortly after receiving the letter whilst moving away from the land to carry out target practice Maitland spied a white object on the water. This turned out to be a shallow punt with two teenagers on board who had lost an oar. He retrieved them from the ocean. They were exhausted, having been in the bay for 36 hours. After two days on board, having been fed they were returned to the shore and their parents. Maitland, op cit., page 10.

11 A handwritten note from Keith, dated 2nd July, received from the *Ferret* on the 6th July. DDHO/7/13/. Croker informed Keith of a passport application in a letter from the Admiralty dated 1 July, 1815: Lloyd, C., *The Keith Papers*, Vol II, Naval Records Society, 1955.

12 Lloyd, C., op cit, p.349, letter written on board *Superb*, 6 July, 1815 to Lord Keith.

13 Lachouque, H., *The Last Days of Napoleon's Empire*, Allen & Unwin, 1966, page 172.

14 Ibid., page 172.

15 The Royal Navy had extensive experience of the Basque Roads. In 1809 Admiral Lord Gambier had bottled up the squadron of Admiral Williameuz in the Basque Roads. This was followed by an audacious attack using fireships and explosion vessels, led by the remarkable Captain Lord Cochrane, better known as 'The Sea Wolf', and the model for Patrick O'Brian's Jack Aubrey.

16 Letter from Maitland to Hotham dated 5 July, 1815 in DDHO/7/13/7.

17 Ibid., DDHO/7/13/7.

18 Letter from Earl Bathurst dated, 26 June 1815, DDHO/7/13/7.

19 Letter from Maitland to Hotham dated 5 July 1815 in DDHO/7/13/7.

20 Lachouque, H., op. cit., pages 190–191.

21 Lachouque, H., ibid, page 194.

22 Letter from Brine to Hotham, dated 9 July, DDHO/7/13/7.

23 Keith's journal, letter to Hotham, for 10 July, quoted in Kerry, Earl of, ibid, Bowood, page 149.

24 Maitland, F., op. cit., pages 28–29.

25 Ibid., pages 36–37.

27 Lt. John Bowerbank in Shorter, C. (Ed.), *Napoleon and his Fellow Travellers*, Cassell, 1908, page 304.

28 Maitland, F., op. cit., 1904, page 44.

29 In 1810 Lucien and his family had been intercepted by a British warship, in the American ship *Hercules*. They spent three months interned in Malta before being transferred to England. Here, using monies he had in a British bank, he bought Thorngrove in Worcestershire where he lived the life of a country squire for the next four years, going to hunt balls at local assembly rooms. Cited in Seward, D., *Napoleon's Family*, Viking Penguin, New York, 1986, page 121.

30 Maitland, F., op. cit., 1904, page 45.

31 Letter to Hotham from Maitland, DDHO/7/13/7.

32 Maitland, F., op. cit., 1904, pages 56–57.

33 They were small decked vessels, only ever intended for coastal work. The idea of them taking Napoleon and his suite, as well as their supplies, seems very impractical. One plan offered by a midshipmen in Rochefort was that with a picked crew he could make for the open sea, overpower a passing merchant vessel and transfer the Emperor and a few of his followers, then head for the United States.

34 Lt John Bowerbank in his journal quoted in, Shorter, C., *Napoleon and his Fellow Travellers*, Cassell and Co., 1908, page 305.

35 Ibid., page 304.

36 Maitland op. cit., 1904, page 80.

37 Ibid., page 81–82.

38 Ibid., page 81.

39 Copy of a letter from Captain Senhouse to his wife, DDHO/7/13.

40 Maitland op. cit., page 84.

41 Copy of a letter from Captain Senhouse, op. cit.

42 Las Cases had been a Naval officer for a brief time before the Revolution.

43 Copy of a letter from Captain Senhouse to his wife, op. cit.

44 Extract or orders given to Maitland off Rochefort on 15 July, 1815. Quoted in Maitland, op cit., pages 95–96.

45 Kerry, Earl of, Confidential Admiralty letter to Keith from Melville, dated 25th July, 1815, op. cit., page 157.

46 Ibid., page 158.

47 On 25 July, 1815, the *Bacchus* would board the American merchant vessel, *Commerce* off the French coast. Officers came on board to examine the papers of the passengers. They found a Spaniard, an American and several Frenchman, including a M. Surviglieri, who remained in his cabin. As Napoleon had already surrendered they had no reason to detain anyone. The man within the cabin was Napoleon's older brother, Joseph, former King of Spain. Described in Stroud, P.T., *The man who had been King*, Univ. Of Pennsylvania Press, 2005, page 1.

48 Maitland, op cit., pages 100.

49 Letter from Ephraim Graebke, Assistant Surgeon on Bellerophon, to his mother, in: Maitland, Frederick, op. cit., 1904, page 242.

50 Quoted in Maitland, op. cit., 1826, pages 110–111.

51 Shorter, C., *Napoleon's Fellow Travellers,* Cassell & Co., 1908, page 296 and in *The Bowood Papers*, page 144.

52 The *Bellerophon* was followed into the bay by the *Myrmidon*, who had the rest of Napoleon's followers on board. Shorter, C., op. cit, page 297.

53 All the extracts by John Smart are taken from Shorter, C., *Napoleon's Fellow Travellers*.

54 Letter to Mr J. P. Taylor, at Newton Abbott, from the Revd Froude of Totnes, NMM.

55 Wright, a naval officer had been arrested in France and charged with landing French agents who were involved in a plot to assassinate Napoleon.

56 Quoted in, Thornton, M., *Napoleon after Waterloo*, Stanford University Press, 1968, page 72.

57 On emerging from his first interview with Napoleon. Quoted in, Thornton, M., ibid, page 106.

58 In a letter to his eldest daughter, dated 25th July in Kerry, Earl of, op. cit., page 155.

59 Maitland, op. cit., 1826, pages 134–135.

60 Maitland, op. cit., 1826, page 143.

61 An enclosure to a letter, dated 31st July 1815, quoted in Kerry, op. cit., pages 164–165.

62 Maitland had known Lallemand when the former had been a prisoner in the *Camelion*, under his command, in Egypt. Cited in Maitland, op. cit, page 41. Savary speaking of his appointment on Napoleon's return from Elba, page 146, also in Maitland.

63 Ibid., 1826, pages 148–149.

64 Ibid., 1826, pages 144–145.

65 Napoleon to Lord Keith, quoted in Kerry, op. cit, page 166.

66 Maitland, op. cit., 1826, pages 152.

67 Ibid., 1826, pages 155.

68 Letter from Lord Keith to his daughter, quoted in Kerry, op. cit, page 167.

69 Maitland, op. cit., 1826, page 161.

70 Sir William Lemon was a Cornish MP and local mine owner.

71 Maitland, op. cit., 1826, page 163.

72 Kerry op cit, page 168.

73 See the letter in the appendices.

74 Maitland op. cit., p182.

75 Lord Keith to Melville, quoted in Kerry, op. cit., page 173.

76 Maitland, op. cit., 1826, page 195.

77 Ibid., 1826, page 195.

78 Ibid., 1826, page 197.

79 In the preface to the 1904 edition of Maitland's memoirs, W. K. D. states that 'On Maitland's declining, in the circumstances, to accept any present of value, the Emperor begged him to keep as a souvenir a tumbler from his travelling case, bearing the crown and cipher of the Empress Josephine.' Page xiii.

80 Kerry, op, cit., pages 176–7.

81 Maitland, op. cit., 1826, page 207.

Chapter Four

His British Admirers

To consign to distant exile and imprisonment a foreign and captive chief, who, after the abdication of his authority, relying on British generosity, had surrendered himself to us, in preference to his other enemies, is unworthy of the magnanimity of a great country; and the treaties by which, after his captivity, we bound ourselves to detain him in custody at the will of the Sovereigns to whom he had never surrendered himself, appear to me repugnant to the principles of equity and utterly uncalled for by expediency or necessity.[1]
Lord Holland

Unfortunately for Holland this heartfelt plea for magnanimity met with a very cold response in the House of Lords in April 1816. The government was pushing through a bill to legalise the detention of Napoleon on St Helena. The country had had enough of Bonaparte even if Holland had not.

Lord and Lady Holland appear as minor characters throughout Napoleon's years in power, the former a great liberal political theorist and the latter more than a little in love with the liberal image that Napoleon had created of himself. Henry Hallam, the historian and member of the Holland House circle admitted at the time:

I once wished that Buonaparte should have found a tranquil asylum in this island; but, when I see the foolish admiration which many persons entertain for that man, and the still more foolish association of his name with the love of liberty, I cannot desire to see his Court, as it were, frequented by all the discontented, as well as all the idle and curious.[2]

Even in Britain, he felt, it would have been necessary to adopt security measures almost as severe as those in place on St Helena. The economic downturn that followed the end of the wars in mainland Britain and the troubles in Ireland were other reasons why it was better that he did not reside in Britain.

Henry Richard Fox, 3rd Lord Holland, was the nephew of that great political beast of the Whig party, Charles James Fox. They had an excellent personal relationship and it was Fox who organised a grand tour of Europe for Holland. In 1794 Holland met Lady Elizabeth Webster in Naples and began a passionate affair which resulted in her refusing to return to England and to her divorce. In 1796 she gave birth to Holland's child and later travelled home with him and they then married quietly in London. The path of their future life together was set. As a divorcée, with an illegitimate child, Lady Holland could not be presented at court. Her situation was then made worse by the revelation that in order to keep Harriet Webster – her daughter by her previous marriage – with her in Italy, she had arranged a sham illness, death and burial for the girl.

Whatever else the Italian business had shown it did reveal clearly how determined she could be. This strength she now gave to her husband. They were to live at their London home, Holland House, a Jacobean mansion in what is now Holland Park, London. Lady Holland began to host political and literary parties that soon ranked amongst the most prestigious in Europe. Despite her initial lack of interest in politics, he seems to have quickly won her over to his passion for political matters. She in turn brought him a fortune and he brought one of the greatest names in British politics. There was also their own wit and presence, one observer likening them to the opposite poles of a magnet, 'he attractive and she repulsive'. Together they hosted the Holland House set who were a significant influence on British political life throughout this period and beyond.

The set was open to all. The one defining qualification for entry being that one had to be interesting, mediocrity was as unwelcome as literary ineptitude. Though it was never so modern or populist in outlook that it supported democracy. As with the insurrection in Spain, Lord Holland saw the Whig landed classes in Britain leading the rest of the nation forward.

For Holland the revolution of 1789 could not be unmade and any attempt to use arms to unseat Napoleon was to be deplored. As far as he was concerned France should be left to resolve its internal problems without external interference. Far better that a deeply flawed Bonaparte dynasty rule France than a Bourbon one, which had ruined France, be restored. Bonaparte was the lesser of two evils. When the peace of Amiens was signed in 1802 both Holland and Fox were pleased, though a little disturbed by what they had seen of Napoleon – Fox and Holland had met Napoleon in 1802. They had both been disappointed with his imperial posturing and dislike of political freedom. He in turn had put himself out to flatter Fox, praising him as one of the greatest Englishmen ever. Napoleon was then both displeased and irritated when Fox had openly interrupted his monologue and criticised his aggressive foreign policy. In Napoleon they saw a man enacting liberal policies across Europe but forever drawing the reins of power back to Paris and himself. What they had hoped for at that stage was a set of events which would echo the English Revolution of 1688.

Holland never seemed aware of the strategic and trade elements within national politics. Here he was, shortly after Waterloo, demanding 'fair play' for Napoleon whilst the wounded from the battle were still recovering or dying. This blinkered approach to politics can be found in his critical reports from Spain in 1808 when

Sir John Moore, began his desperate retreat to Corunna. Writing to England from Spain Holland proposed several impractical schemes for supporting the local juntas and at the same time criticising Moore and his generals. There was no reference to the huge French armies that were bearing down on the British. At the time Lord Auckland writing to London from Spain, declared in exasperation that Holland was prepared to 'sacrifice ten Englishmen in order to save one Spaniard'.

Holland had no faith in the newly restored Louis XVIII who re-entered Paris in 1814, nor in the written constitution which was supposed to give authority to the new king. The Hollands made their way to Paris to see for themselves. The 'ultras', the conservative royalists, were as determined as ever to recover their estates. On his return Holland, speaking in Parliament, revealed what everyone already knew, that the Bourbons were only maintained on their throne by the presence of a foreign army, which had previously fought the French army.[4] The French people also saw that their king was on his throne because of this occupying force. Louis, in turn, pushed by the ultras and a faction of the church, was driven further away from the new middle classes and thus further away from the nation.

That Lady Holland was devoted to the idea of Napoleon is not in doubt but what is more difficult to assess is Lord Holland's attitude the great man. There was never to be a clear answer to this. As far as Holland was concerned, every time he carried out a political or military act, Napoleon was to be judged. If he was found to be illiberal he was condemned and if he promoted the greater good of mankind then he was to be praised. It was not surprising therefore that some people, seeking a simpler label for Lord Holland, took his wife's unwavering hero worship of Napoleon as typical of both.

Understanding Bonaparte and supporting the good he did became more difficult when examining his foreign policy. Strategic and trading threats to Britain remained but there were aspects of his European policies which they believed they could support. In July 1815, a month after Waterloo, Holland wrote from Germany to his sister. He expected to see 'interminable wars' in every part of Europe as people who had benefited from the Napoleonic interlude awaited the return of their previous feudal masters. Specifically he had in mind the Russians and Prussians or the 'northern barbarians' as he called them. To those who had family members serving under Wellington or at sea with the Royal Navy Holland must have seemed very disloyal.

Unlike Lady Holland, Lord Holland was never a blinkered admirer of Napoleon. Having travelled through Spain and admired the liberal elements of that society he believed passionately in the fight against Napoleon and yet in central Europe he praised him for sweeping away the old petty princes who ruled as autocrats. Wherever Napoleon seemed to deny national independence, he was to be opposed and where he overturned feudal rulers he was to be praised. However as a basis for deciding and delivering national policy this approach was clearly extremely indulgent. Almost every other British politician saw no prospect of peace with Napoleon on the throne of France. War alone was the only means of removing him from power and restoring the balance of power in Europe. By their bizarre disregard for the necessities of everyday political life Holland House and its inhabitants spoiled their chances of promoting the interests of Napoleon by creating an impression that they were 'Bonaparte mad'.

Napoleon at different times hoped that Holland would, on the fall of the Tory government, occupy a significant office in government enabling him to intercede and ultimately bring him home to Europe. Holland, contrary to Napoleon's wishful thinking was never to be his puppet, he was well beyond the reach of either Napoleon or political pressure. Consequently he had little political power. As a man his principled passion for politics was respected but he was of little use to the Whig cause as he was not interested in the day-to-day practical politics of negotiation and compromise.

Early in 1817, Holland stood to address the House of Lords on the subject of Napoleon's alleged ill treatment on the island of St Helena. He was well aware that his was a lone voice. He accepted that the government pursued their actions guided by 'necessity', for the safety of the nation and 'the tranquility of Europe':

> Owing, it was said, to the character of the man, and to the events which had occurred in Europe, it became necessary that this extraordinary person should be detained in this extraordinary manner: and an act of parliament was passed for that purpose.

He was not such a 'coxcomb' that he was going to rake over that old ground. Neither, he said, was this to be an attack upon the governor, whom he knew personally to be a 'gallant officer'. He had received a set of complaints, recently smuggled out of the island, entitled *The Remonstrance*. It was the complaints laid out in this document that he wished the government to respond to.

It was a paper, ostensibly written by Montholon, but of course dictated by Napoleon, published on several occasions in Britain and torn apart in the *Quarterly Review*. At the same time, also in circulation in Britain, was a thin and miserable work, entitled: *An Appeal to the British Nation* which even Napoleon denounced as nonsense. Purportedly written by one of Napoleon's servants, Santini, it was later believed that a Colonel Maceroni, who had never been to St Helena, had written the paper.

There were, said Holland, 'rumours and reports in circulation', some of which were more credible than others, that Napoleon had been the subject of 'unnecessarily harsh and cruel treatments'. It was vital he said, that these were investigated and either shown to be false or if not, then rectified.[6]

His principal complaints were:

1. that a recent curtailment of his ability to move about the island had occurred which left Buonaparte in the bleakest part of the island, 'the dampness of which was calculated materially to aggravate the evil of confinement' which was exacerbated by the fact that the best hours for exercise 'were those during which no ingress not egress was permitted to or from the house at Longwood.'[7]

2. Napoleon was not allowed to receive specific books, 'journals, newspapers, and such public prints'. It was a needless aggravation for a prisoner. For a person who had a long life ahead of him 'it was a most cruel and unnecessary hardship'. It would be a great loss to posterity, he said, if Napoleon were unable to access journals and histories that would help give 'an account of the events of his extraordinary life'. But if it could be shown to be necessary for his restraint then he would accept it.

3. That sealed letters addressed to the Prime Minister were not permitted to leave the island. Consequently members of the French party who might have a complaint against the head of the island government were forced to reveal that criticism to the very person whom they accused. Clearly this went against an important principle of law that a prisoner had the right to petition his sovereign when he felt an injustice had been committed against him.

Earl Bathurst, Secretary for War and the Colonies, rose to reply. Bathurst was directly responsible for the management of Napoleon's confinement. Holland he noticed had based his case partly on a paper written by order of Napoleon and signed by Count Montholon, and partly on rumours. Sir Hudson Lowe, he assured Holland, used the same regulations for the control of Napoleon as had Admiral Cockburn.

> Those instructions considered Napoleon as a prisoner of war, and consequently laid down this general rule, that all restrictions should be imposed which were necessary to secure detention, but that no restrictions should be imposed which were not necessary to that detention. This principle he was prepared to show had actuated all the instructions from his majesty's government and all the steps which Sir Hudson Lowe had taken.[8]

He then answered Holland's alleged complaints in two points. The first concerned the ability of Napoleon to communicate with others, either in person or by writing and the other points concerned the personal treatment of the prisoner.

Bathurst pointed out that Napoleon had not been prevented from writing to anyone but that the rule must always apply, of every letter being open for inspection by the governor. Bathurst then reminded the house that the same rule applied to anyone writing to him, that their letters must be sent to his office for reading prior to them being sent on to Napoleon. There is then a hint in the parliamentary record that Bathurst relished his next observation. For the checks to be made on incoming mail, it was of course necessary that

> ... his friends should write to him, and the fact was, that only one of his relations had written to him – namely his brother Joseph, whose letter reached the office in October last, where it was opened, and immediately forwarded to him.[9]

Lord Bathurst after T. Philips. Bathurst had the ultimate responsibility for Napoleon's care and security. It was he who received the endless stream of letters from Lowe assiduously detailing the important and the trivial. Author's collection.

Bathurst then brushed aside the complaint about not being able to write a sealed letter to the Prince Regent – that the rule about open letters still applied. The purpose of this regulation

> ... was to protect the governor against frivolous charges; and, on the other hand, if any grave charge could be adduced, to insure relief sooner than would otherwise be possible, because it would not be necessary to send back to St. Helena to inquire into the truth of it, before steps could be taken to remove the inconvenience complained of.[10]

Bathurst then went onto to state that had such a sealed letter for the Prince Regent reached him he would feel bound to open it. After all, he said: 'In this country, where the ministers are responsible for the acts of the sovereign, he did not know how he could discharge his duty, if he did not make himself acquainted with the nature of such communications.'[11]

Napoleon complained that having requested some books from Europe, those about modern times had been kept back, Napoleon's request for books to complete his library was received in London. Bathurst explained that this list was sent to an eminent French bookseller with orders to supply such of the books as he had, and to obtain the rest from other booksellers. The bookseller had then sent to Paris to purchase those volumes which he could not obtain in London. However some of these, 'which could not be procured were principally on military subjects'. These books, along with an explanation to account for the omissions were then forwarded to St Helena. Bathurst also pointed out that these were not a 'few books' as the letter stated but had the huge value of between £1,300 and £1,400. Bathurst then dealt with the withholding of newspapers from Napoleon, which he admitted to. These were withheld on the grounds of security:

> As to this, he should say, that if the noble mover [Lord Holland] thought that general Buonaparte should be furnished with all the journals he required, he (earl B.) had a different sense of the course which it was proper for him to pursue. And this opinion was grounded on the knowledge, that attempts had been made, through the medium of newspapers, to hold communication with Napoleon.[12]

The mood was then lightened when he addressed Napoleon's apparent exasperation at not being able to correspond under a sealed letter even with a bookseller nor yet his banker or agent:

> He (earl B.) did not deny that, on a correspondence between friends, the necessity of sending letters open was a most severe restriction, because it was impossible to consign to paper the warm effusions of the heart, under the consciousness that that it would be subject to the cold eye of an inspector. But this surely did not apply to a correspondence with a banker. Who had ever heard of an *affectionate* draught on a banking-house, or a *tender* order for the sale of stock?

Bathurst then dealt with the charge that letters from Napoleon and his suite had been opened and read by subaltern officers on the island. This said Bathurst was simply not true. The only connection he could make was that in the haste to equip the ships sailing to St Helena

> Napoleon and his suite … were in want of many necessaries, such as linen and other articles of that kind. It was judged that great inconvenience might be felt, if they were obliged to wait till they could send to this country for them, and accordingly a considerable quantity of such articles were sent out in anticipation of their wants. It so happened, that about the time these articles arrived, Las Cases wrote a letter to Europe, which of course came under the inspection of sir Hudson Lowe, who found that it contained an order for some of those very articles which he had ordered, and which were much at his service; and observed, that it would not perhaps be necessary to send the letter.[13]

Las Cases on discovering that the governor had read the letter castigated him for reading 'a letter directed to a lady', and for offering him presumably more mundane undergarments than he had intended to purchase in Europe. It was a poor attempt to whip up a storm of protest out of nothing. Such, concluded Bathurst, was the behaviour of 'these intractable people'.

Bathurst next dealt with the complaint that letters sent to the officers in Napoleon's suite from their families in Europe had been 'broken open' read by Lowe and then returned to London, without revealing their contents to the intended recipients:

> They had to travel back 4,000 leagues, and these officers endured the mortification of knowing that there existed on the island accounts of their wives, their parents, and their children, of which they could not be informed in less than six months. The heart revolts at such treatment!

Bathurst assured the house that there was no truth in this assertion. He then turned to the claim that Napoleon was restricted in his ability to exercise around Longwood. This only applied to when ships arrived, or as long as they were in sight. During that time Napoleon was restricted to the immediate Longwood plain, which was several miles in circumference and whose boundary he would ride in his coach.[14]

Though Napoleon was forbidden from speaking to any of the inhabitants when these vessels were either dropping anchor or passing by the island, once visitors to the island had landed they could apply for a pass from the governor to visit Longwood. An audience with Napoleon was not a ticket affair however. A separate application had to be made via Bertrand, the Grand Marshal of the Palace for that honour in order to protect 'the privacy of the general from being broken in upon by the curiosity of individuals'. That he could not speak with officers of the garrison, Bathurst answered:

> He had on one occasion entered into conversation with an officer of the 53rd Regiment, in which he bestowed high praises upon that regiment and its officers

(none of which could be too high for their deserts), and then expressed a regret that all intercourse with them was interdicted him. The officer assured him that no such interdiction existed, at which he expressed some surprise, but since that time he had no more frequent communication with them than he had previously, when he supposed the prohibition which he so much lamented, to have existed.[15]

That Napoleon could not move out of his house at the only time that exercise was healthy in that climate:

Now the fact was, that though he had not free passage through the island after sunset, he might at any hours walk in his garden. Sentinels were stationed there after sun-set, and he expressed his dislike to walk when he was thus watched. Sir H. Lowe, with every desire to attend to his wishes, after that fixed the sentinels in places where they would not look on him. Would their lordships wish them to be removed altogether just at the time when it was most likely that he should escape? Let them suppose for a moment, that instead of debating on the motion of the noble lord, that intelligence was brought to them by Sir Hudson Lowe that general Buonaparte had actually escaped. Let them suppose, than instead of sitting to discuss whether a little more or little less restriction should be imposed, that they thus had to examine Sir Hudson Lowe at their bar. How and when did he escape? – In the early part of the evening, and from his garden. Had this garden no sentinels? – The sentinels were removed. Why were they removed? – General Buonaparte desired it – they were hurtful to his feelings, they were then removed, and thus was he enabled to escape. What would their lordships think of such an answer? He begged them to consider the position of sir Hudson Lowe – in what a painful and invidious position he was placed. If general Buonaparte escaped, the character and fortune of sir Hudson Lowe were ruined for ever.[16]

Looking to the choice of residence Bathurst noted that as it had previously been the residence of the Lieutenant Governor he understood that they would not choose 'unpleasant and unwholesome spots'. Bathurst noted that in conversation with Admiral Cockburn, on the day of his initial visit to Longwood, Buonaparte had told him at first sight, 'that he wished to remain there and not to go back to the town'. On being told that it would be impossible for the Lieutenant Governor's family to be removed instantly, he replied that he would manage with a tent in the garden. It was after this, on the return journey that he spied the Balcombe house and proposed that he live in the small ballroom that had been built upon the tiny hill.

What Bathurst either did not know or did not choose to share with their lordships was that Longwood was usually only occupied in the southern hemisphere summer months by the Lieutenant Governor. The particular maritime weather patterns that affect the island result in rolling fog regularly shrouding the south and eastern half of the island. The outlook can change within fifteen minutes from one of blue skies and sunshine to swirling, warm fog. In Longwood garden visibility changes dramatically. Views of the Knoll and the Barn disappear and visibility is reduced to less than a hundred metres.[17]

Bathurst then went on to point out that whilst the alterations to Longwood had taken two months to complete, Napoleon had remained encamped in the ballroom at the Briars, surrounded by a small garden

> … beyond which he never moved without a guard; he did not at any time make a complaint; but he now, for the first time, complained of restrictions on his liberty, when he was allowed to range within a circuit of eight miles, if he pleased unattended.

He then observed that in the matter of having a new house built, Napoleon had remarked that as he expected to be released in two or three years upon a change in government in France or England it was better that only short-term alterations be made to Longwood. Finally, Bathurst moved to the very core of the debate in the House of Lords. What he objected to most of all when discussing these matters was this:

> … every attempt to render his residence convenient was made the foundation of a charge against the governor, and that he watched the moment when an attention was paid to his wishes, to make that very attention a source of complaint.[18]

With regard to the funding of the Longwood establishment, Bathurst pointed out that the Governor's salary was £1,800 per annum to which was added the allowance of £4,700 per annum paid by the Honourable Company for the entertaining of passengers on board Company vessels. Consequently, £8,000 per annum seemed an appropriate amount for entertaining at Longwood where such occasions were few. However, if Sir Hudson Lowe considered that a further allowance was necessary then

> … His Majesty's ministers were inclined to allow it. Sir Hudson Lowe, in answer, said he thought the establishment of general Buonaparte could not be suitably provided for under £12,000 a year. An intimation was immediately given that that the sum of £12,000 was agreed to by His Majesty's ministers.[19]

Napoleon had then entered into negotiation with the governor stating that if he could send a sealed letter to his banker in Europe he would seek to provide his own funding. He then moves on to the wine issue – that there was insufficient available at Longwood. A bottle a day per person was the current allowance 'and that if this allowance was drunk by any of the individuals on the establishment he could get no more. In order to ascertain the expenditure of any establishment it was usual to calculate on a certain quantity of such things as were used for each individual, per day.' In this country a bottle a day was the norm in the army, 'sufficient for themselves and for such company as might be invited to their mess' and for the King's table. Bathurst then calculated that the current allowance for Longwood.

Weak wine 84 bottles per fortnight

Better sort of wine 266 bottles per fortnight, broken down by Bathurst as:

a. 7 bottles of Constantia (or 14 pint bottles)

b. 14 bottles of champagne

c. 21 bottles of Vin de Grave

d. 84 bottles of Tenerife

e. 140 bottles of Claret[20]

When the children were discounted this left his personal suite as nine persons, resulting in 19 bottles per day for nine persons plus Bonaparte!

Bathurst's conclusion when it arrived was consistent with the measures that had been put in place in July 1815. He applauded Lord Holland for his 'good intentions and upright views' but when he turned to Napoleon he saw only the 'most bitter and rancorous enemy that this country ever had':

> If by our negligence Buonaparte were allowed to escape, we would not only incur the censure of those who now called for a relaxation of vigilance and restraint, but our conduct would be liable to misrepresentation throughout Europe: it would be asserted that we intended to allow his enlargement for some purposes of our own.[21]

He then dealt with Napoleon's claim, so eloquently built up in the Themistocles letter that he was not 'the prisoner of England' but someone who had placed himself under its laws. Bathurst pointed out that those major powers he now claimed would have given him asylum in a gracious and kindly manner were the very countries he had invaded and ill-used:

> ... This person should be kept in close confinement, and ... every restriction should be enforced, and every degree of vigilance exercised, that should be found necessary for that purpose. The severe and close durance to which general Buonaparte was subjected was not dictated by motives of revenge, but of security; and he considered any measure justifiable which was necessary to prevent that man from again breaking loose and throwing Europe into agitation. It was a piece of political justice that we owed to Europe and the world. It taught a political lesson that should never be forgotten in this country or any other.[22]

Holland rose and asserted that the noble lord had not produced any evidence. He on the other hand, said Holland, had asked questions in a spirit of inquiry, not censure. Also the lord had not presented the documents to the house but rather had presented extracts, which,

> ... as a man of wit and pleasantry, instead of allowing the justification of the absent to be heard, he cracked jokes upon an individual, whose character and person were in his power. If this was his glory, if this was his triumph, he did not envy him his feelings, or his taste.[23]

Holland, with only the radical Duke of Sussex, brother of the Prince Regent, as his supporter must have known early in the debate that he was fighting a lost cause. The motion was defeated without a vote being taken. There were far more pressing matters to be attended to in Britain: the change from a wartime economy and subsequent unemployment and fears of political unrest were of greater concern to the Tory government. In February 1817, Bathurst revealed in Parliament details of intelligence that indicated

> … attempts made in various parts of the country as well as in the metropolis, to take advantage of the distress in which the labouring and manufacturing classes of the community are at present involved … in a total overthrow of all existing establishments, and in a division of the landed, and extinction of the funded property of the country. It further appears that in these meetings the most blasphemous expressions and doctrines are openly and repeatedly advanced … The design was by a sudden rising in the dead of night, to surprise and overpower the soldiers in their different barracks, which were to be set on fire [and] at the same time to take possession of the Tower and the bank.

This warning was not accepted in all quarters of the house but the government had enough supporters who believed it was so, and they were to continue in power for a long time to come. The complaints of an ex-Emperor, who was generally judged to have precipitated a great deal of this misery, came a poor second when compared to seeking out and suppressing supposed revolutionary dissent amongst the poor.

As for Lady Holland, writing to Mrs Creevey in Brussels in September, she said that 'idle paragraphs' in the pro-government press gave a false impression of Napoleon's followers; that contrary to the impression generated in those papers, they all wished to stay in service on the island. She was 'mortified' that the British had become 'jailors and spies for the Bourbon Government' under the control of Lord Castlereagh.[24]

Notes

1 Holland speaking in the House of Lords opposing the bill to formally detain Napoleon, quoted in Sanders, Lloyd, *The Holland House Circle*, London: Methuen, 1908, page 39.

2 Sanders, ibid, page 40.

3 Quoted in the *Oxford Dictionary of National Biography*.

4 Mitchell, Leslie, *Holland House*, Duckworth, 1980, page 249. Hansard, 19 Feb, 1816, Vol LXVIII, columns 664–5

5 Lord Holland, House of Lords, Personal Treatment of Buonaparte, in Hansard, 18 March 1817, Volume XXXV, column 1138.

6 ibid., column 1140.

7 ibid., column 1141.

8 ibid., column 1148.

9 ibid., column 1149.

10 ibid., column 1150.

11 ibid., column 1150.

12 ibid., column 1151.

13 ibid., column 1151.

14 ibid., column 1153.

15 ibid., column 1154.

16 ibid., column 1155.

17 In August 2004, whilst walking in Longwood garden the author experienced the sudden inrush of swirling fog. In fifteen minutes the entire plain was blanketed and visibility was reduced to less than 100 metres. On arrival at St Helena, RMS *St Helena* hove to, off George Island on the southeast corner of the island. All the coast was shrouded in fog. An hour later, on reaching Jamestown, the fog had not penetrated to that side of the island.

18 Hansard, 18 March, 1817, Volume XXXV, column 1156.

19 ibid., column 1158.

20 ibid., column 1159.

21 ibid., column 1160.

22 ibid., column 1162–3.

23 ibid., column 1165.

24 Maxwell, (Ed) Sir H., *The Creevey Papers:* Volume I, John Murray, 1903, page 267.

Chapter Five

Un Petit Isle

It is clear he is still inclined to act the Sovereign occasionally, but I cannot allow it, and the sooner therefore he becomes convinced it is not to be admitted the better.
Admiral Sir George Cockburn

Cockburn's involvement in the examination of Napoleon's effects and monies was both unavoidable and unknown to him, warranted.[1] Prior to the inspection and removal of the 4,000 napoleons from his luggage Napoleon had ordered his supporters to conceal amounts of money about their persons, money that would be deployed in his struggle against being abandoned and forgotten.[2]

He was to be allowed domestic items such as furniture and plate provided that it could not easily be converted into cash. All his 'money, diamonds and negotiable bills of every description' were to be surrendered, as were those of his entourage lest they be used to engineer his escape. This money would then be held by the British government and paid out on behalf of Napoleon as and when required. Cockburn had clearly found the process of checking the trunks to be embarrassing and quickly left Napoleon's valet and Mr Glover to carry out the task.

Napoleon now knew that he was to be addressed only as General Bonaparte, that when a new vessel arrived at the island his movements were to be limited to his residence and its grounds and that he was not to be allowed to speak to any of the inhabitants at such times. Further, that these regulations were to apply to his followers.

The memorandum also pointed out that should he attempt to escape then he would subsequently separated from his followers and 'placed in close custody'. Any correspondence, either from or to him or his followers, was to be first read either by the Admiral or later the Governor before being passed over. And if it was a letter to the British Government then he was to understand that the Admiral or Governor would be expected to append any observations that they considered would be useful. It was a very ignominious development.

Meanwhile a letter had been despatched from Bathurst to the governor at the Cape, Lt General Lord Charles Stewart, forewarning him that Cockburn might

well ask for additional troops from the Cape. Stewart was to be particularly sure
not to send a regiment with 'foreigners' whose loyalty might be played upon by
Napoleon.[3] Even at the end of July there was a fear that Napoleon still had the
ability to mesmerise those about him and win them over for another mad adventure.

Among the instructions flying out to both soldiers and sailors at this time is
one from Bathurst to the Admiralty where for the first time we see the Prince
Regent taking an interest in Napoleon's imprisonment. The government had
made certain that Napoleon and he would never meet – their fears best summed
up by the oft quoted comment by Keith that had they met they would have been
the best of friends within ten minutes. The Prince Regent was 'desirous'

> ... that no greater measure of severity with respect to confinement or restriction
> be imposed, than what is deemed necessary for the faithful discharge of that duty
> which the Admiral as well as the Governor of St Helena must ever keep in mind, –
> the perfect security of General Buonaparte's person.[4]

Meanwhile the island's Governor, Colonel Wilks of the HEIC, was informed in
a secret letter that until the arrival of the new Governor, Cockburn was to have
sole charge of General Bonaparte:

> ... you will clearly understand that you are to comply with every requisition he
> may consider it his duty to make connected with the safe custody of General
> Buonaparte, and the Individuals above mentioned, placing at the disposal of Sir
> George Cockburn any house or place belonging to the Company, with the excep-
> tion of the Governor's Plantation House, that the Admiral may think proper to
> select with that view.[5]

Already Napoleon was being provided with one of his chief complaints, the
lack of a suitable house. Longwood was not be an ideal home as the fogs roll in
swiftly and regularly. He was also be denied the symbolic home of the governor,
Plantation House, on the sheltered side of the island.

The obvious problem was that here was a sparsely inhabited island with few
large houses. Those which were suitable were already owned and occupied.
Longwood really was the only large structure available. Furthermore, Napoleon
would soon be offered a large elegant, prefabricated bungalow fitted out completely with furnishings and furniture, which he would reject.

Wilks was also informed that if any of the local laws or ordinances required
alteration or removal in order to better secure the General, then he was to comply
entirely with Admiral Cockburn.

Cockburn received details of his squadron which was to proceed to St Helena.
Two troopships would convey the 53rd Regiment of Foot and a detachment
of Royal Artillery, presumably to oversee the training of the resident St Helena
Artillery Regiment. The other sloops, frigates and a storeship would enable him

to put rigorous security measures in place and equip the troops to enable them to work and live in the field.

He would be responsible for security at the Cape, which also provided an administrative base for his squadron and for the waters as far east as Mauritius, as far west as Ascension Island and Tristan da Cunha, as far south as Bouvet Island and north to the Equator.[6] It was a huge area with few islands and fortunately for Cockburn, no favourable winds for those who would contemplate snatching Napoleon from the island.

His orders were most emphatic on one point, if some vessels in his squadron were not ready to sail once Napoleon had transferred from the *Bellerophon* then he was to proceed immediately to St Helena leaving them to follow on when they could. The longer Napoleon lay off the coast of England the more likely it was that persons such as Mackenrot, Lofft and Holland might interfere with the government's plans to have him secured in the middle of the South Atlantic. No one wanted Napoleon to have the opportunity of becoming 'the best of friends' with the Prince Regent or members of the liberal Whig elite.

On 7 August Napoleon, having yet again formally protested through a letter, as he had previously done in conversation, that he was the 'guest' of England and not her prisoner, finally left the *Bellerophon* and went on board the *Northumberland*. Keith meanwhile, determined to have Napoleon sent on his way, ordered the boats of HMS *Tonnant* to supply water to the *Northumberland* and the troop ships, so that she might depart all the sooner rather than calling in along the English coast for further supplies.[7]

Cockburn having formally received Napoleon took him through into the great cabin. Cockburn was to be far more rigid in his interpretation of his orders than either Maitland or Keith had been. Having introduced Captain Ross as the *Northumberland's* captain he then pointedly introduced some of the ship's officers, along with Lord Lowther, Mr Lyttleton and Colonel Bingham and left them standing with Napoleon in the great cabin. From the very beginning the General was treated as a general officer and not as an imperial figure. He was not going to be allowed to set up a small court in the great cabins of the *Northumberland*. Napoleon then asked to see his sleeping cabin, on one side of the great cabin – which he did accompanied by Keith. Napoleon generally did not rise until between ten and eleven in the morning having first breakfasted, read and had himself attended by his valet. Then having dressed he would appear in the public great cabin.

Shortly afterwards Savary and Lallemand accompanied by Maitland, came on board to say their farewells to the Emperor. Over the next two days the other vessels of the squadron, barring the storeship Weymouth, joined Cockburn and at dawn on 9 August the squadron made sail for St Helena.

That evening, after dinner, Napoleon went out on deck bareheaded, the officers of his suite doing likewise. Cockburn on seeing this pointedly removed his hat in salute and then immediately replaced it, making it known to his officers that they were not to remain uncovered in Napoleon's presence whatever the General decided to do. Napoleon, he said,

> ... seemed considerably piqued, and he soon afterwards went into the cabin and made up his party at vingt-un, but he certainly neither played not talked with the same cheerfulness he did the first night: this might, indeed, have been accident, but it appeared to me to proceed rather from downright sulkiness, though I cannot but remark that his general manners, as far as I am yet able to speak of them, are uncouth and disagreeable, and to his *French friends* most overbearing if not absolutely rude.[8]

The next day after dinner, another attempt was made by Napoleon to interfere with the hierarchy on board.

> Immediately after dinner to-day, the General got up rather uncivilly and went upon deck as soon as he had swallowed his own coffee and before all the rest of us were even served. This induced me to request particularly the remainder of the party to sit still, and he consequently went out only attended by his Marechal, without the slightest further notice being taken of him. (It is clear he is still inclined to act the Sovereign occasionally, but I cannot allow it, and the sooner therefore he becomes convinced it is not to be admitted the better.)[9]

Cockburn and Napoleon continued in this state of quiet hostility for several days though the members of his suite were 'certainly behaving as if anxious to gain my good opinion'. Then on 15 August, Napoleon's birthday, Cockburn congratulated him, drank his health and walked on deck with him for some time. Another factor in Napoleon's amiability may have been due to the better weather which they now enjoyed:

> Buonaparte's behaviour is improving and I am always ready to meet him half-way, when he appears to conduct himself with due modesty and consideration of his present situation, after dinner to-day I had a good deal of pleasant conversation with him; in the course of which some of the most remarkable circumstances he mentioned were, he assured me upon his word and honour (as Comte de Bertrand had done before), that he had not had any communication or invitation from any other Marshals or Generals, or from any other person in France, when he returned to it from Elba, but that the public papers conveyed to him such an account of the state of France as induced him no longer to hesitate in taking the steps he did.[10]

Napoleon confessed that he had paid too much attention to the Jacobins in Paris and should instead have followed his own inclinations in matters of policy; that the Allies had forced him to move too quickly with his army, therefore not enabling him to weed out those disaffected men, 'and he attributed solely to the disaffected officers of his army the Waterloo disasters'.

Napoleon told Cockburn that he had known that the blue masses on his right flank had been Prussians but 'contented himself' with believing that Grouchy was close behind and ready to pounce upon them. It was then that those disaffected officers spread the cry of '*suave qui peut!*' on the battlefield.

Yet again he lamented Wellington for deciding to fight such a decisive action on 18 June. This battle had been his best hope of crushing the British completely, thus enabling him to turn his attention to the Austrians as the Prussian Army, having already been defeated on 16 June, would have probably retired into Prussia. He felt sure that a significant defeat of the British would have resulted in the fall of the government in London resulting in an administration more favourably disposed towards him. Such an administration would have afforded him the chance of 'concluding an immediate general truce; which was really his first object, as France was hardly equal to the effort she was then making'.[11]

Napoleon then expressed his disappointment at not being allowed to live in England – particularly as he had been prepared to give '*his word of honour*' not to interfere in any way in the affairs of France. In this edition of Cockburn's diary the words were printed in italics.

He then told Cockburn that the Emperor Alexander had urged him, whilst they were at Erfurt together, to legitimise his throne by 'setting aside Josephine' and marrying a Russian princess, whom Napoleon believed to be the Princess Ann. The matter rested there for a while but later, he sent a representative to Russia to reopen negotiations and the whole matter was then beset with difficulties on the Russian side, which resulted in his ministers urging him to consider an offer of the hand of an Austrian princess in marriage. He then assured Cockburn that he could not face placing himself under the protection of the Emperor Francis, after the manner in which he had behaved during the last campaign. Despite the harsh and unfair treatment he had received from the English he took some comfort from the fact that he was now under the protection of British laws and his fate was not controlled by the mere whim of any one man, as it may have been if he had gone anywhere else.

Cockburn continues to describe Napoleon as being more at ease on board. On 18 August, the brig which Cockburn had sent to Guernsey returned with some 'French papers and gazettes' for Napoleon and here there are no observations as to their effect.

He told Cockburn a story about the late Queen of Naples who, he claimed, had urged Maria Louise that if she really cared for her husband, despite her father forbidding her to make contact with Napoleon on Elba: 'My child, when one has the happiness to be married to such a man, papas and mammas should not keep one away from him whilst there are windows and sheets by which an escape to him might be effected.'[12] An interesting piece of advice, particularly given that by this time Count Niepperg was firmly established as Marie Louise's unofficial consort. Soon she would give birth to their first daughter. Palmer believes that Napoleon was already aware of her relationship with Niepperg and that he had wisely decided not to acknowledge it. Any reference to Niepperg in conversation set him up to be laughed at in the future. Far better to say nothing and minimise the damage.[13]

Not for the last time Napoleon assessed the monarchs and peoples whom he had both defeated and negotiated with. The Russians and Poles were far braver than the rest of the European races save for the French and English; Francis 'had neither abilities nor firmness of character'; the King of Prussia was '*un pauvre bête*'; Alexander was 'a more active and clever man that any of the Sovereigns of Europe, but … was extremely false.' Cockburn says he spoke in effusive terms of Mr Fox and Lord Cornwallis and also of Captain Usher, the Royal Navy officer who had taken Napoleon to the isle of Elba.

Cockburn noted the change in his dining habits. On board he ate and drank a great deal, preferring meat 'highly dressed' and never touched vegetables. Cockburn wondered whether with his lack of exercise and poor diet, his health might suffer by the time they landed.

On 20 August service was held and Cockburn was surprised that none of the French party attended out of curiosity. At dinner Napoleon questioned the chaplain about the differences between the Anglican and the Roman Catholic faith and later retired to his cabin, being aware that none of the British officers would play cards on a Sunday.

The rest of the diary continues in this vein, apparently pleasant conversation at dinner, usually followed by a walk on the quarterdeck afterwards and then cards. On approaching the island of Madeira, Cockburn became aware of the French party making great efforts to complete letters to be sent back to Europe.

On 24 August they lay to off Funchal and the British Consul was invited on board for dinner. Napoleon impressed Cockburn with the great number of questions he asked Mr Veitch about the island's economy. On 26 August he talked to Cockburn after dinner about the issues raised in the French newspapers which had come aboard earlier. He was sure that the Bourbons faced further troubles as they had been returned to power by the Allied powers marching their armies into France; and he wondered what had occurred to his brother Jerome.

The next day, Cockburn had them directed to Tenerife so that Napoleon might see the peak as well the Canary Islands. Unfortunately it was very hazy and so little was seen. Then for several days the French party were affected by a heavy swell which kept them in their cabins with seasickness.

In conversation regarding the alleged poisoning of the sick French soldiers in Jaffa in 1798, Cockburn confirms that all the sick French soldiers save for three of four were dead of their disease when Captain Beattie of the Marines, at that time on the *Theseus*, entered the town. He then talks about the Queen of Prussia and how she had sought to persuade him at Tilsit to leave Magdeburg to Prussia, which, had she arrived earlier, she might have succeeded in doing, 'by reason of the great advantage an extremely clever and fine woman of high rank must always have when personally urging any suite she has much at heart'. He continued for the entire dinner that night to fend off her entreaties to him to yield Magdeburg to Prussia and caused the treaty to be signed that next morning without any change in it.

As they sailed further south the daylight hours shortened and Napoleon took less exercise in the darkness and consequently Cockburn walked with him less, 'his people have kept more closely around him during those evening walks'.

On one of their walks Napoleon assures Cockburn that had he reached London he would have concluded a treaty 'offered on moderate terms' though as Cockburn himself mentions he did not explain what he meant by the term 'moderate'. In another conversation he explains that the only reason he had invaded Russia was to make Poland independent and to ensure that Alexander joined in completely with the continental system against England. On another occasion, he reveals that he had paid people in Russia to travel about the country urging the peasantry to rebel against the Tsar and consider him as their potential saviour.

At another time Cockburn speaks of the moment when, talking of the intelligence he procured through English agents, Napoleon especially mentioned Mr Goldsmith the editor as being someone who had passed information to France and on one occasion had obtained an interview with him at Boulogne. Cockburn:

> I mention this because I have determined to note down herein every particular this extraordinary man tells; but it is right I should at the same time remark that there was something of a malicious cunning in General Buonaparte's manner whilst making this statement which induced me very much to doubt the truth of the whole story, and I was rather inclined to think he made this assertion (which was in public, at my table) either with a view to make us fancy all Mr Goldsmith had written against him was merely as a cloak to cover his (Goldsmith's) own treasons, or (which is more probable) he hoped by such a statement so made, and therefore likely to be repeated, that he might cause public suspicion to fall on Mr Goldsmith, which might therefore draw him into difficulties, and thereby offer General Buonaparte some chance of being revenged upon him for the unqualified abuse he has so lavishly heaped upon the General and his family. He further observed that he believed Mr Goldsmith was possessed of some talent, although a consummate rogue, and he then immediately turned the conversation to other matters.[14]

Lewis Goldsmith was the editor of the Anti-Gallician *Monitor*, which had published a large number of outrageous and scandalous stories about Napoleon and his court prior to his fall.

On 4 September he spoke about his plans to invade Ireland. He was confident that there were many Protestants as well as Catholics who were well disposed towards him. He stated that he had no intention of separating the people from their religion but simply had the object of separating Ireland from England.

On crossing the equator, General Bertrand came to Cockburn to ask if Napoleon might gain exemption from the usual ceremonies by distributing amongst the seamen 'one or two hundred napoleons'. Cockburn, not surprisingly, refused this offer, seeing it as merely an attempt to ingratiate himself with the seamen, citing the scale of money paid by his officers and proposed that 'he might give as far as five napoleons'. Bertrand then returned to Napoleon with this information and Cockburn apparently heard no more.

Notes

1 Instructions from the Secretary of State, 30 July 1815, COC/1 NMM.

2 Marchand, L-J, *In Napoleon's Shadow*, 1998, Proctor Jones Publishing, p.328. Thornton, M. J., in *Napoleon after Waterloo*, 1986, Stanford University Press, quotes Las Cases as receiving a money belt from Napoleon containing the diamond necklace that his stepdaughter Hortense had given him when he left Malmaison.

3 Copy of a Letter from Bathurst to Stewart, Downing Street 31 July 1815, COC/2, NMM.

4 Enclosure, Bathurst, War Department to the Admiralty, copy, dated 31 July 1815, COC/2, NMM.

5 Secret letter: copy of instructions to the Governor of St Helena dated 1 August 1815. COC/4, NMM.

6 Melville and Yorke, Admiralty appointment as naval commander-in-chief, at St Helena and the Cape to Cockburn, dated 31 July, 1815. COC/3 NMM.

7 Thornton M. J., op cit, p. 197.

8 Cockburn, Sir G., *Extract from a Diary of Rear Admiral Cockburn,* Simpkin, Marshall & Co., 1888.

9 Ibid, pages 10–11.

10 Ibid, pages 12–13.

11 Ibid, 16 August, 1815, pages 25–26.

12 Ibid, page 30.

13 Ibid, page 38.

14 Palmer, A., *Napoleon and Marie Louise: The Second Empress*, Constable, London, 2001, p. 208.

15 Cockburn, op cit, page 74.

Chapter Six

The first few weeks

The English or rather Welsh character of the scenery, is kept up by the numerous cottages and small white houses; some buried at the bottom of the deepest valleys, and others mounted on the crests of the lofty hills. Some of the views are striking, for instance that from near Sir W. Doveton's house, where the bold peak called Lot is seen over a dark wood of firs, the whole being backed by the red water-worn mountains of the southern coast. On viewing the island from an eminence, the first circumstance which strikes one, is the number of the roads and forts; the labour bestowed on the public works, if one forgets its character as a prison, seems out of all proportion to its extent or value.
Charles Darwin *Voyage of the Beagle*, London, 1845.

The *Northumberland* first saw the island on 14 October 1815, but it would be another day before they arrived at the southeast or windward side of the island. The island does have a magnetic influence over those who view it from the sea simply because there is nothing else to look at on the ocean. This is how James Prior, naval surgeon described it two years before Napoleon arrived:

It is impossible to approach and see this singular island, for the first time, without wondering how the deuce it got there. A vast mass of rock rising abruptly from nearly the centre of the Atlantic Ocean, jagged and irregular, cut and slashed as it were, cut into pieces by the great hatchet of nature – too large to be passed without examination, and too small and unfruitful, and badly situated, to be of much use.[1]

Most British diarists of this period invariably described the interior of the island as having more colour and vegetation than they had supposed. Often the island became a metaphor for the turbulent times that the great man represented. The island is described as being 'brooding' and often as generating a 'melancholic' reaction in themselves. The same impression is easily generated today, as the maritime climate of the island results in the southern half being covered in cloud for at least the first half of many days. Those clouds create the smudgy grey shroud of which those diarists spoke. Surgeon Walter Henry, arriving with the 66th Regiment of Foot in July, 1817 had this to say:

> I had associated shade and verdure with St Helena; and classed it with Juan Fernandez and other delectable spots, dotted here and there in the midst of immense tracts of ocean, for beneficent purposes, by the hand of Nature. It was therefore with no small disappointment I beheld the ugliest and most dismal rock conceivable, of rugged and abrupt surface, rising like an enormous black wart from the face of the deep. Not a blade of grass or trace of vegetation could be perceived from our ship, as we sailed round to get to leeward of the Island.[2]

These clouds swirl over the high ground on the windward side of the island, which is also the site of Longwood House. Longwood had, until Napoleon's arrival, been the summer residence of the Lieutenant-Governor of the island, Lt Colonel Skelton and used as an escape from the summer heat of Jamestown. This climatic phenomenon would play a crucial role in the depression that closed in upon Napoleon and would be used by him to repeatedly illustrate the idea that St Helena was a very unhealthy place.

Although named as a bay, James Bay is no more than a shallow ellipse on the side of the old volcano, with a narrow, flat bottomed valley at its centre. There is no great stretch of beach, only a thin line of rocks between the sea and the town promenade hemmed in by the steep-sided volcanic cliffs. Today, as then, all vessels anchor off this point as the only viable coastal settlement on the island, Jamestown. Prior, in the same diary entry:

> But the charm of novelty erased this impression; we compared it to a good-natured man with a repelling countenance, whose heart, though kind was veiled under a rough exterior. The approach to the anchorage leads round Sugar-loaf Point; here ships send their boats ashore to declare their names, their destination and country, without which they are fired on and at and not suffered to anchor. Batteries now appear in every direction; guns, gates, embrasures, and soldiers continually meet the eye; so that instead of being, as we might suppose, the abode of peace and seclusion, it looks like a depot for the instruments of war. It was the last day of the year when we anchored. Unlike the heavy opaque atmosphere of your English Decembers, the sky was serene and cloudless; and tropical sun, moderated by the trade, or south-east wind, made the prospect better that nature perhaps intended it.[3]

On the morning of 15 October HMS *Northumberland* finally dropped anchor and the fort fired the customary salute in honour of Admiral Cockburn, which was returned by the warship. HMS *Havannah* also dropped anchor along with the transports containing the 53rd Regiment of Foot. Napoleon had arrived four months to the day since he had crossed the border into Belgium at the start of the Waterloo campaign.

The brig *Icarus* and the frigate *Havannah* were already in the Jamestown roads, after storms had separated them from the rest of the squadron near the Azores. They had made better time and arrived several days earlier. Napoleon however was not to land until the evening of 17 October when Cockburn had found suitable temporary lodgings for the General and his suite.

Marchand saw Bonaparte rise surprisingly early on 15 October. His master dressed and went on deck as he could not see the island very well from his cabin. He had his small spyglass in his hand. Once on deck Marchand handed him a sketch of the island. Marchand could only see the square tower of the church above the wall that screened the town from the promenade. Only the large government building known as 'The Castle' seemed to have any vegetation around it. Everything else was a 'large rock devoid of any vegetation'.

Napoleon stayed on deck only for a few moments and then returned to his cabin 'without comment, allowing no one to guess what was transpiring in his soul'. Cockburn and Colonel Bingham then went ashore to locate a residence suitable for the General and his suite. For the next two days Cockburn undertook to organise temporary accommodation for Napoleon. On each of those days islanders gathered opposite the squadron of ships until nightfall, hoping for a sight of Napoleon embarking for the shore. Then, after the sudden fall of the tropical night, they would leave the seafront along with their disappointment. Prior again:

> [The town] is formed by one principal street, of some length, extending directly up the valley, with here and there, intersections, tolerably broad, paved, clean, and resembling an English village, thorough, neat and compact. The houses are small and white-washed; they consist principally of shops and lodging-houses, the former retailing the wares of India and Europe at an advanced price, the latter giving a temporary home to passengers in the India fleets. It also contains a church, a residence for the governor, a theatre built in 1809, a tavern, barracks, and (what would be better in any other situation) a burying-ground. Several batteries and posts surround it on all sides. The head of the valley gives origin to a fine stream of water, which, besides supplying the inhabitants, is conducted to the beach for the use of the shipping.[4]

The island had received little notice of either the battle of Waterloo or of the arrival of the 'Disturber of the Peace'. It did not possess the resources with which to enhance a large residence on the windward side of the island suitable for such an illustrious resident. The house at Longwood was used specifically for occupation during the summer months (January to April) by the Lieutenant Governor, when the heat of Jamestown became uncomfortable. There was little or no seasoned timber for building, no great suppliers of household goods nor any body of craftsmen on the island. It was most fortunate that the squadron of warships that had brought Napoleon to the island, each had their teams of qualified craftsmen on board as part of their normal establishment.

The principal function of St Helena was to act as a supply base for the vessels of the Honourable East India Company. Any other function or amenity received little or no attention from the directors of the company in Leadenhall Street, London.

Admiral Cockburn's orders directed him to keep the General on board the flagship until his detention could be 'assured' but Marchand says that the Admiral behaved in a more humane manner than his orders required. On the evening prior to leaving the *Northumberland*, Napoleon received Captain Ross and asked him to pass onto both the officers and the crew of the *Northumberland* his thanks for his treatment on board the ship. Then at seven o'clock, some time after the tropical night had fallen, he made his way into the gig and was rowed ashore beneath the stars of the southern hemisphere.

On shore, amongst those hoping to get a glimpse of the ex-Emperor was Elizabeth 'Betsy' Balcombe. She wrote her account almost thirty years later:

> It was nearly dark when we arrived at the landing place, and shortly after, a boat from the *Northumberland* approached, and we saw a figure step from it on shore, which we were told was the emperor but it was too dark to distinguish his features. He walked up the lines between the Admiral and General Bertrand, and, enveloped as he was in his surtout, I could see little, but the occasional gleam of a diamond star, which he wore on his heart. The whole population of St. Helena crowded to behold him, and one could hardly have believed that it contained so many inhabitants. The pressure became so great, that it was with difficulty way could be made for him, and sentries were at last ordered to stand with fixed bayonets at the entrance from the lines to the town, to prevent the multitude from pouring in. Napoleon was excessively provoked at the eagerness of the crowd to get a peep at him, more particularly him as he was received in silence though with respect. I heard him afterwards say how much he had been annoyed at being followed and stared at 'comme un bête féroce'.[5]

Today the walk from the landing point to the boarding house is barely three minutes but amidst the crowds described by Balcombe it must have seemed a greater distance. Soldiers held them back as he walked across the seawall, under the town gate, across the parade square and into the first house beside the botanic gardens. This would be the only occasion during his imprisonment on the island that Napoleon would walk along the seafront in Jamestown. The building may have been one of the best in the principal street of the town but it was still only a boarding house whose principal rooms overlooked the street. It was not free from inconvenience, as Napoleon could not make his appearance at the windows, or even descend from his bedchamber, without being exposed to the 'rude and ardent gaze of those who wished to gratify their curiosity with the sight of the imperial captive.'[6]

There were no gated gardens to keep the curious at bay, either at the front or the rear of the building. He climbed several steps to the front door, entered and then ascended to the principal bedroom on the first floor. Once in this room, along with his small staff he was a prisoner for the night, unless he wished to face the townspeople. In the drawing room, on the ground floor, Cockburn explained to the General that this was only a temporary measure whilst the building work was carried out at Longwood. He assured Napoleon that he would see to it that the building work would be completed as quickly as possible, even though he was short of resources.

By 8 o'clock everyone was inside the lodging house. Once Cockburn had left, Napoleon's servants removed the hidden money belts they had brought ashore. The French 'Mameluke', Louis Etienne Saint-Denis, known as 'Aly': 'I had two for my share. I had put them around my waist and 50,000 francs was a considerable weight to carry during a large part of the day; consequently I felt greatly relieved when I could get rid of my burden. My hips were flayed.'[7]

Marchand had arranged his master's room 'according to his customary habits as much as possible'. Not surprisingly Napoleon slept badly. He called for a covered lamp and read a book. He spoke to Marchand about the 'impracticality' of the Porteus house and his wish to move into Longwood as soon as possible: 'It will have to be in a very inadequate shape indeed for me for me not to find a way to lodge there.' Today the house no longer exists though the site is now occupied by another building. However the street and buildings surrounding the Porteus site are much as Napoleon knew them in 1815.

At eight o'clock next morning Cockburn and Napoleon left Jamestown on horseback. Today, looking from the windows of the Consulate Hotel at the far end of the high street one is immediately impressed by the closeness of the valley side, across the road. Back yards jut out from the buildings opposite but even some of these rise up as they are built into the valley wall itself. Beyond them is the steeply rising wall of the valley. Casting the eye up, you meet only a narrow strip of sky.

Almost four months to the day after Waterloo, Napoleon was riding along the only completely surfaced road in the only town, on a small island in the South Atlantic Ocean. He was accompanied by Bertrand, Saint-Denis and the Admiral's staff officer. They rode up the high street to the fork in the street and taking the left hand one, climbed slowly out of the town and up the side of the valley. The street soon deteriorated into an earth track. Half way up the valley Napoleon saw a house below, on his right, clearly separated from the small town, surrounded by its own gardens. On enquiring, he was told it belonged to a Mr Balcombe, an employee of the East India Company. This house then disappeared as the road them veered to the left to climb over the top of the ridge and the town was left behind. The party was seen climbing up the valley side. Betsy Balcombe:

> The next morning, we observed a large cavalcade moving along the path which wound round the mountain, at the base of which our dear little cottage was lying, almost hidden in its nest of leaves. The effect of the party was very picturesque. It consisted of five horsemen; and we watched them with great interest, as, following

the windings of the road, they now gleamed in the sun's rays, and were thrown into brilliant relief by the dark background behind, and then disappearing, we gazed earnestly until, from some turn in the road, they flashed again upon us. Sometimes we only saw a single white plume, or the glitter of a weapon in the sun.[8]

After this climb out of the town they rode on for a little over three miles, following the level road which curled around the head of Sane Valley – the location of Napoleon's grave for almost twenty years. The road then opened out onto the Long Wood plain to their front and Dead Wood to their left. Beyond the plain the horizon was dominated by the great hill known as the Barn and beyond that, the sky. Below that sky lay the Atlantic Ocean and nothing else.

Napoleon was invited into Longwood House by Cockburn, who conducted a tour, mentioning all the work which was to be carried out prior to his moving in. Napoleon was evidently not pleased. There was a great deal that needed doing to bring the farm house up to a point that would befit even 'a general officer of the highest rank'.

Longwood is at a high point on the island and so had no running water available. A detailed map of the island surveyed and drawn in 1811 shows a water tank on the plain, close to both the East India Company gardens and Long Wood House. However this was simply a collection point for barrels of water brought up from the town.

That map also shows the wood that screened the house and gardens from the prevailing winds. Unfortunately these were gum trees, which in appearance are like sparse pine trees. They were well spaced out and provided neither efficient shelter from the rain nor an adequate windbreak for the house. At least two contemporary pictures show a thin scattering of these trees close by the house. The trees grew at a distance from each other and had no leafy canopy under which people could stroll in shade. According to Marchand, when the Emperor visited Longwood, the south easterly wind blew quite strongly cross the plain.

The Emperor could only see one advantage – that the extensive plateau would enable him to go riding and even take carriage rides, 'if they were willing to cut paths through the woods of gum trees that stood a short distance from the house'. Even in this hope, he would soon be disappointed.

When Napoleon cast his customary penetrating gaze over the landscape he would have noted the fort to the west dominating the view. Almost wherever he went on this plateau it would be in view, a constant reminder that he was a prisoner. In 1815 there was only a small fort on the knoll. The current fort is of Victorian construction but built on the same site.

Marchand claimed in his memoirs that the Emperor had been the victim of a 'barbaric process' in the allocation of Longwood, 'when there was such a charming one on the opposite side of the island'. He was referring to the governor's residence, Plantation House. This grand Georgian house is still the residence of the governor today. It is occupied all year as it lies on the sheltered side of the island. It nestles at the head of the valley, which then, as now, had fields for grazing and cultivation and some woodland. It was a far more pleasing location for a home than Longwood, but it was the official residence of the governor of the island and was declared by the government to be the only building that Napoleon should not occupy.

The wife of the Lieutenant Governor, Mrs Skelton, provided lunch and at three o'clock Napoleon called for his horse and the party began their ride back to Jamestown. Returning over the ridge Napoleon once again saw the Briars sitting above the town and asked to visit it, saying that providing the owners were agreeable, he would like to occupy the pavilion beyond the house. Looking down from the road he would have seen a town house in small yet well maintained gardens and beyond it a smaller one-storey building beyond it, the roof of which swept out over it almost in the manner of a Chinese pagoda. Betsy thought it 'a beautiful little cottage'.

It was a very simple two-storey structure with a small upper floor area. At either side was a single-storey wing with two long windows in each. The Briars could have been the home of an impoverished clergyman. It was not a grand country house, though its setting was quite delightful, overlooking the town and surrounded by well tended gardens.

At two o'clock the two naval surgeons, O'Meara and Warden, called at the Briars and were questioned a great deal about Napoleon. They assured the family that they would find him 'pleasing and agreeable' but the young girl Betsy still thought of him 'only with fear and trembling'. Two hours later Napoleon's party was seen approaching the Briars. The Balcombes all came out onto the lawn (save for the father, William, who was in bed suffering from gout) to greet their illustrious visitor. Betsy wanted to 'run and hide' but her mother persuaded her to stay because she could speak some French:

> The party arrived at the gate, and there being no carriage road, they all dismounted, excepting the emperor, who was now fully visible. He retained his seat and rode up the avenue, his horse's feet cutting up the turf on our pretty lawn. Sir George Cockburn walked on one side of his horse and General Bertrand on the other. How vividly I recollect my feelings of dread mingled with admiration, as I now first looked upon him whom I had learned to fear so much. His appearance on horseback was noble and imposing. The animal he rode was a superb one; his colour jet black; and as he proudly stepped up the avenue, arching his neck and champing his bit, I thought he looked worthy to be the bearer of him who was once the rule of nearly the whole European world!
>
> Napoleon's position on horseback, by adding height to his figure, supplied all that was wanting to make me think him the most majestic person I had ever seen. His dress was green, and covered with orders, and his saddle and housings were of crimson velvet richly embroidered with gold. He alighted at our house, and we all moved to the entrance to receive him. Sir George Cockburn introduced him to us.
>
> On a nearer approach Napoleon, contrasting, as his shorter figure did, with the noble height and aristocratic bearing of Sir George Cockburn, lost something of

the dignity which had so much struck me on first seeing him. He was deadly pale, and I thought his features, though cold and immovable, and somewhat stern, were exceedingly beautiful. He seated himself on one of our cottage chairs, and after scanning our little apartment with his eagle eye glance, he complimented Mamma on the pretty situation of the Briars. When once he began to speak, his fascinating smile and kind manner removed every vestige of the fear with which I had hitherto regarded him.[9]

Almost all of the contemporary pictures of the Briars show both the family home and the pavilion up against the hills and the famous heart shaped waterfall. It is a very charming view. On turning around to face the sea, the view from the veranda of the pavilion is even more stunning. The pavilion looks across a subtropical garden, the luxuriance of which is emphasised by its being framed by the barren volcanic sides of the Jamestown valley. Here the viewer would physically dominate the valley, looking both down the valley and out to sea. The pavilion had an attic room, which would accommodate both Las Cases and his son, whilst Napoleon would occupy the single large room below.

Napoleon was not even the master of his own garden. Looking over the walls of the fort at Ladder Hill today as sentries did then, one can see the entire area of the Briars. Only one contemporary watercolour shows both parts of the Briars and the fort – the others concentrating on the two properties, the waterfall and often the tent, which would be set up in front of the pavilion. The lush garden was described by Betsy:

An Eden blooming in the midst of desolation. A beautiful avenue of banyan trees led up to it, and either side was flanked by evergreen and gigantic lacos, interspersed with pomegranate and myrtle, and a profusion of large white roses, much resembling our sweet briar, from which, indeed, the place derived its name.[10]

Here, she says, there was such an abundance of fruits that it provided a profit of between £500 and £600 annually – a very substantial sum in 1815. Captain John Barnes in his general history of the island mentions that the Briars was noted for producing 'varieties of the best fruits; viz. mango, apples, figs, guava, pomegranates, oranges, lemons, grapes, peaches, &c. in abundance'. Today there is no trace of that garden or the house. The site is now occupied by a small swimming pool but the stone pillars which supported the gates are still there, as is the lane along which Napoleon walked his horse.[11]

All of the horsemen, according to Betsy, except Napoleon, dismounted at the gates and walked into the garden of the house. He walked his horse across the lawn whilst Admiral Cockburn and General Bertrand walked at either side of him. With some difficulty he dismounted at the house and the Balcombes moved forward to receive him. The Admiral made the introductions, chairs were brought and Napoleon sat outside on the lawn. Betsy recalls how he looked much as the portraits portrayed him:

The portraits of him give a good general idea of his features; but his smile, and the expression of his eye, could not be transmitted to canvas, and these constituted Napoleon's chief charm. His hair was dark brown, and as fine and silky as a child's, rather too much so indeed for a man, as its very softness caused it to look rather thin. His teeth were even, but rather dark, and I afterwards found that this arose from his constant habit of eating liquorice, of which he always kept a supply in his waistcoat pocket.[12]

The view from the pavilion garden today is splendid. The variety of flowers in the garden are made vibrantly colourful through their contrast with the volcanic valley sides. From the garden in front of the pavilion Napoleon would have looked down onto the lower garden in front of the Briars house. He would have seen both the children and the adults, beneath him, before they climbed the steps up to 'his' garden. Any horseman approaching the house would have to ride through the main gates and into the lower garden first. No one could directly approach the Emperor without first negotiating those few hurdles. Here at least, he had some distance from the people of the island.

The garden, according to Betsy, had a thick prickly hedge around it, from which the property took its name. Beyond the garden plateau in front of the pavilion was another garden area. Here again he could find a little peace away from the curious. However, not all sightseers would be disappointed. The principal tower of the Victorian fort at High Knoll occupies the position of the earlier tower. The pavilion of the Briars and its garden can be easily seen from there. Soldiers could peer down into the valley and see Bonaparte as he strolled in the garden. Surprisingly, given the active policy of complaining about anything and everything, none of Napoleon's companions ever mentions the presence of the fort. Behind the pavilion is the waterfall. It does not always cascade. When heavy rains come and fall over the lip it is a delightful sight as the water falls into the stream below, to be carried through the valley and out to sea at Jamestown.

Having surveyed the site, Napoleon declared that he wished to stay in the pavilion rather than endure another night at the Porteus lodging house. Mr Balcombe in response offered to evacuate the main house but according to Marchand the Emperor reiterated, once this offer had been translated, that he would be most comfortable in the pavilion.

When the Admiral arrived Balcombe found that he was appointed Navy Agent, in which capacity it was his duty to act as 'purveyor to Bonaparte'. Balcombe had a direct link to the Royal Navy having, according to Betsy, served at the battle of the Nile, only being compelled to leave the Navy as a consequence of his 'unreasoning hot headed temper'.

A letter to Balcombe, addressed from the House of Lords and dated 5 August, had also arrived with the squadron. The writer was Sir Thomas Tyrwhitt, secretary and confidant to the Prince Regent: 'Ministers will not pledge themselves to purchase any particular spot, but ... all is to be left to the choice of the two commanders, as to what place is best adapted to confine Napoleon comfortably but

Parade Square and the Porteus House in the background on the right *c.*1890. This
is the only photograph to show the front of the Porteus House. Courtesy of the St
Helena Archive.

severely.'[13] It goes on to suggest that the Briars might be chosen as the future residence for Napoleon. Chaplin proposes that Balcombe was chosen by Napoleon
to be his purveyor, whereas this letter shows that the matter had already been
decided in London at a very senior level. It seems unlikely that Napoleon had
any influence over the appointment of any British member of his domestic staff.
Everyone who was appointed to assist him was vetted by some agency of the
British government. Why should the British government believe that General
Bonaparte would keep his word that he had finished with politics? He had been
sent into exile on Elba barely a year previously and had returned to Europe in
the following spring leaving a trail of destruction across the plains of Belgium.
Previous to this he had been given opportunities to come to an accommodation
with the Allies in 1813 and yet he had squandered each one. Those experiences
had taught the Allies that there would never be any peace with France unless
Napoleon was removed as head of state.

Physically, Napoleon was in decline. However, this had not seemed so to the
governments and monarchs of Europe in the summer. He had demonstrated his
military genius with a startling opening to the Waterloo Campaign. Clearly he
remained a dangerous opponent. He was to be cut off from any means of communicating directly with Europe. By removing monies from his staff, their ability
to bribe seafarers to carry clandestine correspondence would be curtailed. It was

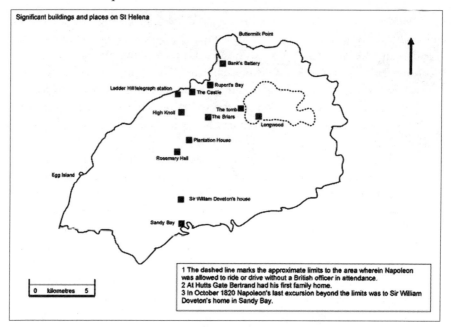

Significant buildings and places on St Helena

1 The dashed line marks the approximate limits to the area wherein Napoleon was allowed to ride or drive without a British officer in attendance.
2 At Hutts Gate Bertrand had his first family home.
3 In October 1820 Napoleon's last excursion beyond the limits was to Sir William Doveton's home in Sandy Bay.

a vain hope. Napoleon had already smuggled gold ashore and St Helena would leak like a sieve when it came to getting secret correspondence off the island.

It is likely that the Honourable East India Company headquarters at Leadenhall Street had already provided Balcombe's name to the government. Copies of all significant records concerning the running of East India Company possessions were held in London. Tyrwhitt mentions a 'very strong letter indeed' from Beatson, 'recommending you to Sir George Cockburn, as Naval Agent. This letter goes in this cover to him, and I sincerely hope it will answer the purpose intended'.[14] Beatson was General Beatson of the East India Company who had recently completed five years as governor of St Helena Island. An energetic soldier, administrator and agriculturalist, he had encouraged the development of farming to make the place as near self-sufficient as possible.

William Balcombe was a man with a sound business background. He occupied the position of a senior manager on the island and had carried out his duties in a very efficient manner. The records showed that he was to be relied upon. How wrong they were.

Betsy's memoirs paint an idyllic picture of life with Napoleon. However, she admits that as a child she did not keep a diary. She does not claim that this diary presents an inventory of daily life with Napoleon but rather impressions of specific instances which she managed to put into the correct chronological order some 23 years after his death.

Several diarists comment on the genuine pleasure Napoleon got from being in the presence of the Balcombe children. That afternoon, seated on the lawn of the Briars, Napoleon invited Betsy to join him. He had already been told that she spoke some French. He quizzed her in his usual quick style about the chief cities of Europe. When he asked her what the capital of Russia was and she replied that it had been Moscow but that it was now St Petersburg, he, 'fixing his piercing eyes' on her, demanded to know who had burnt it. The child, not surprisingly, was overwhelmed by his stare and said nothing. On his repeating the question, fearing to offend him she stammered that she did not know. He laughed and she went on to say, 'I believe, sir, the Russians burnt it to get rid of the French.' Napoleon laughed again.

Marchand summed up the situation in the little country house succinctly. The Emperor was severely limited in his movements but at least he was actually free to move about and the rest could be forgotten.[15] It was a temporary home made more comforting by the presence of four children. For the first time since leaving Elba he was in the presence of innocence, in the form of those children. In the corridor at the back of the pavilion, his two personal servants would sleep on thin mattresses which Saint Denis believed were from the *Northumberland*. Las Cases and his son occupied the six-foot-square attic room above the Emperor.

If he was restless Napoleon could rise and read. The view from the pavilion gave out onto the ocean framed by the volcanic edges of the James valley. If he wished to walk he had the enclosed garden with its fruit trees and flowers, screened by a thick hedge. Beyond that lay an interval of perhaps half a mile before the straggling margins of the town. Behind him stood the waterfall and the hills. At the Briars he could recover a little of his humanity. Once he had stepped on board of the *Bellerophon* his imperial dignity had been deflated. This process had then accelerated on board the *Northumberland*. His private baggage had been inspected and his monies removed. His personal staff had been largely withdrawn and he now knew that he was to have no access to Europe. He had lost an army, a country and a throne, for a second time. He was to have no private correspondence with anyone in Europe. Yet here perhaps there was some rest. There is an impression when reading the memoirs of both Betsy Abell and Louis Marchand that Napoleon did indeed use this time to recuperate.

That first afternoon Bertrand, the Grand Marshal of the Palace, returned to the lodging house and ordered Marchand to take Noverraz with him and move the Emperor's personal camp equipment to the Briars. Cipriani, the butler, was ordered to prepare the Emperor's dinner in Jamestown and to have it taken up to the Briars. Marchand says he was relieved at this change as the cramped situation of the town was so at odds with the habits of his master.

On arriving Marchand saw the Emperor sitting outside of the pavilion chatting with the Admiral. He thought the location of the pavilion very pleasant, the waterfall creating a light mist as it fell. Mrs Balcombe and her two 'charming daughters' assisted in providing what furniture they could. But the island then as now was not rich and 'the Emperor found around him the furnishings of a field tent.' The Emperor's bed was assembled and a table was set up in the middle of the room over a rug.

A dresser offered by Mr Balcombe was used to display Napoleon's travelling kit, which 'decorated the room a little'. The silver washstand created by the craftsman, Biennais arrived and was set up, along with the portraits of Marie-Louise and the King of Rome. Curtains were improvised at the four windows and the room was as furnished as it could be. That night Saint-Denis, Noverraz and Marchand slept in the corridor at the back of the pavilion. They were wrapped in their coats and slept on mattresses which had been sent up from the town.

Both Marchand and Betsy mention Napoleon continuing with the routine established aboard the *Northumberland*, with the dictation of his memoirs his great occupation. To that end things were arranged so that work written one day could then be fair copied by the next morning for any subsequent alteration and redrafting the next. Betsy:

> The emperor's habits, during the time he stayed with us, were very simple and regular. His usual hour for getting up was eight, and he seldom took anything but a cup of coffee until one, when he breakfasted, or rather lunched; he dined at nine, and retired about eleven to his own rooms.[16]

For the first two days the Emperor's meals were delivered by slaves, who brought them up from Jamestown. After two days of cold meals Marchand reorganised things. He arranged for one of the domestic staff to cook at the pavilion using a small oven which the slaves used at the back of the pavilion for cooking their own food. This arrangement also had the advantage, says Marchand, of not disturbing Mrs Balcombe. Two days later, Pierron, the butler and Lepage, the chef, moved into the Briars. The Emperor's table linen and silver were also brought up from the town. (Later, the plate will play a part in Napoleon's war against the British government.)

Shortly afterwards, the Royal Artillery officer Captain Greatly who had travelled on the *Northumberland* moved into the Briars. With him were two orderlies, probably NCOs taken from the artillery detachment that Greatly commanded. Here was an obvious source of irritation for Napoleon, a daily reminder that he was a prisoner. No matter how much care he took to avoid being in the Emperor's way, Greatly always was, and this had unfortunate results; it marked the beginning of the deterioration in relations between the Admiral and the Emperor.[17]

Cockburn still had to provide stringent security until the permanent governor arrived in the New Year. Marchand says that the sergeant and men were withdrawn and Captain Greatly was put into civilian dress. However, Greatly was still there to observe the French, He was withdrawn later, but only to be replaced by another orderly officer, Captain Macky of the 53rd Regiment. There would always be, as the July memorandum made clear, an orderly officer living close by, whose principal task was to monitor, not to attend upon, the General.

> The General must be always attended by an officer appointed by the Admiral or Governor, as the case may be: – if the General is permitted to move beyond the

boundaries where the sentries are placed, the officer should be attended by one orderly at least.[18]

In view of the letter to Cockburn, the removal of the orderlies attending Greatly was a clear concession. Though the prevailing winds, which blow from the south-east to the north, plus Cockburn's complete authority over all the vessels belonging to the island, meant he could confidently bend the rules in the memorandum. The coastline was patrolled day and night and no strange vessel would be allowed to approach the island without being stopped and investigated. Even the island fishermen would be affected by these new security measures.

There could not be a repeat of the escape from Elba. Napoleon had left that island in the vessels of his tiny navy. Here he had no control over any vessel, large or small, rowing or sailing. When Napoleon had escaped a few months previously, the unfortunate Captain Adye commanding HM Sloop *Partridge* had been at sea, cruising. This would not happen again. On both sides of the island, to the south and north there would be an armed sloop cruising on permanent patrol, with the authority to interdict any passing vessel. In the St Helena roads the flagship, of greater firepower, would be available.

The small French party, men and women, were under observation wherever they went in Jamestown. But remember Elba. Was he about to spring from St Helena as he had done there? How could anyone be certain? The man was brilliant. With a miserable squadron of ships he had avoided the Royal Navy in the Mediterranean. Then he had landed and with barely a thousand men, advanced on Paris, gathering up almost all of the army units that had been sent to arrest him. The government instructions to Admiral Cockburn were clear, General Bonaparte was to be afforded every luxury due to his rank, provided it did not conflict with keeping him secure. If the Admiral felt that the General's security on the island could not be guaranteed then he was to be re-embarked. This had been made clear to Cockburn in July in the memorandum detailing the procedure for examining Bonaparte's property.[19]

Even if they were not being followed, the French were being observed. How could it be otherwise? There was part of the newly arrived infantry battalion quartered in the town, whose sole purpose was to prevent the removal of General Bonaparte from the island. Every day they saw some of the people whom they were to stop, should an attempt be made to free General Bonaparte. There were also the soldiers of the existing Honourable East India Company garrison. These comprised a single infantry battalion, the Saint Helena Infantry Regiment and a single battalion of artillery, the Saint Helena Artillery Regiment. Part of each unit was quartered in the town. Instead of protecting the island from the threat of invasion, as they had done year in and year out, they too were now under the control of the crown, subject to the same regulations and rules as the King's troops.

The small French party were aliens on a very small island. Most of them spoke no English. They had been sent to a tiny community whose principal activity was servicing the merchant shipping of the Honourable East India Company.

There was little other economic activity on the island. Jamestown was home to part of the military garrison. The administrative headquarters of the island were based in the Castle. Both of these buildings were barely two hundred yards from the Porteus House. Only the small botanic gardens separated the house from these buildings. Officers, soldiers, sailors and military orderlies passed the Porteus House every day.

Today the small town has the same street plan as it had then. Barnes' excellent map, surveyed in 1811, can confidently be used today to navigate across the island. There are only three principal streets in the town. Many of the same buildings that Napoleon had ridden past still occupy the high street. Where the high street forks, one road leads to Longwood and the other into the upper part of the town below the Briars. Wherever the French strolled they would meet the British soldiers, both the King's and the Company soldiers. Some were busy with their new garrison duties, others marching up to or from Longwood, and some reconnoitring the island. Amidst them were the officers, craftsmen and labourers from the Royal Navy ships carrying their tools and materials up to Longwood to carry out the repairs and improvements.

Napoleon, like everyone else, could largely settle into a daily routine, begun on board the *Northumberland*. He rose early, often but not always, dressed, took a stroll in the garden, took a cup of coffee and perhaps briefly strolled again. Sometimes according to Betsy he would have his papers taken across the main lawn to an area beyond the ornamental fish pond. Here at the end of the grape trellis an arbour had been created:

> To this spot, which was so sheltered as to be cool in the most sultry weather, Napoleon was much attached. He would sometimes convey his papers there as early as four o'clock in the morning, and employ himself until breakfast time in writing; and, when tired of his pen, in dictating to Las Cases. No one was ever permitted to intrude upon him when there, and this little attention was ever after gratefully remembered.[20]

It would seem unlikely that Napoleon would sit with his pen for very long, as none of the other diarists mention him writing alone. Wherever he was, the tent or the arbour, the business of the day would invariably begin with Las Cases reading a fair copy of yesterday's dictation, written before breakfast, by Las Cases's son. This Napoleon would check. Then he would recommence his dictation. The Italian Campaign was dictated to Las Cases, the Egyptian Campaign to General Bertrand, to General Montholon the Empire and to General Gourgard the Consulate, Elba and the Waterloo Campaign. As the dictation grew, so too did the need for more fair copying and Marchand and Saint Denis found themselves writing for the Emperor. Napoleon did attempt to write himself but

> His hand could not follow his thoughts that were so quick, concise, and full of fire; his fingers did not respond to the speed of his imagination. Then he attempted

The Briars and the pavilion. Today the house has gone but the pavilion has been sensitively restored by the French Consul.

abbreviating, but in such a fashion that it was illegible to everyone, and sometimes even to himself.[21]

After lunch he would stroll in the garden again with his companions before working again and later he would converse with his companions whilst walking among the short avenue of trees that was dubbed 'the philosopher's avenue'. Then dinner would be announced, 'His Majesty's dinner is served.'

In the first few days at the Briars he would send Las Cases to the main house to enquire whether or not the Balcombe family were at home. If they were then the Emperor would join them for a simple family evening where the two girls and Betsy in particular would be drawn into the conversation and entertainment. Marchand remembers

... Mrs Balcombe, kind, sweet, and affectionate, and two young ladies of whom the younger, Miss Betsy, promised to become pretty. Both of them were pleasant and gracious; they spoke a little French; as Count Las Cases spoke perfect English, relations were established with this family. The Emperor sometimes went to their house to be amused by the naïveté of these young people, and to partake in a game of whist that they offered him.[22]

The Emperor would have attended more of these pleasant evenings at the Balcombe's but people eager to see him found out about them and called at the Briars hoping to see him. This understandable desire to see the great man would follow Napoleon to Longwood and beyond – even the trees around his grave would be stripped for souvenirs.

Betsy recalls that first evening where she sang the Scottish air 'Ye banks and braes' and was complimented upon it by Napoleon. He then responded with a French song, *'Vive Henri Quatre.'* He began

> … to hum the air, became abstracted, and leaving his seat, marched round the room, keeping time to the song he was singing. When he had done, he asked me what I thought of it; and I told him I did not like it at all, for I could not make out the air. In fact Napoleon's voice was most unmusical, nor do I think he had any ear for music; for neither on this occasion, nor in any of his subsequent attempts at singing, could I ever discover what tune he was executing.[23]

The song was composed by the popular French composer Grétry who had been awarded pensions from both Louis XVI and Napoleon and shortly before his death in 1813, the Legion of Honour. Grétry probably exemplified the best sort of popular music for Napoleon – written by a Frenchman but in an Italian style.[24]

Shortly after this musical interlude the Emperor retired for the night and thus ended his first night at the Briars. Betsy delightfully adds to the impression of Napoleon having no ear for music by describing a friend, whom she does not name, who, when visiting, delighted in singing Italian songs which

> … she loved, indeed 'not wisely, but too well', for her own attempts in the bravura style were the most absurd burlesque imaginable. Napoleon however, constantly asked her to sing, and even listened with great politeness; but when she was gone, he often desired me to imitate her singing, which I did as nearly as I could, and it seemed to amuse him.[25]

He declared that even French music was poor in comparison to Italian opera.

Shortly afterwards, Sir George Bingham came to pay a call. He was shocked to discover how little room Napoleon had in the pavilion and suggested that his soldiers could erect a marquee on the small lawn in front. Napoleon accepted this idea and the tent became the dining room and his study. It was connected to the pavilion by a covered way. At one end stood a small bed with green silk hangings on which Gourgard slept. Between the two internal rooms of the tent an imperial crown was cut into the turf of the lawn and over this imperial symbol walked Napoleon.[26]

One of those who was as keen as any to see Napoleon was Archibald Hamilton, Captain of the HEIC vessel *Bombay Castle*. On 6 November, sailing from the Cape for St Helena, he saw a warship cruising off the south west or weather side of the island, which was clearly going to intercept them. Hamilton knew nothing of the battle of Waterloo or the recently signed peace treaty with the Americans and wondered whether this was an enemy privateer.[27]

At eight o'clock the warship hailed the *Bombay Castle* and proved to be the *Icarus*, a brig of 18 guns, commanded by Captain Devon. An officer boarded the *Bombay Castle*, checked documents and passed on the remarkable news of Napoleon being a prisoner on the island. He also informed Hamilton that he would find the rest of the naval squadron there along with another warship cruising on the leeward or northern side of the island, whilst the *Ceylon*, would be seen anchored off Egg Island, helping to build a battery position there. He told Hamilton that from now on only the vessels of the Company along with naval vessels might seek shelter in the Jamestown roads. Hamilton signalled the island, and came in, 'after some demure about allowing us to proceed to the anchorage on account of our being associated with the late insurrection in Bombay and Java'.

He immediately made his way to the *Northumberland* to pay his respects to the Admiral but found he was ashore. Captain Ross then showed him the cabin which Napoleon had occupied during the voyage. Going on shore he met the Governor but was told that the Admiral was 'in the country'.

> I was like any one else extremely anxious to see the extraordinary man: And Mr Balcombe at whose house, the Briars, he lived asked me to dine with him on Wednesday, and that as Buonaparte came in every evening from the detached cottage which he occupied to play cards and amuse himself with the family I should be given [access] to him in the evening – I was very happy to accept this invitation.[28]

The Monday night before his invitation to dine at the Briars, he and Captain Richards of the *Zephyr* returned to their lodgings. Richards had just dined there and had played whist with Buonaparte. Richards explained that he had asked, through Las Cases, a great many questions of him. He also told Hamilton that Bonaparte had played very carefully, taking a great deal of money from him during the evening.

On Wednesday, full of anticipation, Hamilton went up to the Briars accompanied by his brother and a Mr Pennington. When they arrived they discovered 'so large a party assembled that I had little hopes that Buonaparte would join the party in the evening.' Not surprisingly, Napoleon refused to cooperate. As the house party sat at dinner, Hamilton became aware that Napoleon was taking his customary walk in the garden accompanied by Las Cases. Hamilton got up from the table and saw

> that he was grown corpulent and did not walk with at least with ability – he was dressed as usual in the uniform of the National Guard, green with small epaulettes, white waistcoat, nankeen breeches.'[29]

This would have been his usual undress uniform of a colonel in the mounted Chasseurs of the Imperial Guard. Las Cases walked beside him with his hat off and as they walked they conversed. Hamilton observed that later Las Cases had his hat on as they walked together. This may have been a concession by Napoleon as Hamilton also noted that Las Cases seemed to 'suffer much from the cold in his head'. Hamilton also noticed Betsy:

> Buonaparte was much in the part of joking with the younger Miss Balcombe, a most surprising girl who said anything that came apparent; the family had introduced several people to him – with whom he conversed fondly and with good humour – This evening Mrs Smith, a great fat woman and her daughter in law, a large woman and the eldest Miss B – intercepted them as they came up the walk, to the Emperor who made them a polite bow and passed on. When Miss Balcombe heard that her friends had not had the honour of consorting with the Emperor, she insisted on introducing them again and the fat lady and her daughter were again introduced, when the Emperor passed on with displeasure she took no notice of them – Mrs B upon this observed she had no idea of him giving such airs with her friends.[30]

For the rest of the evening Hamilton waited in vain. Later he learnt that the Emperor had told the Balcombes that he had not agreed to meet such a large party of people. Fortunately for Hamilton, his ship was not leaving the island for another three days. Later, after most of the other guests had departed, Balcombe told him to come to the house again, on Friday evening. Hamilton was to bring only Mr Pennington with him. Balcombe assured him that as they were the only invited guests they would probably meet Bonaparte after all. So for the rest of the evening the guests had to be content with hearing tales of Bonaparte from Mr Balcombe.

Alas, on returning on Friday evening with Pennington and his brother, Hamilton found that the house party was again a very large one. Not expecting to see Napoleon, Hamilton went to walk in the garden before dinner and suddenly realised that Napoleon was there. Hamilton says he did not wish to stare at Napoleon and so retired, Napoleon doing the same. Later Hamilton spotted him again, walking on the lawn before the main house.

At this point in the evening Balcombe took Hamilton the thirty yards up to the pavilion to show him Napoleon's living quarters. Looking into the tent he saw the dining table 'where the Emperor dines and also writes and sat afterwards'. He was also shown the 'N' which had been cut into the grass and the beautiful Sèvres dinner service he used.

However, he was still disappointed at not having met the Emperor and said so to Balcombe. With another unannounced large party in the house, the Emperor would never show. Also there were three persons 'in regimentals' which made it almost certain. Balcombe proposed a final plan. Hamilton was to come up alone, on Saturday evening, saying nothing to anyone prior to arriving. The great man would probably be at home – playing cards with the family. Hamilton agreed to this. There was a slight modification, Hamilton came to breakfast next morning and had a good view in the daylight of Napoleon's temporary home.

Hamilton left declaring that he would return for any last instructions from the ladies, before leaving for England in the morning. He arrived back at the Briars some time after eight o'clock, and stood by the door of the drawing room where

Sketch of the main house and the pavilion at the Briars, taken from Betsy Balcombe's book.

he could plainly see the Emperor seated at cards with Mr Balcombe and his two daughters. They were playing whist:

> Buonaparte's partner was the eldest Miss Balcombe & Mr Balcombe played with youngest daughter, a young scamp of fifteen – Las Cases and his son attended as usual and General Gourgard was upon a visit tonight.[31]

The orderly officer, Captain Mackay was also present, as was Mrs Balcombe:

> I was of course taken up with really as much as possible in contemplating this extraordinary man, without appearing to please myself for that purpose – He was laughing and joining with the girls all the time he played.[32]

He was dressed as his usual green undress uniform. Hamilton added that he seemed 'rather corpulent' and rather clumsy. In describing his head he did so as others have done: 'His eyes were grey and blue, a very handsome nose, a most handsome shaped mouth …' Hamilton also took time in his diary to describe Napoleon's hands, alluding to their feminine nature. Whilst he was observing Napoleon, Balcombe

> … took an opportunity to get up about the Madeira and asked me to take to take his cards; and I became seated at a small card table playing at Whist with a man who little more than the year before at head of a Powerful Empire with almost despotic powers, and commanding the greatest and finest Armies that any empire ever possessed had nearly subjugated Europe – And who after many [problems] had again

been crowned emperor in Paris & had again commanded Powerful Armies not quite months ago – No retrospect of those circumstances seemed to distract him at this time, he appeared neither thoughtful or sad but continued in perfect good humour joking and gay disputing with Miss Betsey about the game, demanding payment.[33]

After she had refused to make the payment demanded, he turned to Las Cases who then enquired of Hamilton whether there were special courts in England concerned with commercial bankruptcies. Napoleon addressed Hamilton directly in French, wanting to know what water his ship drew. On being told it was 23 feet Napoleon seemed impressed, whereupon General Gourgard informed him that the ship was not like HMS *Northumberland*. This was Gourgard reminding the Emperor that the *Bombay Castle* was a large, heavily laden merchant vessel and not a naval one.

After the questions, Napoleon stood, spoke politely with the ladies, made a bow to every person present and left. Hamilton says he was standing by the door as Napoleon left and so shook hands with him. Shortly afterwards, with his list of requirements from the ladies, he left for Jamestown.

At the end of the letter there is a note, dated 18 March 1840, in which Hamilton remembers the questions Napoleon asked him. These questions concerned the number of guns his ship carried, the crew, the value of the cargo, what it was and what duties would be payable to the government. Later he met with Mr Haws, a passenger on the *Bombay Castle*, and, 'on comparing notes we found that he did not ask me one question which he had previously put to Mr Haws'.

One of the strangest incidents recounted in the Abell diary is the account of the 'punishment' of Las Cases. A few days after settling at the Briars, Napoleon, apparently taunting Betsy that she ought to marry Las Cases junior, held her hands whilst the teenager was told to kiss her. This he did. Upon being released Betsy flew at the boy and 'boxed le petit Las Cases' ears most thoroughly'. Presumably the adults present thought the amusing incident had ended. Not so for Betsy – she was 'determined' to revenge herself on Napoleon.

Later as they walked in single file down the steep slope which separated the pavilion from the lawn, she waited for Napoleon, Las Cases, his son and her sister Jane to pass. Then she sprang. She collided with the younger Las Cases, who staggered into his father until even 'the Emperor, who although the shock was diminished … still had some difficulty … in preserving his footing'. Betsy was delighted but Las Cases was genuinely furious at the way the Emperor had been 'insulted'. He seized her by the shoulders and pushed her hard against the rocky bank. It was now her turn to be shocked. She 'burst into tears of passion':

'Oh, sir, he has hurt me.' 'Never mind,' replied the emperor, 'ne pleure pas – I will hold him while you punish him.' And a good punishing he got. I boxed the little man's ears until he begged for mercy; but I would show him none; and at length Napoleon let him go, telling him to run, and that if he could not run faster than I, he deserved to be beaten again. He immediately started off as fast as he could, and I after him, Napoleon clapping his hands and laughing immoderately at our race round the lawn. Las Cases never liked me after this adventure, and used to call me a rude hoyden.[34]

What an abandonment of imperial protocol! His grand chamberlain dashing across the lawn pursued by a thirteen-year-old colonial girl. If all of this is true and even if only part of it was, what a fine distraction for Napoleon from his position.

Following the story of the dash across the lawn Betsy says that Napoleon would never lose his temper with her, or 'fall back upon his rank or age' to avoid a confrontation. For her he was always keen to participate in 'every sort of mirth or fun with the glee of a child'. He was

> ... almost as a brother or companion of my own age; and all the cautions I received, and my own resolutions to treat him with more respect and formality, were put to flight the moment I came within the influence of his arch smile and laugh.[35]

Another good example of this relationship concerns a ball gown. Betsy had asked Napoleon to intercede with her father over his refusal to let her attend her first ball. Napoleon had done so, permission had been granted and a dress prepared. They were playing whist in the cottage, Jane playing with Napoleon and Betsy with Las Cases. The cards did not flow and so Napoleon asked Las Cases to deal them again. Whilst he did this, Napoleon turned to Betsy and enquired about her dress. She immediately left the room and returned with it. It was to be her first ball and this was her first ball dress and she was 'not a little proud of it'. Napoleon complimented her on the dress, and, the cards being ready she placed the dress on the nearby sofa and returned to the game.

Napoleon then declared that they would not play for sugar plums as they usually did. Instead he would wager a Napoleon on the game. Betsy says she had a pagoda which 'made up the sum of all her worldly riches', and she pledged that. However, as the game progressed Napoleon attempted to draw Betsy's attention away from his cards and to signal important cards to his partner, Jane. Betsy told him to stop cheating, but it was not to be and at the end of the game, Betsy seized his hands and reminded everyone what he had done over the course of the game. At this point, he 'laughed until the tears ran out of his eyes, and declared he had played fair, but that I had cheated, and should pay him the pagoda.' Suddenly he snatched up the ball dress from the sofa and ran out of the house. Betsy was left, in her own words, 'in terror lest he should crush and spoil all my pretty roses'. She then set off in pursuit but he escaped dashing through the marquee and into the pavilion – locking it behind him. She assailed the door with 'remonstrances and entreaties' but the laughter from behind gave her the only answer she was to receive that night. The next day brought no further response to her requests for the return of the dress. The moment arrived, the horses were ready and the black boys stood ready with the tin cases which held the dresses, apart from Betsy's. As she dithered about whether to go in her plain dress or not go at all, Napoleon appeared 'running down the lawn,' carrying the dress, 'Here Miss Betsy, I have brought your dress; I hope you are a good girl now, and that you will like the ball; and mind you dance with Gourgard.'[36]

He accompanied the horses until they came to the end of the bridle road and paused to look further down the valley at a house on the far side of the stream. As they parted company he was told it belonged to Major Hodson of the Company's service. He decided that he would visit. Whilst the Balcombes made their way to the Admiral's ball, Napoleon, followed by Las Cases and his son, descended down a path usually followed only by slaves into the valley. Major Hodson recalled the event in a letter written a few months later:

> One evening he took a walk to the end of the wall at the side path road, and seeing that I was at home with my family and no others he ventured down with Las Cases. I, of course, went out to meet; he came into the house, looked about, and seemed very well pleased with it and the garden, which he walked over, paid Mrs Hodson a great many fine compliments, and took a great deal of notice of the children ... He was particularly struck with the youngest boy (who, bye the bye, is handsome), and said he is a fine boy, and knew he was the most wicked of them all, although at that moment he looked perfectly the reverse. He happened, however to be quite right. After staying a good while with us I mounted them both on horse-back, and they returned to the Briars in the dark. He gave the servants who attended him home some napoleons.[37]

Chaplin says Charles, the eldest of those children, recalled many years later that Napoleon had tweaked his nose during the visit – which was always a sign of affection with children. The Hodsons were to dine at Longwood on 4th January 1816. Major Hodson was nicknamed 'Hercules' by Napoleon on account of his imposing stature. Hodson would be one of the few people who would attend both the funeral in 1821 and the exhumation in 1840.[38]

It then being dark and the way back being steep they returned on borrowed horses. This excursion seems to have been on the spur of the moment for Marchand had no idea where the Emperor had gone. In the morning Napoleon appeared delighted with his visit. For Marchand there was 'something behind this pleasure', which was to have outwitted the orderly officer, Captain Greatly. However, the regulations were being tightened. In his memoirs Marchand lists the Port Regulations and the curfew, which had the French party back in town by nine o'clock every evening. Possibly on the day of the dress incident, Napoleon decided to ride out, to explore some of the island. Horses were sent for from the town and Las Cases and Saint-Denis prepared to accompany him. As he was about to leave he was informed that the orderly officer had new instructions, which meant that he would also have to accompany Napoleon on horseback wherever he rode over the island. He had the horses sent back. He would not compromise his political dignity. As far as he was concerned he was not a prisoner.

The principal gardener of the Balcombes was a Malayan slave, a man known as Toby. He had apparently been captured by pirates many years before and brought to the island as a slave. Betsy says that Napoleon 'took a fancy to old Toby' and asked if he might purchase him from Mr Balcombe and give him his freedom. This was not allowed, though who forbade it is not recorded in her account. It may have been the governor, Admiral Cockburn, but why he would prevent this act of generosity is not clear. This thoughtful act is in contrast to Napoleon's policy whilst First Consul. During the insurrection against French rule on the islands of the West Indies in 1802 he suppressed the attempt by the black slave population to set up a republic along French lines.[39]

> As the time drew near for Napoleon's removal from the Briars to Longwood he would come into the drawing room oftener, and stay longer. He would, he said, have preferred altogether remaining at the Briars, because he beguiled the hours with us better than he ever thought it possible he could have done on such a horrible rock as St. Helena.
>
> A day or two before his departure, General Bertrand came to the Briars and informed Napoleon that Longwood smelt so strongly of paint, that it was unfit to go to. I shall never forget the fury of the emperor. He walked up and down the lawn, gesticulating in the wildest manner. His rage was so great that it almost choked him. He declared that the smell of paint was so obnoxious to him, that he would never inhabit a house where it existed; and that if the grand marshal's report were true, he should send down to the admiral, and refuse to enter Longwood.[40]

Betsy had seen this rage and as she approached him

> … he changed his manner, and in a calm tone mentioned the reason of his annoyance. I was perfectly amazed at the power he evinced over his temper. In one moment, from the most awful state of fury, he subdued his irritability, and his manners became calm, gentle, and composed.[41]

Napoleon then ordered Las Cases to investigate the grand marshal's report next morning. On his return, Las Cases informed him that the smell of paint was so slight as to be scarcely perceptible. Bertrand was then upbraided for making an exaggerated report. The next morning Cockburn arrived to escort Napoleon to his new home. Betsy describes his farewell to the family. She was to come and see him at Longwood – and often. Turning to her father he said,'Balcombe, you must bring Missee Jane and Betsy to see me next week, eh? When will you ride up to Longwood?' Balcombe assured Napoleon that they would visit the very next week. He then enquired after Mrs Balcombe who was not present – she was ill in bed, and sent her apologies. Napoleon then 'darted' upstairs and sat at her bedside, declaring that, if they would have let him, he would rather have stayed at the Briars than leave for Longwood. He then presented Mrs Balcombe with a gold snuffbox. For Betsy there was 'a beautiful little bonbonnière' that she had often admired. In presenting it he declared that she could always offer it as a token of love to the younger Las Cases. With that she fled the room in tears and flung herself on her bed and wept.

Not only did Betsy see Napoleon the very next week but with her father being appointed both Navy Agent for the island and General Bonaparte's purveyor, she would visit Longwood on an almost weekly basis. They generally arrived at one, had breakfast with him and returned in the evening. From then on she recalled 'He was more subject to depression of spirits than when at the Briars, but still gleams of his former playfulness shone out at times.'

He attempted to teach her to play billiards, though she found this rather boring and spent more time attempting to hit his finger rather than pocketing the balls. On another occasion they found him firing his pistols at a mark and he invited her to shoot, declaring afterwards that he would make her the captain of a corps of tirailleurs.

Some months after his departure Betsy was taken ill. O'Meara attended her and Napoleon enquired after her health repeatedly. When she was convalescing he sent pastries made by his own confectioner, La Page, to tempt her and restore her to good health.

Betsy was convinced that it was the arrival and subsequent disputes with Sir Hudson Lowe that led to the decline in Napoleon's health. And as his health worsened so did that 'playfulness' which in her opinion marked his time at the Briars.

Betsy's memoirs are short. She did not keep a diary and she admits that as a teenage girl she did not realise how momentous those days on St Helena were. All the incidents she reports she has placed in the correct order but she regrets there are others which she never wrote down as she could not be certain exactly when they had taken place.

Notes

1 Prior, J., *Voyage along the coast of Africa to Mosambique, Johanna and Quiloa to St Helena in the Nisus frigate*, Sir Richard Philips & Co., 1819, page 83.

2 Henry W., *Trifles of a Surgeon's Life*, page 143.

3 Prior, J., op. cit., page 83.

4 Ibid., page 84.

5 Abell, Mrs, *Recollections of the Emperor Napoleon on the island of St Helena*, John Murray, London, 1844, page 15.

6 O'Meara B., *Napoleon in Exile or A Voice from St. Helena*, Volume 1, Jones & Company, Sixth Ed., 1830, page 10.

7 Saint-Denis, L. E., (Trans. Hunter Potter, F.) *Napoleon from the Tuileries to St Helena*, 1922, page 165.

8 Abell, op cit pages 16–17.

9 Ibid., pages 19–21. This less than flattering description of him was to be toned down in the later edition of her memoirs. By that time she had received a grant of lands in North Africa from Napoleon III.

10 Abell, op. cit., page 10.

11 The pavilion has been given to France by the late Dame Mabel Brookes, herself a direct descendant of the Balcombe family, and is now in the care of the Honorary French Consul, Michel Dansoineau-Martineau. The gardeners under the active direction of Martineau have restored the garden area immediately outside of the restored pavilion. After Napoleon's death, it, along with Longwood, was given over to other uses. The international interest in restoration work would not flourish until the twentieth century.

12 Abell, op. cit., pages 32–33.

13 Abell, op cit, page 3.

14 Ibid., page 3.

15 Marchand L. J., (English Edition), *In Napoleon's Shadow*, Proctor Jones, 1998, page 350.

16 Abell, op cit, 1844, page 41.

17 Marchand, op. cit., page 353.

18 Instructions from the Secretary of State by Command of the Prince Regent dated 30 July 1815. COC/1, NMM.

19 Ibid., COC/1.

20 Abell, op. cit., p. 67.

21 Marchand, op. cit., p. 355.

22 Ibid., pages 353–4.

23 Abell, op. cit., p. 37.

24 Harewood & Peattie (Eds.) *The New Kobbe's Opera Book*, Putnam, 1997, page 286.

25 Abell, op cit, p. 38.

26 Ibid., p. 35.

27 Hamilton, Archibald, Commander (H.E.I.C.) Captain's Log Book, HMN/87, NMM.

28 Ibid, HMN/87, NMM.

29 Ibid, HMN/87.

30 Ibid, HMN/87.

31 Ibid, HMN/87.

32 Ibid, HMN/87.

33 Ibid, HMN/87.

34 Abell, op. cit., p. 50.

35 Ibid., p. 52.

36 Ibid., p. 64.

37 Letter in the Appendix of Brooke, T. H., *History of the Island of St Helena*, Kingsbury, Parbury and Allen, 1824, page 266.

38 The Hodson family had strong connections with the island. In the Anglican church of Jamestown is an impressive memorial to Captain Benjamin Hodson who was probably a close relative who had died the previous year whilst serving with the St Helena Artillery. Major Hodson's wife was a daughter of Sir William Doveton, one of the three executive members of the island's council.

39 Fregosi, Paul, *Dreams of Empire*, Hutchinson, 1989, page 203. Slavery, as an institution had the approval of many on both sides of the English Channel. Sir Hudson Lowe was to be instrumental in stopping it on St Helena.

40 Abell, op. cit., pages 103–104.

41 Ibid., page 104.

Chapter Seven

Longwood House

I hate this Longwood. The sight of it makes me melancholy. Let him put me in some place where there is shade, verdure, and water. Here it either blows a furious wind, loaded with rain and fog, *che mi luglia l'anima* [which cuts me through]; or, if that is wanting, *il sole mi brucia il cervello* [the sun broils my brain], through the want of shade, when I go out. Let him put me on the Plantation House side of the island, if he really wishes to do anything for me.
Napoleon on the house at Longwood, O'Meara.[1]

The maritime climate of the island automatically leads to fogs swirling in to Longwood plain in a very dramatic manner. In July whilst walking in the gardens at Longwood house and then walking across and into Bertrand's garden, the author timed the arrival of thick fog, which obliterated the view of the Barn in fifteen minutes. Prior to its arrival the view from Longwood house lawn to the north had been one of blue sky and sunshine. Within two minutes of it arriving the author's clothes were covered in a fine warm mist. This was the very weather of which Napoleon complained to O'Meara whilst he was working on the history of his life.

The almost constant rain or fog, with the strong wind continually blowing over the bleak and exposed situation of Longwood, has contributed much to keep him indoors, and disgust himself with his present residence.[2]

Napoleon declared that he would much rather live on the leeward side of the island, which is warmer and suffers less from the wind. A year later, O'Meara records that the fog was so thick, and the weather so bad that the daily signal of, 'alls well' could not be sent from Longwood, which necessitated an orderly dragoon taking the message on horseback.

Barnes says that in 1815 'the recent eradication of the wild sheep' would lead to more vegetation growing and consequently more water would then be retained in the ground, enabling trees to flourish. The few accurate watercolours of the period that have been painted on the spot show few trees. Today as then,

Jamestown on the north side of the island and Plantation house to the east can have substantial rain in the morning whilst Longwood plain has only experienced the clouds passing over. Today, this difference in rainfall can be clearly seen in the amount of woodland on the north eastern side of the island. Plantation House, then as now was surrounded by relatively lush parkland and banks of mature trees. This growth was further encouraged by the relative lack of wind. The Trade Winds brought in the fog from the south over Longwood whilst the ridges of the island protected Plantation House and the areas around it. In 1816 there is a complaint made to Captain Poppleton, the Longwood orderly officer that that the wind has extinguished the lamps at the front of the house.[3]

Temperatures taken in Town and at Longwood for 1812, 1813 taken from Barnes:

	Town	Longwood
January	76	68
February	78	71
March	79	72
April	78	70
May	77	67
June	75	65
July	73	65
August	72	64
September	71	63
October	73	62
November	73	63
December	74	64

The rainy season lasts from July or August for six to ten weeks. The statistics offered by Barnes in the table above are similar to those given by Mellis in his book, published in 1875, where he quotes a table of temperatures for the period 1841 until 1845.[4]

Napoleon was determined to fight for the freedom to ride across more of the island, and so he remained cloistered at Longwood as a protest. Everything was to be turned into a complaint. The Russian commissioner Count Balmain on landing at St Helena had been particularly struck by the 'ascendancy' or influence which Napoleon had over everyone on the island. No one, possibly save for Admiral Cockburn, dared to treat him like an equal. Balmain saw as well as Lowe that Napoleon sought to divide and conquer all around him. He was pleasant and affable with Admiral Malcolm and at the same time rejected any positive communication with the Governor.

The difference between the Admiral and the Governor was, in Balmain's opinion, that Admiral Malcolm was more subtle in his approach:

From his very first visit he had it understood that the surveillance of the prisoner in no way concerned him, and that only the sea up to the Isle de France belonged to him. It was merely another means of pleasing Napoleon. He has been exceedingly modest and quite a lady's man, so that his tactics have succeeded and he is today a favourite. He is sought out, he is flattered; interviews are sought with him lasting entire hours. As a matter of fact this predilection has for its real object only to seduce him or to mystify other people. But the Admiral is not the man to make a mistake.[5]

The Admiral was not concerned with the day to day affairs of the island, only when those matters concerned the ocean. Malcolm in his diary openly speaks of his disagreements with Lowe. There were issues between them concerning the irregular supply of food to the island from the Cape and more significantly, Lowe's suspicions that Malcolm was being duped by Napoleon.

Admiral Cockburn on the other hand had openly and systematically thwarted any attempt by Napoleon to establish court etiquette on board the *Northumberland*. At dinner, on Napoleon rising from the table and going out on deck after one of his typically short meals Cockburn had pointedly asked the rest of the company at table not to rise and leave. On learning that British officers on board were removing their hats in his presence and remaining bareheaded, as his staff did, he pointedly went out onto the quarterdeck, doffed his and then replaced it.

Napoleon was to repeatedly claim after Cockburn had left St Helena that though he had experienced disagreements with him, Cockburn 'had never vexed him with trifles' which was less than honest. Cockburn had vexed him with his lack of deference. The more that he was referred to as 'General' or 'Napoleon Buonaparte' the more he would invoke his imperial and royal past. As O'Meara reported, 'The more they lessen me, the more I will exalt myself.'

Balmain's assessment of Lowe was equally crisp:

He tries to satisfy Bonaparte. He treats him with respect and ceremony, does not complain of his brusque manner, tolerates his caprices, in short achieves the impossible. But he will never be anything except his scourge. The mind of one is still restless. He is a wandering genius who, in the circumstance where fate has reduced him, wishes to take his flight and seeks perhaps to make converts for himself. The other opposes to this strong will merely an inexhaustible fund of commonplace ideas and a cold suspicious nature, a repulsive exterior with however, the best intentions in the world, and a tyrannical precision in fulfilling his duty. To sum up, he who only knows how to command is at the mercy of him who knows only how to obey. Hence there is no manner of displeasing his jailer which the prisoner has not tried.[6]

Those who asked for an interview at Longwood were first sifted and examined. What could they offer to Napoleon? How might they assist the captive in his quest to be moved to Europe? Passing politicians and senior government officers who were on their way to report to the government in London were courted. Those from whom little advantage might be gained were put off with a declaration that the Emperor 'was indisposed' whilst others would be received along with a number of other visitors and perhaps be spoken to briefly by Napoleon.

With those he sought to influence, such as Mr Ricketts, a distant relative of the Prime Minister, Lord Liverpool, were carefully courted. Ricketts was proffered a list of reasons as to why Liverpool should have him moved back to Europe. This was how these audiences were conducted:

> At his audiences Napoleon appears in a green hunting coat quite well worn, with silver buttons in the shape of stags, wild boars, and foxes; white trousers and stockings with oval buckles of gold. His everyday hat is under his arm. He wears the plaque of the Legion of Honour and carries a snuff box in his hand. Never does he invite his guests to be seated unless he himself is lying down. He fears lest any one assume Cockburn's example of self-assurance, which he is careful to prevent by himself always standing. Sir Pulteney Malcolm has had at Longwood interviews lasting three or four hours, during which they finally because of fatigue leaned upon the table or against the wall, and nothing can persuade him to relax on this point.[7]

By late 1816, according to Balmain, Longwood was 'without being either large or magnificent' filled with fine mahogany furniture. There was also now a large tent in the garden, created from a ship's sail and stacked on the quayside in Jamestown there was the prefabricated structure for a large bungalow. Napoleon though dismissed the idea of a new permanent structure:

> But whether he hopes for some sort of a change in his position or whether he wishes to annoy Sir Hudson Lowe, no one has yet has been able to persuade him to consent to it. His expenditures are only what the English Government allow him and it is not known whether or not he has private means; since his fall he has said or done nothing which might give any clue. It is supposed however, that he has some, and that they are placed in England under an assumed name.[8]

Napoleon, on his initial inspection with Cockburn had been distinctly unimpressed with Longwood. Here was a summer home which was poorly equipped to allow Napoleon to live, as the Prince Regent suggested, as a British general officer who was fond of good living. In 1815 Barnes described it as 'an insufficient dwelling, being only a set of rooms thrown together at different times without attention to order or convenience'.[9]

The island had received no real warning of his arrival. In this tiny community there were no large shops where furniture, wallpaper and fittings could be bought. Unless arrangements had been made in London to supply the convoy with the particular articles Longwood required then everything had to be ordered in advance. What was available had to be either bought from the islanders themselves or manufactured by the tradesmen of the naval squadron. This problem led Cockburn to galvanise the workmen on the island:

> No exertions were spared by Sir George Cockburn to enlarge and improve the old buildings so as to render it capable of containing so great an increase of inmates …

and Longwood, for nearly two months presented as busy a scene a has ever been witnessed during the war, in any of His Majesty's dockyards.[10]

The Admiral, says O'Meara, 'indefatigable in his exertions, was frequently seen to arrive at Longwood shortly after sun-rise'. Lieutenant Blood and Mr Cooper, carpenter of the *Northumberland*, with several other craftsmen from here lived at Longwood House, Blood and Cooper living under the old sail set up as a tent.

On 8 December Cockburn had called at the Briars, bringing both letters and newspapers from the transport ship which had arrived from Europe. He informed Napoleon that the repairs to Longwood were now complete and that consequently he wished Napoleon to propose a date for his move to it. Napoleon declared that he would go to Longwood the next day but on reaching it found the smell of new paint too 'noticeable' and declared that he would move in the day after.[11]

On the 10 December, 1815, six weeks after settling at the pavilion next door to The Briars, Napoleon left. Admiral Cockburn escorted Napoleon on horseback to his permanent residence. They would have climbed up the volcanic, valley side which then, as now, was generally free of vegetation. Riding along the ridge top they would have gazed down upon Geranium Valley, unaware that less than six years later it was to contain Napoleon's body.

Marchand, Napoleon's valet, was already at Longwood preparing to receive his imperial master. Noverraz had joined him having accompanied an ox cart which carried the necessary furniture and items for Napoleon's first night. At three o'clock Marchand heard a drum beat and knew that the Emperor had reached Hutts Gate, where there was a subaltern's guard. Minutes later Napoleon, dressed in the familiar green uniform, escorted by some of the officers of his suite and the Admiral, arrived at Longwood.

After looking around his apartments, Napoleon told Marchand to substitute his field bed for the one which the Admiral had obtained for him and made use of the deep bath which had been built into his new quarters, 'into which he had jumped with childish joy'. This was eventually to be replaced with a smaller one from London, which was taken to France some time after Napoleon's death but returned.

Napoleon took great pleasure in bathing and it must have been a genuine relief for him to have this huge bathtub, after weeks at sea where he had experienced only a single private cabin and then the cramped conditions of the pavilion at The Briars. The pavilion after all was just that – built for entertaining and without a bathroom. All water heating had to be done on a small, simple range outside, at the side of the building.

On leaving his bath, Napoleon climbed into his bed for a while before dressing in civilian clothes. Marchand declared in his memoirs that the Emperor declared that he would never again wear uniform. Yet pictures do show Napoleon in uniform two years later, whilst others show him in civilian dress with the ornamentation of an imperial star on his breast and sometimes the tricolour cockade in his hat.

Napoleon had entered the refurbished and extended building through his garden and up the four stone steps, onto the narrow veranda. These stone steps remain the most original parts of Longwood House.[12] Stepping through the outer double doors Napoleon stood in his reception room. Here the billiard table was set up. Billiards did not interest him but the large surface of the table would enable him to unroll maps whilst he dictated his memoirs. Sometimes as he peered at the maps and dictated he would idly roll billiard balls across this table.

British visitors to the island would enter this room from the veranda prior to being announced to 'His Majesty'. Prior to any audience taking place with visitors to the island it would be made perfectly clear that if they chose not to address Napoleon as 'Your Majesty' they would not gain an audience with him.

Lt Basil Jackson, though frequently at Longwood, in an administrative capacity hardly ever saw Napoleon. Then one day after several months he was riding close to the house:

> On turning a corner, I came upon three figures advancing, the centre person wearing his small cocked-hat square to the front, the others, one walking on each side of Napoleon, bare headed. Turning a little aside to get out of the way, I took off my hat and made a low bow, which was returned by Napoleon raising his. He was dressed just as we see him in his portraits, viz., with a green cut-away military coat, white waistcoat, breeches, and silk stockings; of course he bore the tri-coloured cockade, and the star of the Legion of Honour.[13]

As a subaltern officer his potential usefulness to Napoleon was minimal. Consequently his attendance at a brief audience was based entirely on his arranging for Major Emmott of the Engineers to accompany him. His only other meeting was when he accompanied Lowe on his initial meeting with Napoleon. His usefulness to Napoleon's officers was great as Jackson had a good command of the French language and was at Longwood on a regular basis. He was responsible for the maintenance of the Longwood buildings. He did meet Bertrand often as he was involved in supervising the construction of the Bertrand's house, which is just fifty yards from Longwood. His diary also reads as if he were a little captivated by Madame Bertrand and delighted to ensure that the verandah for her new home should be as well constructed as he could manage.

Jackson also displays a great deal of respect for Bertrand and thought him a discreet and sensible man who did not necessarily possess a great deal of ability; this from a 21-year-old subaltern. We also have a fine description of Bertrand:

> [He] wore a military dress, which was truly French from far above his head to his feet; for his cocked hat was of the loftiest, while his legs were encased in jack-boots reaching to mid thigh. A blue coat thrown open so as to show an expanse of white

Napoleon leaves Malmaison for the coast in an unmarked carriage. Napoleon's demand that he left France in his own carriage probably lost him his best chance of escape and saw him lodged at Longwood House.

waistcoat, across which was displayed the blue ribbon of the Legion of Honour, and nankeen small clothes completed the dress of General Count Bertrand. He seemed a man on the wrong side of fifty, perhaps he was fifty five; his hair like Marmion's was 'coal black and grizzled here and there'. He wore a melancholy, depressed look, shrugged his shoulders like most of his countrymen, and his demeanour was quiet and impressive.[14]

Count Bertrand was either 42 or 43 years old at this time and Jackson just 21. This goes some way to explaining his assiduous verandah building. He also gives us a sketch of Montholon, whom he got to know. Montholon had to apply for any repairs to the Longwood buildings through Jackson. Montholon was: 'rather short, standing under five feet seven inches; he never wore a military dress, but always appeared in jack boots like Bertrand. His age about forty, and he was good looking, with dark complexion.'[15] He was also on friendly terms with General Gourgard and paid him frequent visits, as Gourgard seems to have coped least well with the monotonous existence at Longwood.

Napoleon's private apartments lay behind the drawing room. Through the rear door was the dining room which was initially occupied by the bed Admiral Cockburn had supplied. A door immediately to the right led into Napoleon's study and second bedroom. During his sleepless nights he would retire to the bed here after leaving the one next door. In this room he would also dictate. Emmanuel Las Cases, in his sketch of the Longwood house shows a table in

A select few of those granted an audience with Napoleon received a gift like this snuff box or a small piece of porcelain. Acceptance of such a gift was a source of great consternation to Sir Hudson Lowe. When the officers of the 20th Regiment accepted books for their library, Lowe insisted they return them. The Royal Regiment of Fusiliers still hold them today in their Lancashire headquarters. Image courtesy of the Greens Howards Regimental Museum.

The back of Ney's snuffbox. Image courtesy of the Greens Howards Regimental Museum.

Jamestown; one of the better period engravings, which still does not capture the scale of the waterfront. Large vessels could not come alongside and there has never been a sandy beach on the north side of the island.

Ladder Hill to the right of Jamestown; on the cliff edge is the modern signal flagpole on the site of the Georgian telegraph station. Signals sent from the Castle below in Jamestown could then be rebroadcast to the other stations across the island, including Longwood. Signals could also be sent out to vessels approaching the anchorage. Behind the signal station is High Knoll.

The left hand side of Jamestown; the two government buildings known as the Castle are the large, white-walled buildings immediately behind the town wall. The site of the Porteus House is directly behind the Castle.

Jamestown from Ladder Hill, showing the southern end of the town; the street layout is exactly that which Napoleon would have observed as he rode up the valley on his first day.

The High Street, Jamestown, looking from the Consulate Hotel across to the Wellington Hotel, which has the four dormer windows.

Napoleon Street at the top of the high street in Jamestown. Napoleon passed by these houses and shops as he ascended the hillside on his journey to view Longwood during his first day on the island.

The start of the Chinese quarter at the southern end of Jamestown. By 1818 over 600 men lived here. They were employed on short-term contracts as labourers, gardeners and craftsmen.

The line at Lemon Valley. The defences here are typical of those across the rest of the island; artillery positions with a wall from behind which a small infantry force could keep a much larger enemy force at bay. The layout matches the one sketched on Barnes' map of 1811.

Sandy Bay on the south side of the island, a wide bay with a protective harbour mouth. The extensive defences ruled out its use by any raiders who hoped to snatch Napoleon.

The Castle at the Cape; from here Governor Lord Charles Somerset monitored the activities of those Frenchmen who had been sent off St Helena and anyone else who attempted to correspond with the island.

HMS *Trincomalee*, a naval link with St Helena and Napoleon; *Trincomalee* was built in India and is now at Hartlepool in the North East of England. She called at St Helena on her way home, delivering much needed livestock to the island. Image courtesy of the 68th Regiment and the Trincomalee Trust.

Cape Town, where those being sent to Europe sailed initially. The Cape supplied much of the food required on the island.

Plantation House, home of Sir Hudson Lowe.

The pavilion at the Briars. This single-room building was situated on a promontory within the large garden of the house. From here Napoleon looked out on the valley and town below.

The author at the Briars. The tent was placed where the camera is. The Imperial Eagle was also cut into the turf at that spot.

The view from the pavilion at the Briars looking out towards James Town and the ocean.

Longwood; Napoleon's small private apartments were in the right wing. Today the wooden structure about which he complained has been replaced with breeze blocks, along with the wooden verandah and window shutters. The stone steps are original.

A side view of the reception rooms at Longwood. Marchand, his faithful valet, lived in one of the tiny and leaky attic rooms above Napoleon's private rooms. The garden has been stocked with hardier plants than those Napoleon planted.

Napoleon's principal bedroom, with views into the garden and of the road from Hutt's Gate. His study also had a bed permanently set up, enabling him to move into the other room during his restless nights.

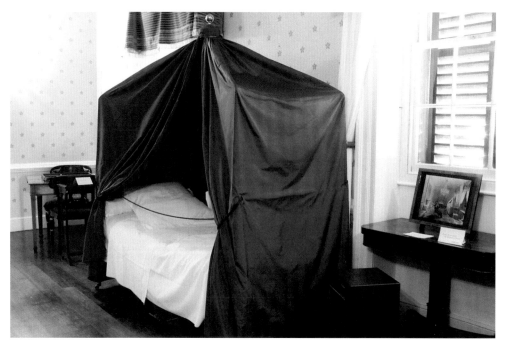

The final position of his bed in the drawing room in 1821. From here he would have looked out to the double doors of the billiard room.

The restored deep bath that was a place of relaxation for Napoleon in the first period of his time on the island and later would provide a form of pain relief.

The back wall of Napoleon's study. Here he would often sit with a pile of books scattered before him. The wall hangings were originally nankeen, helping to hide the damp in the walls that so plagued the front of the house.

The dining room; Napoleon sat with his back to the fire with a view of the garden and usually an empty seat to his right. This was sometimes offered to an honoured guest as it was intended as a symbol, demonstrating the absence of the Empress.

The drawing room at Longwood. He would stand or lean here in order that guests remained standing in apparent deference to him. No one sat unless invited and very few were.

The improvised altar that was used by Napoleon towards the end of his life.

The view from the drawing room into the billiard room; this was the view that Napoleon would have had during his final days.

The billiard table Napoleon used for his maps when dictating and upon which he would be laid when his autopsy was carried out. It was around the walls of this room that the officers of the 20th Regiment of Foot stood when Napoleon granted them an audience.

The Napoleon oak on the front lawn, beneath which he would sometimes dine.

The fish pond at Longwood in the Chinese garden; there is also an earth-covered pavilion in this garden, decorated inside in Chinese style.

The path down to the grave from the Longwood road along which the bearers carried the coffin. After the funeral the willow tree that overhung it was slowly stripped of its branches as sightseers took them as mementos.

The grave with the unnamed slab and railings taken from the new house. There is something almost chilling, or moving perhaps, about the fact that these were some of the railings Napoleon complained of – declaring that they were being erected to imprison him inside the new building.

Napoleon on St Helena; this image sums up his physical state very well. Sick during the Waterloo Campaign, Napoleon would only regain something of his old energy during his 'gardening phase' on the island. Author's collection.

the middle of this room. The Emperor would sit facing the window whilst Emmanuel Las Cases sat opposite him. His father would sit at the end of the table facing the dining room, taking dictation on different subjects to those his son took.[16]

The further room to the west was Napoleon's principal bedroom and breakfast room. Here he would eat at a small table and use the small sofa which was turned towards the fireplace. O'Meara described this room in detail:

> The walls were lined with brown nankeen, bordered and edged with common green bordering paper, and destitute of surface. Two small windows, without pulleys, looking towards the camp of the 53rd regiment, one of which was thrown up and fastened by a piece of notched wood. Window curtains of white long cloth, a small fireplace, shabby grate, and fire irons to match, with a paltry mantel-piece of wood, painted white, upon which stood a small marble bust of his son. Above the mantel-piece hung the portrait of Marie-Louise, and four or five of young Napoleon, one of which was embroidered by his mother. A little more to the right hung also a miniature of the Empress Josephine, and to the left was suspended the alarm chamber-watch of Frederic the Great, obtained by Napoleon at Potsdam; while on the right the consular watch, engraved with the cypher B, hung by a chain of the plaited hair of Marie Louise, from a pin stuck in the nankeen lining. The floor was covered with a second hand carpet, which had once decorated the dining room of a lieutenant in the St. Helena artillery. In the right hand corner was placed the little plain iron camp-bedstead, with green silk curtains, upon which its master had reposed on the fields of Marengo and Austerlitz. Between the windows there was a paltry second-hand chest of drawers: and an old book-case with green blinds stood on the

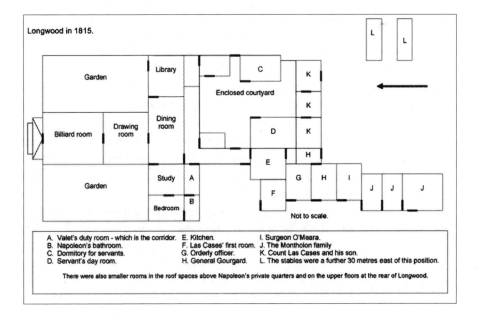

Longwood in 1815.

A. Valet's duty room - which is the corridor. E. Kitchen. I. Surgeon O'Meara.
B. Napoleon's bathroom. F. Las Cases' first room. J. The Montholon family
C. Dormitory for servants. G. Orderly officer. K. Count Las Cases and his son.
D. Servant's day room. H. General Gourgard. L. The stables were a further 30 metres east of this position.

There were also smaller rooms in the roof spaces above Napoleon's private quarters and on the upper floors at the rear of Longwood.

left of the door leading to the next apartment. Four or five cane bottomed chairs painted green were standing here and there about the room. Before the back-door, there was a screen covered with nankeen, and between that and the fire-place, an old-fashioned sofa covered with white long cloth, upon which reclined Napoleon, clothed in his white morning gown, white loose trousers, and stockings all in one, a chequered red madras upon his head, and his shirt collar open without a cravat. His air was melancholy and troubled. Before him stood a little round table, with some books, at the foot of which lay, in confusion upon the carpet, a heap of those which he had already perused, and at the foot of the sofa, facing him, was suspended a portrait of the Empress Marie Louise, with her son in her arms. In front of the fire-place stood Las Cases with his arms folded over his breast, and some papers in one of his hands. Of all the former magnificence of the once mighty emperor of France, nothing was present except a superb wash-hand stand, containing a silver basin, and water jug of the same metal in the left hand corner.[17]

Behind the sofa lay the bathroom, well-liked by Napoleon. Here throughout his captivity he would relax, eat, read and converse. The other door led into the waiting room for his valet. The corridor beyond this tiny room led to the servants' working rooms grouped around a courtyard on the eastern side of the irregularly shaped complex. The rooms to the rear of the servant's rooms were occupied by Gourgard, Montholon, Las Cases, the British Orderly Officer and Napoleon's physician.

Longwood is a collection of awkwardly shaped rooms. Napoleon's private rooms seem particularly small. His two main rooms barely measure around ten feet by fourteen each; not much for the man who called the Piazza San Marco in Venice 'the finest drawing room in Europe' – and made it his own. For some of his personal staff, conditions were even more cramped. Marchand had a room above Napoleon in the roof with little standing space. Emmanuel Las Cases shared a small bedroom with his father to the rear of the muddy courtyard. In the hot summer the tar on the paper and shingle roof became soft and moved. Then when the rains came, water seeped into their rooms.

These irritations were not for want of effort on the part of Admiral Cockburn. What few resources there were to hand Cockburn had gathered, along with a large party of sailors and tradesmen from the *Northumberland*. They had worked hard to render Longwood 'shipshape and Bristol fashion'. Napoleon had his servants housed with him along with his suite of officers and Bertrand, who had asked to live in better style than the tiny rooms proposed at Longwood, was eventually to live a short distance beyond the lawn of Longwood.

During these early days at Longwood Napoleon would drink his customary cup of coffee and then shave himself, using the silver washing basin whilst standing between the window and the fireplace. A valet would hand him the razor, brush and soap whilst another held a mirror before him. Afterwards he would have his entire torso brushed 'vigorously' by one of the valets before finally applying eau de cologne. In these early days Napoleon would take his morning ride, sometimes as early as 6 am. He wore a green hunting coat with a velvet collar, adorned with silver buttons, white kerseymere breeches and waistcoat, a black cravat and top boots. He would be accompanied by the Master of the Horse, General Gourgard and often Las Cases as well. The other officers would sometimes accompany Napoleon in turn. In these early days Napoleon had a circuit of perhaps twelve miles around Longwood over which he could ride unaccompanied by a British officer. This included the road out towards Alarm House, most of Deadwood Plain up towards the Barn and Flagstaff and south along the edge of Fisher's Valley. Young says that it was Colonel Wilks who proposed these limits to Cockburn. In these early days he did make use of this area for riding unaccompanied. His usual rides were taken in Fisher's Valley and up the slope beyond to Miss Mason's or out to Hutt's Gate and beyond to Alarm House.

After his morning ride Napoleon would bathe. He would sometimes take his breakfast in the bath, hot water being poured in to maintain the temperature, whilst he dictated or conversed with the officers of his suite. After bathing, wrapped in a dressing gown he would sit, taking breakfast if he had not already done so, possibly inviting one of his officers to join him. If he breakfasted in the garden he would do so in a tent or under a tree – one of which is still known as Napoleon's tree.

After breakfast O'Meara would attend for conversation and then dictation would be given. Napoleon would walk up and down either with his hands clasped behind his back or with one hand in his tail coat pocket. Las Cases had apparently invented a system of shorthand that enabled him to keep up with Napoleon's fast speech. All his followers took some part in the dictation.

The library he used as his reference source was built up slowly. The list of books was posted to England from Madeira, but they did not arrive until June 1816. Meanwhile Lowe sent up to Longwood several copies of the Annual Register and a number of books in French. Thereafter books arrived in batches, often sent by his principal British admirer.[18]

Napoleon was a voracious reader. When the library was finally broken up volumes belonging to the British Government were catalogued and sold in Jamestown. Others were sold at Sothebys in London in July 1823. Some would be taken by Bertrand back to France. Other books in the care of St Denis and willed to Napoleon's son would never be delivered as the Austrian court refused to accept them.

Lowe sent newspapers up to Longwood, though he was at times, according to Gorrequer, worried about the pro-Napoleon sympathies of some of the newspaper articles. When new books arrived Napoleon would spend the day indoors, reading late into the night, reclining on the sofa in front of the fire in the bedroom.

In the afternoon Napoleon would go for a drive in his carriage accompanied by members of his suite. He was driven by the brothers Achille and Joseph Archambault through the thin wood to the east of Longwood house or out to the Bertrands at Hutt's Gate. An alternative was to walk in the wood, or the garden immediately around the house, accompanied by most of his suite.

Could he have escaped at this time? Did he consider escaping at this time? The answer to both these questions is, as O'Meara commented, no. Any attempt to flee into one of the narrow valleys and then down to the rocky shore would have been extremely difficult physically for him to manage. Even today, footpaths down to the seashore often peter out on the barren hillsides and can be very difficult to negotiate even on a sunny day. Quite how any rescue party would have managed an overweight, unfit man in the deep darkness of a tropical night is difficult to imagine. And of course by late 1815 there were pickets and detachments of troops at all of the potential landing places.

Though of course the British were not dealing with just any middle-aged man. They were containing the most remarkable man of the age, some say, of any age. So every foreign vessel had been expressly prevented from landing at the island. Cockburn no doubt deployed his battalion of King's infantry along with his warships and two small St Helena regiments to cover any gaps in the island's defences. Napoleon was already being shadowed by a British sergeant and an officer at the Briars. There were manned batteries in most of the valleys of the island. Any approach towards St Helena would during daylight hours be spotted far out to sea and the curfew both of local fishing craft and amongst the island inhabitants was already in place. And there were the smaller but powerful warships on patrol either side of the island, day and night.[19]

At dinner Napoleon would sit with his back to the fireplace. This fire was usually very hot and the the room very stuffy. This was made worse, Sir George Bingham says by the great use of candles in the room, as when he dined there on 8 January, 1816:

> It was a most superb dinner, that lasted only forty minutes, when we retired into the drawing room to play cards. The dessert service was Sèvres china, with gold knives, forks and spoons. The coffee cups were the most beautiful I ever saw. On each cup was an Egyptian view, and on the saucer a portrait of some Bey, or other distinguished character. They cost twenty-five guineas, the cup and saucer, in France. The dinner was stupid enough; the people who live with him scarcely spoke out of a whisper, and he was so much engaged in eating that he hardly said a word to anyone; he had so filled the room with wax candles that it was as hot as an oven. He said to me, after I had entered the drawing-room, 'You are not accustomed to such short dinners.' He has generally one or two officers of the 53rd to dinner, or rather supper, for it is half-past eight before he sits down.[20]

Bingham seems to have had a leisurely dinner compared to some. The young Emmanuel Las Cases wrote 'Our dinner hardly lasted eighteen or twenty minutes. Then the Emperor sent away his servants, practising his English, "Go out; go to dinner." The Emperor would then ask his dinner companions whether they wished to 'go to a comedy or a tragedy' and Emmanuel would fetch the chosen work from the library beyond the dining room. The group would then move into the drawing room and Napoleon would read to the group.

On 20 June, 1816, Admiral Malcolm was presented to Napoleon along with Lowe. Malcolm introduced some of his naval officers and Lowe introduced Colonel Wynyard, his Military Secretary. The Governor later remarked to Malcolm that he had been pleased with the interview. Before they left Lowe informed Bertrand that the commissioners from France, Austria and Russia had arrived and were keen to have an audience with General Bonaparte. Bertrand then asked whether they had any letters for the Emperor, to which Lowe replied that they had none as they were there on the island simply to verify his existence, not in any other capacity. Three days later Napoleon's letter in reply landed like a grenade on the Governor's desk. He protested against the Treaty of Paris, of being held on the island, of being regarded as a prisoner, of being addressed as 'General' and of being denied the title of 'Emperor'. He reminded the governor that the Emperors of Austria and Russia and the King of Prussia 'were under an obligation to him'. He also objected to the manner in which he was denied access to the people of the island and also to the very manner in which the governor exercised his authority.

A very important document for our understanding of what happened on St Helena is *A Diary of St Helena: The Journal of Lady Malcolm*. It is clear that Lady Malcolm was her husband's amanuensis and that he was the real author. There are many interviews recorded with Napoleon when she was not present. Wilson also points out that the oldest copy of the diary was in his handwriting, not in hers. Its value is that it was written 'on the spot' and without the hidden and sometimes not so hidden agendas of the inmates of Longwood and the Briars. There is a clear view in them of the suspicious as well as the dutiful side of Sir Hudson Lowe. Malcolm was present at Lowe's last interview with Napoleon when the latter had spoken most offensively against the Governor. Sir Hudson was exercised over the friendly conversations Malcolm had with Napoleon – convinced that Napoleon was manipulating Malcolm in order to spite Lowe.

On 25 June Lady Malcolm accompanied the Admiral. They rode from Plantation House to Hutt's Gate, where they found Napoleon's carriage waiting for her. Lady Malcolm then rode with Madame Bertrand to Longwood. The postilions were so aggressive in their driving that near the gate the horses took fright and nearly tipped them into the Devil's Punch Bowl. Madame Bertrand spoke of her social life in Paris and contrasted it with 'this frightful solitude', adding that she hoped that they would return to England in October as each month there seemed like a year. Lady Malcolm quizzed her about the reports that Napoleon had punished her for too much socialising with the English, by refusing her permission to come up to Longwood for some time. There is no reply recorded in the diary.

At Longwood the Malcolms were shown into an outer room and introduced to Montholon, Count Las Cases, his son and General Gourgard. Then the inner door was opened and they met the Emperor. He was charming. He invited Lady Malcolm to sit with him and he asked her about the voyage. How did she occupy herself? Had she had been sick on the passage? Was it her first voyage? How did she amuse herself – did she embroider? Napoleon asked for the news from Europe and the Admiral told him about proposed reductions in the armies to peace establishments and

> ... in England of the repeal of the income tax. Bonaparte said that a proof to him of its being a good and productive tax was, that almost every person complained of it, which showed that all paid. The Admiral fully acquiesced, saying that he was one of the few admirers of that unpopular measure, and that we should again resort to it.[21]

He then talked to Lady Malcolm about the poems of the Scottish poet Ossian and about poems he had read in translation. Lady Malcolm's description of Napoleon's dress at these audiences echoed what Balmain had been told:

> He was dressed in an old threadbare green coat, with green velvet collar and cuffs; silver buttons with a beast engraven upon them, his habit de chasse (it was buttoned close at the neck); a silver star of the Legion of Honour; white waistcoat and breeches; white silk stockings; and shoes with oval gold buckles. She was struck with the kindness of his expression.[22]

It was all so contrary to the fierceness she had expected. She saw no trace of great ability, 'his countenance seemed rather to indicate goodness'. The refusal to replace his coat was also part of his war against the 'English'. He refused to have any of his coats repaired or replaced with British cloth.

On 24 July the Admiral met with Napoleon and they talked alone at length about naval matters and the Waterloo campaign. Malcolm and he spoke about Nelson's brilliance. Malcolm declared:

> Lord Nelson [was] the greatest sea officer who had appeared; in which commendation Bonaparte agreed, and then said that in many instances the French had well defended the honour of their flag, but had never done anything very brilliant at sea.

Napoleon concurred. When they spoke of Waterloo, Napoleon asserted that two causes had lost him the battle, Grouchy's failure to check the Prussians, and his great charge of cavalry, though heroic, being made half an hour too soon.

He was asked why he did not cross the border into Belgium and then cut the British off from the sea. Bonaparte explained that Blucher was an hussar and Wellington an officer of method, 'who would not move his army without reflection, nor without his supplies'. If he had first attacked the British, the Prussians would have attacked him at 'full gallop' and as everything depended on the first clash, he thought it preferable to begin with the Prussians.

Napoleon said that if he had won the battle, there would have been a change of ministers in England, and they would have made peace with him. Malcolm disagreed because whoever was in power generally followed the same course of action:

Bonaparte said that he believed that to be the case, for he remembered to have heard a story of a leader of opposition making a violent speech when a change of ministry was expected. The minister called out, 'Take care what you say, you may be in the majority tomorrow.'

He then spoke about the Bourbons, saying 'that they would never tranquilize France'. Malcolm asked him what, if anything, they could have done to re-establish themselves. Napoleon said that the King should have addressed the French people thus:

> You have had a great revolution during which great atrocities have been committed, but the nation has done great things. You appointed a great man your emperor: he did great things for France, and added to her glory. Circumstances have occasioned you to offer me the crown. I accept it on the terms you propose. Changes have taken place that render it neither desirable nor possible that things should return to their original state, when my family reigned over you. Therefore, as you have thought proper to create a fourth dynasty, I shall now consider myself as the beginner of the fifth.[23]

He concluded that now they sat on a 'smothered volcano, and no person is content'. They then moved onto a discussion of when Britain might have brokered a peace with him; which led to Napoleon laughing out loudly and frequently. Meanwhile both groups of officers waited in the billiard room until they were finally admitted to a brief audience.

Malcolm next had an audience on 25 July when he took up some newspapers which had arrived via the *Griffon*. After discussing affairs in France Napoleon began to berate the Governor again. Malcolm attempted to point out that the Governor was anxious to make him as comfortable as possible. His sharp reply was: 'He has not the character of an Englishman. He is a Prussian soldier. He is clever and cunning. He writes well and will make good statements to his government.'[24] Napoleon talked about that awkward character trait of the Governor that irritated both the French and his own staff officers:

> Bonaparte allowed that it was manner more than matter, that so frequently vexed him. He instanced some things that had been done by way of civility, but the manner prevented them being received as such. 'In short he cannot please me. Call it *enfantillage*, [childishness] or what you will, so it is.'[25]

He also objected to being escorted by a British orderly officer when out riding. The officer might object to his speed or destination. And as for letters, even local ones, having to be sent open to the Governor, he thought this unacceptable. Malcolm replied that when some local notes had been sent to the inhabitants, some of his suite had 'abused the indulgence'. Malcolm does not follow this comment with an explanation but presumably as local civil letters would be expected to be filled with just that, civil pleasantries only, these were not and were viewed by the governor as vehicles for public complaint against his authority.

Napoleon complained about the British Government and expressed the belief that the Prince Regent was in their hands. He was sure that if the old king had been well he would have been better treated. Napoleon seemed never to appreciate the complementary powers held by the monarch and Parliament. Though it is probably fair to say that the Prince Regent was still in that self absorbed state that characterised so much of his life prior to becoming king. It was not so much that he was outmanoeuvred by the government, but that Napoleon, the prisoner on a faraway island, no longer interested him. The Prince Regent was surrounded in London by all the heroes of Waterloo. More absorbing and draining for him were all the responsibilities of being Regent at a time of national economic distress. He also had worries over his daughter, and his wife, who would soon become involved in a scandal that would eventually be played out in public in the House of Lords. For Napoleon the worst single possibility that haunted him constantly had occurred. He had been forgotten by the Prince.

Napoleon continued complaining about Lowe and then he turned to the matter of the island. Why had he not been incarcerated in the Tower of London or any prison other than the island? Malcolm spoke of the island's advantages but Napoleon would not agree with any of them. He then declared that he would not live three years on the island, to which Malcolm replied that he hoped he would as his history would surely take much longer than three years. At this Napoleon laughed and began to talk of the Commissioners:

'If I saw them as Commissioners, it would be acknowledging that I was a prisoner to their masters, which I am not.' He then broke out into invective against the two Emperors, and said that he had letters from them that would fill volumes, and one of these days the world should see them. 'And what could I say to the Austrian Commissioner, who comes from my father-in-law without a kind word, or even to say my son, his grandson, is alive, from a man who pressed me to marry his daughter, and to whom I twice restored his kingdom? And how am I to address the Russian, whose Emperor has been at my feet, and who called me his best friend? I am less embarrassed with the Frenchman. Louis owes me nothing. But it does not signify seeing them; why were they sent?'[26]

All of these complaints were to be repeated endlessly. The Prince Regent may have lost interest in him but he was determined to remain in the European public arena. It was neatly summed up by Malcolm who commented that 'he was not displeased to have grievances'.

The next meeting was on 10 August when Admiral and Lady Malcolm drove up to Longwood to discover Napoleon in his carriage with Madame Montholon. Napoleon stepped out and invited Lady Malcolm to join him whilst the Admiral and Madame Montholon made ready to follow in the

Admiral's carriage. The two postilions then set off along Fishers Valley 'at a hand gallop' with General Gourgard on horseback acting as Napoleon's equerry. As they rushed through the trees Lady Malcolm did wonder if they were going a little too fast for safety. But given the monotony of his life, it was not surprising that he should encourage the Archambault brothers on several occasions to provide a little excitement with their driving.

They spoke about the island as the Admiral had been rowed around it on the previous day – presumably taking note of potential landing places and the state of the defences. On their return to Longwood Napoleon pointed out the tent that had been pitched by sailors from the *Newcastle*, 'at the request of the Governor', of which Napoleon much approved. This was presumably to give him somewhere outside to walk and sit out of the sun.

Lady Malcolm apologised on behalf of her brother, John Elphinstone, who, on his ship calling in at St Helena on his return from China, had been too ill to attend an audience. Napoleon recalled that Elphinstone had sent some silks and a chess set to him. This was the chess set with the imperial cypher upon it to which Lowe objected. Lady Malcolm reminded Napoleon that they were under an obligation to Napoleon for tending to her brother who, as a Captain in the 7th Hussars had been wounded during the move from Quatre Bras to Waterloo. Napoleon on seeing him had ordered his surgeon to tend to him.

On 16 August the Admiral rode to Longwood and saw the French officers gathered round an ice making machine with Mr Darling the upholsterer, who had accompanied the prefabricated New House out to the island, carrying out the experiments. Napoleon said that he had encouraged the study of chemistry in France and that he had seen the great chemist Sir Humphrey Davy in Paris. Napoleon then reached out in an effort to take the thermometer out of the cup containing the frozen water and in his haste snapped the thermometer. He laughed, commenting on his clumsiness and invited the Admiral to join him for a walk in the garden.

They spoke about ship design, the action at the Nile, Captain Barre who later commanded the *Rivoli* in a 'gallant action' and the best manner for arming ships of the line. Napoleon enquired whether the English would force the Portuguese to give up slavery. Malcolm pointed out that any Portuguese who attempted to trade with British colonies were seized and their slaves freed in Sierra Leone, where they were fed for a year before being given help to set up as farmers. Napoleon approved of this, saying that it might spread into the interior.

Malcolm's next visit was in the company of the Governor. On 17 August Lowe had gone to Longwood to raise the matter of 'Bertrand's impertinence' and of the Longwood expenses. Lowe had previously written to Bertrand pointing out the 'impropriety' of Lady Bertrand in attempting to have a sealed letter delivered to Montchenu by an inhabitant of the island. Lowe had received 'a violent and improper answer'.

Sir Hudson had received orders to limit the Longwood expenses to £8,000 per annum. He calculated that this was not possible and had decided to allow

£12,000 per annum until he heard from the government in London. The extra money was to be paid initially by Sir Hudson Lowe himself. What he needed to discuss was the significant retrenchments required at Longwood, for currently expenses were running at £17,000 per annum. Napoleon declined to see him, saying that he was in the bath, and that Lowe should communicate directly with Bertrand. Sir Hudson then rode up to Hutt's Gate. Bertrand met him at the door of his house. Sir Hudson proposed discussing the matter inside: 'Bertrand abruptly took the papers, and said he would lay them before the Emperor; the less communication, either verbally or in writing, Sir Hudson and himself had, the better.'[27]

The next day Lowe and Malcolm met at Hutt's Gate and rode up to Longwood. There they saw Napoleon walking in the garden with Madame Montholon and Count Las Cases. Napoleon 'endeavoured to avoid them' whilst Montholon came over to intercept them. Lowe informed Montholon that he wished to speak to Bonaparte. Montholon took the message and returned saying, 'the Emperor waited for us'. According to Malcolm, 'Bonaparte took little notice of Sir Hudson, but received the Admiral in his usual manner, and conversed with him for a few minutes on common subjects. Sir Hudson then addressed Napoleon, describing his meeting with both Bertrand and Montholon and expressing his desire to speak directly with Napoleon in order to accommodate his wishes as far as was practicable. He then referred to the manner in which he had been slighted by Bertrand.

There was silence for a few minutes as they both continued to walk back and forth. Napoleon was evidently contemplating an answer. Finally he looked at the Admiral, not the Governor and said:

'Count Bertrand is a man well known, and esteemed in Europe; he has been distinguished, and has commanded armies. He,' (nodding at Sir Hudson), 'treats him like a corporal. Madame Bertrand is a lady well born, who has been accustomed to the first place in society; he does not treat her with the regard that is her due; he stops her letters, and prevents her seeing those that wish to visit her, except under restrictions.' Then, turning to Sir Hudson, he continued: 'Since your arrival we have experienced nothing but vexations. Your instructions are the same as Sir George Cockburn's – he told me so – but you execute them with fifty times more rigour. He vexed us with trifles. I had reason to be displeased with some of his proceedings, but we never conversed that we were not satisfied with each other: but there is no talking to you – you are quite untractable. You suspect everything and everybody. You are a Lieut.-General, but you do your duty like *un consigne*; you never commanded any men but Corsican deserters; you vex us hourly, by your little ways; you do not know how to conduct yourself towards men of honour, your soul is too low. Why do you not treat us like prisoners of war? You treat us like Botany Bay convicts.'[28]

After he had stopped talking, Sir Hudson replied 'with much coolness' that he very much desired to render his position as comfortable as possible but that Napoleon actively prevented him from doing so. The argument escalated, with Napoleon declaring that there were some people who were honourable and others who were not. The Admiral stepped in at this point when matters were about to get worse and assured both of them that their cases were much misrepresented one to the other because they were being interpreted by third parties. Napoleon was not to be mollified and turning to Malcolm said:

> 'Do you know he has had the meanness to keep from me a book, because on its cover I was designated Emperor, and he has boasted of having done so.' 'I boast?' said Sir Hudson. 'Yes,' added Bonaparte; 'Colonel Keating, late Governor of Bourbon, told me so.'[29]

Again the Admiral assumed the role of honest broker attempting to explain the 'misinterpretation' to the satisfaction of both men. As the agent of a government which had forbidden the use of the imperial title of Emperor amongst the English, Sir Hudson was unable to deliver the book.

Napoleon countered that the governor had sent him letters addressed to the Emperor. Sir Hudson agreed with this, pointing out that these letters came from Napoleon's own family and not from Englishmen. Napoleon had not finished and ploughed on. Lowe, he said, had spoken about the contents of letters which he had seen prior to them being delivered to Napoleon; the entire island knew that his aged mother had written that she would come to St Helena and die with him. Lowe denied this and Napoleon snapped back that he had done it, as Mr Balcombe had mentioned it to him. The Admiral interjected in an effort to calm the combatants. He knew that Sir Hudson 'held sacred the contents of all letters that came open to him'. Napoleon then moved on to other grievances; that he was denied the civility of writing a gallant note to Lady Malcolm as the letter had to be open, that should he wish to invite an officer of the 53rd Regiment to dinner on the day of meeting him, it was impossible as permission had to be obtained from the Governor. Sir Hudson attempted to answer this but was cut short by Napoleon who snapped back with one of his oft quoted retorts:

> I am an Emperor in my own circle, and will be so as long as I live; you may make my body prisoner but my soul is free. Europe will hereafter judge of my treatment, and the shame of it will fall on the English nation; even the poor sentinels of the 53rd regiment weep at my unworthy treatment … You ask me for money to pay for my living; I have none; but I have plenty of friends, who will send me whatever sum I required if I could write to them. Put me on rations if you please. I can dine with the officers of the 53rd regiment, and if not with them, with the soldiers.[30]

Sir Hudson was not to be cowed and pointed out that he had been selected for this post and so would do his duty. Napoleon demanded to know if he was ordered to, would he assassinate him? Lowe, still remaining calm, replied that he would not and that he would remain to carry out his duty and his instructions.

Napoleon was still not finished. The only way Lowe would be at peace, he suggested, would be if he had Napoleon bound 'hand and foot'. He then threatened the Governor with a letter, which he hoped would be known 'in all Europe'. Lowe seems to have replied calmly, and possibly this irritated Napoleon even more and led to him abusing the British Government, and declaring that Lord Bathurst had a blind hatred of him, which was why he had appointed Lowe to his position. Finally Lowe spoke with the same indignation as Napoleon:

> Sir Hudson replied, 'That makes me laugh.' 'What laugh, sir!' said Bonaparte, turning to the governor Sir Hudson with a look of surprise. 'Yes, sir,' answered Sir Hudson; 'I say what I think; I say it not only makes me laugh, but it excites my pity, to see how misinformed you are with respect to my character, and for the rudeness of your manners. I wish you good morning.' Sir Hudson then quitted him abruptly without further ceremony. Bonaparte stopped his walk, apparently much surprised by this sudden retreat. The Admiral said, 'I must also wish you good morning.' Bonaparte returned his bow, and desired he convey his compliments to Lady Malcolm. During this conversation Sir Hudson never for a moment lost his temper; Bonaparte frequently, particularly when he addressed Sir Hudson. They walked to and fro in the garden, and could not fail to be overheard by Count Las Cases, Madame Montholon, and Major Gorrequer, who continued walking at a little distance.[31]

Malcolm is convinced that as soon as they had left Longwood, Napoleon repeated the conversations to his suite, who over the next few days repeated them across the island. The situation was then made worse for Sir Hudson as he insisted that his replies, 'which did him much credit', should be kept secret along with everything else which passed at Longwood. But as Malcolm pointed out, everything that occurred at Longwood was known across the island. The Longwood servants had 'free access to the camp of the 53rd Regiment'. Malcolm also noted that Cipriani, the maitre d'hotel, went to Jamestown daily to shop escorted by a soldier who did not speak his language. The implication was clear. Here was a Corsican, an intelligent, communicative man, who adores his master; a willing agent who disseminates negative stories about the Governor and returns to Longwood with 'all he can hear'.

The relationship between Lowe and Napoleon continued to be icy. On the 23 August Sir Hudson received the letter from Montholon referred to earlier, which had been dictated by Napoleon. Lowe wished to keep its contents secret but again copies were made at Longwood and offered to any visitors who called. Fortunately for the Governor none were taken away. On 28 August Bonaparte ordered Montholon to write to Lowe saying that he wished to end the practice of issuing passes to inhabitants, officers or strangers, as 'they rambled about the grounds and annoyed him'.

The Admiral also decided not to visit Longwood after the arguments there as a mark of his disapproval of Napoleon's behaviour toward Lowe, until he called briefly before leaving for the Cape on 22 September. Lowe did not want him to visit but left the matter in his hands. Malcolm's visit was brief, and Napoleon did not refer to Malcolm's absence over the preceding weeks.

Malcolm returned on 23 November. Here the tone of the diary changes as this time marks the beginning of a 'coolness' between the Governor and himself. There had been a disruption to the system for supplying the island with food, caused it would seem in part by the Admiral's interference with loading processes at the Cape.

On 25 November the Admiral went from Plantation House to Longwood, and the Governor 'again expressed how desirous he was to render Bonaparte's situation more comfortable, but that he was prevented by Bonaparte's conduct towards him'. After a short interview with Napoleon, Malcolm went to visit Madame Bertrand. On leaving their house he met Sir Hudson with his Staff and some dragoons. 'Sir Hudson told the Admiral he was come to arrest Las Cases for having endeavoured to bribe a slave to convey letters to Europe.'[32]

On 4 December Malcolm took his wife to visit Madame Bertrand who was then close to giving birth. Napoleon, on hearing of their presence at Longwood, sent a message to say he was unwell and could not see them. The note also said that he had not been out of the house since the new riding restrictions had been placed on him on 9 October and that he would not leave it until some of them were repealed.

On 18 December the *Orontes* arrived from the Cape with Piontkowski and the three servants of Napoleon who had been banished from the island. On 28 December, during another visit to Madame Bertrand, O'Meara had taken the Admiral aside, to ask him if he wished to see Napoleon. The Admiral said no.

'But,' said the doctor, 'do you bring no message from the Governor?' 'No,' said the Admiral, 'we merely called to see Madame Bertrand.' Dr. O'Meara then mentioned that there had been a proposition between the Governor and Bonaparte that the Admiral should mediate an accommodation of their differences. The Admiral replied that such a proposition must come from Sir Hudson. The Admiral never heard from the Governor on the subject nor does he know at this moment why the idea was not followed up; Dr. O'Meara informed him at one time that both parties acquiesced. Buonoparte was suffering at this time from want of exercise, which he persisted in not taking. The sentinels had been removed, but by some unfortunate mistake not so soon as he was informed they were, and when he went out one day he saw one and returned instantly.[33]

On 11 January Malcolm spoke with Lowe about obtaining an audience for Captain Wauchope. Malcolm's entry has Lowe agreeing to this proposal saying 'he wished Bonaparte might have the gratification of receiving visits, or any other gratification consistent with his security'. So Malcolm went up in the afternoon and spoke with Napoleon for three hours, prior to his introducing Captain Wauchope. At this point in the diary Malcolm declares that his visits after his return from the Cape became less frequent as they 'gave rise to unpleasant ideas in the Governor's mind'. Lowe was either envious of Malcolm's ability to maintain a relationship with Napoleon and piqued that he himself could not, or, more likely, suspicious that Napoleon was influencing Malcolm in some way against him. At the interview, Malcolm noticed that he appeared 'thinner and his eyes rather sunk, but considering that he had not taken any exercise since October, except in a small room, he was in better health and spirits than could be expected'.

The Admiral next visited at Longwood on 31 January to see Madame Bertrand and her infant, 'a fine child'. The following day, Lowe, along with Sir Thomas Reade, called on the Admiral and after some discussion about supplies from the Cape the interview became an interrogation:

> 'At your interview with Bonaparte, did anything occur of which his Majesty's Government should be informed?' The Admiral replied, 'Nothing.' Had Sir Hudson expressed a desire to be informed of the conversation, the Admiral would have had much pleasure in detailing it to him; but to be interrogated in that mode was repugnant to his feelings.[34]

On his next visit on 7 March Napoleon was 'in excellent spirits, reading English papers that had been delivered by the store-ship'. He spoke about England and yet again, of how, if Old George had been well, he would have been better treated than he was at present. He also commented that the Prince Regent ought to remember the 'flattering messages' he had sent him at the Peace of Amiens. Napoleon spoke on several other topics but his most notable comments concerned the act of Parliament which had confined him. He mused on whether Parliament could delegate its powers to the Governor and believed that it could not. Malcolm assured Napoleon that Parliament could indeed delegate the power to interpret the regulations to the Governor, which was a reference to the impending expulsion of Las Cases.

Napoleon then complained about him not being allowed to see the Austrian botanist Welle, 'who had come from and was going to the residence of his wife and son' until Malcolm quietly pointed out that Welle was found to have secretly brought letters to Napoleon and his suite.

Napoleon was in a reflective mood, considering for a moment how he might repair his relationship with the governor: 'The Governor does not understand my character, he has never seen me but when I was irritated and then I spoke folly.' Malcolm urges Napoleon to consider speaking openly with the Governor who had 'considerable talents' and 'great attainments'. They could be reconciled if they only had 'a free personal conversation'. There was no decision reached about effecting a reconciliation between the two of them and instead Napoleon moved on to talk of Lord Bathurst's hatred towards him.

Malcolm, his wife, Captain Festing RN and Captain Stanfell RN visited on 25 March 1817. Having first called on Madame Bertrand they were invited to an audience with Napoleon in the billiard room. Napoleon, on discovering that Stanfell had just come from the Cape enquired after Las Cases and was told that he was then living at the Governor's country residence, Newlands, at the Cape.

Stanfell told him that the remarkable Dr James Barry (who at death was found to be a woman, after a career of 40 years in the British Army) had greatly assisted the recovery of young Las Cases.

On 3 May they discussed Spain during the wars, the Copenhagen expedition and the exchange of prisoners. Napoleon demurred at the comparison made by some Englishmen of himself and Cromwell, which was not just as Cromwell was put in position by the army and he was called to the throne by 'the voice of France'. (In fact the comparison was unjust for very different reasons: Cromwell refused the throne!) Whilst commenting on the French Revolution, Napoleon would not accept the Admiral's assertion that the Bourbons would eventually be accepted by the people.

Malcolm again offered an opening for a reconciliation between Napoleon and Lowe when he suggested that on Lord Amherst arriving from China, perhaps here was an opportunity for Lowe and he to talk in the presence of a third party. 'Bonaparte made no particular reply, but said he should like to see strangers, but he would not till the humiliating restrictions were changed.' There was still to be no reconciliation.

On 19 June Malcolm and Lady Malcolm with Captain Jones of the *Julia* and Major Boyce of the Marines visited Napoleon again. Napoleon took the Malcolms into one of his private rooms to show them the bust of the King of Rome. They discussed his features, with Napoleon remarking, when Lady Malcolm had commented on his curls, that 'he has fair hair like a Scotchman'. There was another such bust, he said, which was intended for the Empress.

> Sir Thomas Reade had told the captain he ought to have thrown it overboard. The Admiral did not believe Sir Thomas had said so – he could not give credits to such reports – Sir Thomas had enemies, and things were told of him which were not true. Bonaparte replied that some officers had heard him, and turning to Lady Malcolm, asked her if it were not barbarous. She replied it was so barbarous that she did not believe that Sir Thomas capable of it … Bonaparte appeared much pleased with the bust.[35]

Napoleon asked Malcolm if he had read Lord Bathurst's speech of 18 March, the reply to Holland's enquiries made in the House on 13 March. Bathurst's replies, he said, were 'full of falsehoods',

> … for either the Governor had not written the facts or Lord Bathurst had misstated them, for in the speech were calumnies and misstatements. The Admiral replied that the speech of Lord Bathurst was not correctly given in all the newspapers, and perhaps in none; he had seen only one, and he understood it was very differently stated in others.[36]

It may well have been misrepresented in some newspapers but Bathurst had adequately refuted the claims made in the Remonstrance, Napoleon had directed

Montholon to draw up and smuggle him off St Helena. Napoleon then offered to show the Admiral the opening part of the very letter but the Admiral refused to see it, saying that he had no authority to interfere in any way respecting the treatment of Napoleon and his entourage. Malcolm once more urged a reconciliation with the Governor, who, he repeated, was anxious to do all in his power for him. Bonaparte frequently interrupted the Admiral to say that it was not so and that Sir Hudson deceived him, that he had no wish to make his situation agreeable.

There then followed several complaints against the governor – that he was a 'cunning man', that he had changed the content of the letters which Napoleon had wished sent to England and that he was 'tortured to death by pin-point wounds' inflicted by Lowe. All of this climaxed in a ringing prophecy:

> I have worn the imperial crown of France, the iron crown of Italy; England has now given me a greater and more glorious than either of them – for it is that worn by the Saviour of the world – a crown of thorns. Oppression and every insult that is offered to me only adds to my glory, and it is to the persecutions of England I shall owe the brightest part of my fame.[37]

The Admiral assured him again that 'he was quite mistaken' as to England's intentions. The government wanted him kept securely, 'but with attention towards his comfort'. Malcolm records here for the first time that he openly criticises Napoleon, saying that 'he had himself to blame'. Napoleon then turned to thank the Malcolms for their attitude to him and after all the carefully crafted statements intended for posterity, its simple openness is quite affecting: 'You wanted nothing from me; I have no longer the power to do any person service; you come from the goodness of your hearts.'[38]

He then returned to the matter of his title and his status as a prisoner of war, claiming with an unusual modesty that no other prisoner of war had ever merited so much effort to detain him. With regard to the matter of having a new house built, given the rate at which things progressed on the island 'it would take six years to complete it,' by which time he would 'dead or removed before it was finished'. This was to be another theme to which he returned on several occasions.

On several occasions he would talk of being relocated to either Rosemary Hall or Colonel Smith's residence – both of which were close to Plantation House and consequently on the more sheltered side of the island. Napoleon here seems to have offered an olive branch to the Governor after the towering biblical outburst earlier. He is quoted as saying that he did not blame the Governor for sending the servants and Piontkowski from the island, as he knew he was ordered to do so by his government. Neither did he object to the reduction in the provisions given to Longwood as his plate could be sold to give them what they required.

The olive branch was not long proffered. Napoleon then found an example of Lowe wishing to keep everything secret on the island to complain of. He complains about the railings that have arrived for his new house, which Malcolm points out are ornamental:

'He [Lowe] did not wish it to be known that iron railings had come out to shut me up, like a bird in a cage, yet all the island knew it.' The Admiral remarked that the iron railing was ornamental for the intended house, and there could be no secret, as it was landed and put with the other materials.[39]

A small section of these ornamental railings can be seen in the photograph of Napoleon's island tomb. Given the confusion surrounding the landings of stores on the quay and the paucity of storage yards and warehousing they would indeed have been on display for the entire island population to see – as cast-iron ornamental railings and not as parts of a cage. The Malcolms then left, with the Admiral promising to return prior to his giving up the command of the naval squadron.

Malcolm then writes immediately after about a further disagreement with the Governor, which arose when Captain Jones, who had attended the interview, spoke with 'a staff officer'. This officer was presumably Sir Thomas Reade, effectively the Governor's assistant, who, according to Malcolm, misreported some of the conversation at Longwood. This then led to Lowe accusing Malcolm of 'concealing matters of consequence which had been promulgated by Captain Jones'. Only now did he realise, at the end of his service on the island, 'that there was a system of spies on the island, and that every trifle was reported to the Governor. With open candid Englishmen this is detestable, and must cause incalculable evil.'[40]

Malcolm had one last interview at Longwood on 3 July when he accompanied his successor, Admiral Plampin, on handing over command. Malcolm then left the island and missed the strange affair of the arrest at Longwood and the deportation of Las Cases.

What did he say of Napoleon and Lowe outside of his diary? In a letter to Admiral Cockburn, his predecessor, he wrote:

I sincerely wish they had left you Governor and Ministers would now be better pleased. Sir Hudson tires them to death with volumes on trifles – the only mode to pursue with Buonaparte is to be unchangeable in your regulations and to let the whole world know how you think proper to treat him, this is your mission but it has not been followed.[41]

On the 25 November 1816, Sir Hudson, accompanied by Captain Blakeney DAAG, Mr Rainsford the Inspector of Police and orderly dragoons rode to Longwood. There Captain Poppleton, the orderly officer was asked to accompany Mr Rainsford to Las Cases's quarters. Here they found only his son, who said that his father was with the Emperor. They waited and on his arrival Las Cases was arrested, along with his son. Las Cases was not allowed to see the

Emperor. Sir Thomas Reade, Lowe's very zealous deputy, states that as they left the house Las Cases said laughing: 'So I am arrested in consequence of Scott's information, I knew the Governor had sent him to me.'[42] Scott was not part of any plot to trap Las Cases; rather he had suffered from an attack of conscience and had confessed all to his father. His father had immediately set off for Plantation House with one of the silk pieces in his possession.

There is an undated set of notes concerning the interrogation of James Scott, following the arrest of Las Cases. Young James had been Las Cases's servant at Longwood. The young man had a white father serving in one of the St Helena regiments, whilst his mother, whose name is not given, was a black slave. James was having to leave service at Longwood after the declaration that only white persons could work as domestics there. His father was to pay a significant fee for his son to be declared a free man in the following January, which would support the idea of James contemplating a career of domestic service in England. In consequence Las Cases said that he would give him a letter of recommendation to friends in England. In the notes taken at the interrogation James Scott is referred to as the Examinant. Las Cases:

> … desired Examinant to leave his Waistcoat and [told him] that when he returned the recommendation should be given to him. In a week afterwards the Examinant did return with some linen and the Count gave him the Waistcoat telling him at the same time that the recommendation was concealed in it. When the Examinant went home he ripped his waistcoat and found a piece of Silk in it with Writing which he gave to his father who said he would take it to the Governor directly.[43]

Some time after his father had left Scott found another piece of writing. This he gave to his half-brother telling him to hand it to his father. A little while later he discovered a third piece of writing and in his frightened state 'hid it under a stone in the grass'.

Scott revealed that Las Cases told him his friend Lady Clavering would get him a place once he was in England or find him a place herself, and give him five pounds; that she would write to him in milk and that it would be possible to read the letter if it were held before the fire.

On being questioned he assured the panel that he had never taken any letters to any person on the island. He had only ever taken one message and that was to Rosemary Hall for the lady who lived there. The message was to ask if the lady knew Las Cases's family in Paris. She did not. He was then asked if he had seen Las Cases handling money. He replied that he had seen him with some some gold and silver coins. Asked who he had seen speaking with the Las Cases, he mentioned Sir George Cockburn, several navy officers and Dr Warden.

The action decided upon by the panel was that James Scott was not to go beyond the fence boundary of his father's farm in Sandy Bay until called for by the Governor and that the Governor would write to the government asking for further instructions in the matter.

The next page is dated almost a year later and sadly confirms the restrictions placed upon James at the original interrogation:'he shall not go up to Longwood'. Further that he would always attend upon the Governor when called upon to do so. There is also a brief investigation of Mr Warden through questioning James, in March 1817. Balmain thought that Las Cases had engineered the entire matter:

> The affair is shrouded in mystery. Some say that the famous handkerchief affair was only a ruse of his own invention to get himself arrested and to leave Bonaparte while appearing to yield to force. Others believe that the project was a serious one, but that, since it did not succeed, Las Cases had the good sense not to return to Longwood, and thus escaped an insupportable exile.[44]

When the Marquis de Montchenu asked for sight of the letters – there were apparently two, one to Lady Clavering and one to Lucien Bonaparte – Lowe refused, saying that the matter might be explained to the French Ambassador in London and that Montchenu could apply to there.[45]

In February 1817, Balmain noted that Napoleon was taking no exercise and received no visitors save for Admiral Malcolm:

> It is now six months since Bonaparte has been seen or received strangers, with the exception of Admiral Malcolm, and nearly three months since he has gone out of the house, even to take the air. He lives alone, without taking any exercise, in a climate where undue repose and solitude easily affect one's health and may cause death.[46]

Montholon says they were never informed why Las Cases had been taken away and offered this explanation to Balmain:

> He used to write to a Lady Clavering, his former mistress. Perhaps he used some secret means to get through a letter and to inform her in detail of what concerned him personally. It was no purpose whatever that the Governor made such a fuss about it, for he never had any idea of escaping.[47]

In a letter of explanation to Bathurst, Lowe explained that Scott was told to leave his waistcoat with Las Cases after he had been discharged from Las Cases's service, as the new regulations regarding the removal of 'slaves and persons of colour' from the service of the French group had come into force. He was then to call for it some time later prior to his leaving for England. According to Lowe, Scott was 'desired not to open the lining' until he had reached England; a just about irresistible invitation to look.

From Scott's interview transcript it seems he had only been taken partly into the plot. The clumsy instruction for him to leave the waistcoat and collect it later clearly made him a minor accessory to something clandestine. Was the plot too clumsy to be true? It would have been easy to avoid the instruction to Scott not to examine the waistcoat by telling him simply to wear it when he met Lady

Claverling, perhaps as a means of identification. It all looks suspiciously deliberate: an attempt by Las Cases to leave the island with his son.

What he probably never considered in all of his planning was the remarkably consistent sense of duty that Lowe continued to exhibit during these trying times. Even though Las Cases had been arrested and removed from Longwood, Lowe would still offer him the opportunity to remain with his master. Las Cases said a little before this time, 'My happiness consists in contemplating a hero, a prodigy', but the strain of living within the embittered walls of Longwood had proved too much.[48] He was to be shipped off to the Cape, and placed in the governor's summer residence, 'Newlands' whilst Lowe wrote home to the government for instructions.

Napoleon's reaction was to use the opportunity to prepare an open letter, ostensibly to Las Cases but which was primarily intended to advertise the supposed pitiful conditions under which he was imprisoned. He commiserated with Las Cases for his being 'kept in secrecy' since his arrest and 'deprived even of a servant of your choosing'. He had in fact been directed to Major Harrison's cottage beyond Longwood and later his furniture from Longwood was taken to Rose Cottage, which he shared with a British officer and his servant. The 'servant of your choosing' was of course Scott, who was under arrest for taking part in the scheme. Napoleon admitted in this letter that La Cases had written to Lady Clavering many times previously. Montholon knew that she had been Las Cases' former mistress.

Napoleon said in the letter that the whole matter was deliberately kept obscure in order to 'to hide this criminal conduct' even from the British government. Napoleon described the day of the arrest:

> With ferocious joy they seized your papers (among which it was known there were several which belonged to me), without any formality, in the room next to mine. I was advised of it a few moments afterwards; I leaned out of my window and saw that they were taking you away; a large number of officers were prancing around the house; and it reminded me of nothing so much as South Sea Islanders dancing around the prisoners whom they were about to devour.

The removal of Las Cases had been a significant loss for Napoleon. He alone spoke, read and understood English to a sophisticated level. Nonetheless, Napoleon ordered him to leave for Europe. The Governor could not prevent it. For Napoleon it would be 'a great comfort' to know that Las Cases was safe. And if Las Cases were to meet Marie Louise and his son, he was to embrace them both on his behalf. He had received no news of them for two years. As mentioned earlier, he had not even been allowed an interview with the German botanist (Welle) who was then on St Helena and who had seen them both in the garden at Schonbrunn. This was a genuinely sad note on which to end the open letter but like almost everything that emanated from Longwood, there was a large degree of contrivance. Balmain remarked a little later:

The grief which Bonaparte felt at the loss of Las Cases seems to have entirely disappeared. He is gayer than ever, and seems in splendid health, except that he has become a little thinner. It is said that Mme. Montholon has now become his secretary. He continues to receive no one, and hardly ever goes out of his house.[49]

Enough of the secret correspondence between Finlaison and O'Meara survives to throw a little light on how the affair of the waistcoat was manipulated from Longwood. The silk had been written upon and sown into the waistcoat with another letter being handed to him, which he was to 'secret in some other part of his dress'. He was then to return for further letters some days later. At home, Scott had shown the letters to his father, a Sergeant in the St Helena Regiment. He in turn spoke with a neighbour, Mr Barker, and together, despite James's reluctance, they escorted him to the Governor.

Lowe then met O'Meara, informed him of the matter and told him to say nothing at Longwood whilst he organised with the inspector of police the arrest of Las Cases and the sealing of all of his correspondence. Accoring to O'Meara Napoleon declared that he was at a loss to explain how Las Cases could have got into such a mess and he despaired of him deciding to send a young and ignorant man like Scott to England. Napoleon wondered what the letters were about and then decided they probably concerned the injustices they faced in the island. Perhaps one was to his banker in London. After all, he had four or five thousand pounds there. He considered that they could not be of much consequence, 'as Las Cases is too much attached to me to undertake anything of moment without consulting me'. Napoleon wondered if, as Las Cases was losing his eyesight 'and can scarcely read or write since his son's illness', allied to his miserable accommodation, he had been driven mad, which would account for his folly in writing the letters.

Certainly, his son's illness, the long hours of writing and editing, their poor living conditions and the potential loss of his sight probably all contributed to his decision to leave the island. On that basis his selection of the illiterate Scott was a good one. He had been caught. He in turn had been arrested and now he was to be deported along with his son.

Two days later Bertrand went to Plantation House to claim the papers as being the property of Napoleon – all of which were returned save for the journal. A few days later Bonaparte became agitated, claims O'Meara, as he thought that the Governor was having a copy made and he became 'melancholy and angry'.[50]

Napoleon, according to O'Meara, was very agitated by the idea that the governor would probably seize all his other papers and muttered about destroying all of his work rather than have this happen. Lowe assured O'Meara that any paper deemed by Las Cases to belong to General Bonaparte, 'was immediately put by and respected'. Lowe had O'Meara witness the procedure of resealing the papers. Las Cases himself sealed up the trunk after examining some of them. O'Meara informed Napoleon of this and for several days he was calm. Later a letter from the young Las Cases also reassured him that his papers had been respected.

O'Meara then gives Finlaison a summary of the points found in the letters. The one to Lucien Bonaparte gave 'a highly coloured' account of events since they came on board the *Bellerophon*; various complaints about their situation on the island; and the harsh treatment they receive from Sir Hudson Lowe. The letter to Lady Clavering asked her to pass other letters to 'two or three', about which O'Meara knew nothing more than that they were to begin a correspondence with French people in London, with a view perhaps to placing 'certain paragraphs in the news paper, if they could not effect sending letters'.

O'Meara was convinced that Las Cases had set himself up 'purposely to be discovered, in order that he might be sent off the island'. This seems likely. All others who had been approached to convey, either overtly or covertly, messages to Britain had been either officers of naval or merchant vessels or wealthy passengers. It had been a very clever piece of ineptitude. The Governor had even offered Las Cases the choice of returning to Longwood or leaving for the Cape pending the decision of the government. Las Cases decided on the latter. His break with Napoleon was swift, for Napoleon wished to see him before he left but would not do so under the condition of having a British officer present.[51]

At the end of May 1817, the *Baring*, a storeship, arrived laden with stores under Captain Lamb (a half-pay lieutenant). On board, the gunner, Radovich, had charge of a white marble bust of Napoleon's son, which he had received from a merchant in London, along with a letter.

On 10 June Lowe informed Bertrand at Longwood that Lady Holland had sent out some things for Madame Bertrand's children and some books. Although they had not come through the minister's office he would send them up. He then mentioned the bust of Napoleon's son, which had also arrived without the sanction of the minister's office. It had travelled from the sculptor on Leghorn via London in the care of the Baring's gunner. It was being offered at a hundred guineas, which he thought was too high a price for a bad statue, but offered to send it up. Bertrand said that Napoleon would be 'extremely glad to get the statue of his son' and that it would be worth a million to him.

That evening, on discovering that O'Meara had known of its arrival for several days, Napoleon wanted to know why he had not spoken of it. O'Meara, quite reasonably, declared that he was waiting for the Governor to inform him of its arrival. Napoleon then admitted to O'Meara that he too had been aware of its arrival for several days. Napoleon added:

> I know that his Prime Minister Reade ordered it to be broken. I suppose that he has been consulting with the admiral, or that little major (Gorrequer) about it, who have probably explained to him what an atrocious and horrible act it would be, and that it would brand his name with ignominy forever, or that his wife has heard of it, and has read him a lecture at night about it.[52]

On being asked, O'Meara assured him that he had not heard anything about the proposal to break it up. However, in the letter he admitted to Finlaison that he had heard 'several days before and from several people' that Reade had proposed breaking it up to Captain Lamb. Next day it was sent up and later O'Meara came to view it. It was two-thirds life size 'and extremely well sculptured'. Napoleon was astonished that O'Meara did not believe that the Governor was involved in the plan to destroy it: 'When I attempted to justify the Governor and to assert that I did not believe the accusation, he repelled me angrily and said it was in vain to attempt denying a known fact.'[53]

According to O'Meara the idea of the bust being broken up emanated from Sir Thomas Reade. He was approached by Captain Lamb for guidance about what to do with it as it had been brought on board without his knowledge. He knew now that it was intended for Bonaparte and asked for advice about what he should do next. Reade 'viewed the business in a very serious light', and had told him that it 'was a very awkward circumstance' to say nothing about it, not to allow the gunner to disembark and that he had 'better break the statue in pieces or throw it overboard'. The story grew because 'Reade is greatly disliked by most classes in St Helena, [it] was in a few hours widely circulated, and with many exaggerations, because the theme of conversation universally, and was as universally believed.'[54]

The next day Captain Lamb asked Captain Johnson of the *Ocean* and Captain Dacre of the *Experiment* not to repeat what he had told them of Reade's advice. It was too late. Captain Johnson 'had been very successful in his exertions to disseminate it everywhere' so much so that Bertrand wrote to the Governor asking that Lamb be admitted to Longwood to talk about the bust. A second letter had the Governor agreeing to an interview.

He explained that the bust had not been sent up, due to the illness of the gunner. He also attempted to forestall any enquiries about the proposal to destroy it by denying that it had ever been suggested. O'Meara is adamant, Sir Hudson Lowe knew nothing of the idea.

A few days later Napoleon saw Lord Amherst and told him he believed that Reade had indeed proposed the destruction of the bust. The Governor later arranged for Radovich the gunner to go up to Bertrand's house at Longwood. The only stipulation was that Captain Poppleton the orderly officer should be present during any interview. When Napoleon discovered that Poppleton had to be present, he refused to see him. Montholon then came to see Poppleton to find out whether Poppleton would insist on being present if the Emperor wished to see the sailor. On Poppleton saying yes Radovich was dismissed. Napoleon had a new source of irritation. The Governor had offered an interview with one hand and then withdrawn it with the other.

Three weeks later Napoleon sent a letter to the Governor enclosing £300 with which to reimburse him for the cost of the bust and the losses he claimed he had incurred when he had first arrived at St Helena.

A few days after this Captain Heaviside of the HEIC arrived from Canton. He had 'a most superb set of chessmen and table' and a number of other items made on behalf of the Honourable John Elphinstone. They were sent as a mark of gratitude for Napoleon's direct intervention at the battle of Quatre Bras in probably saving the life of his brother, Captain Elphinstone of the 7th Hussars. The governor promised to send them up to Longwood but on opening the cases he found that the counters all had a letter N with a crown above them as did the carved work basket. On those grounds Sir Hudson Lowe decided to withhold them until he had received instructions from home.[55]

By this time it was clear to Balmain that Surgeon O'Meara was playing a double game, though he probably did not realise at this stage how disloyal O'Meara was being to the Governor:

> O'Meara is the secret agent of Sir Hudson Lowe at Longwood. This doctor is a clever and discreet man. He informs Bonaparte of what is said and done on the island in order to have access to him. At the same time he keeps a record of his slightest action and words. Without seeming to do so, he pokes his nose in everywhere, and it is through him that they learn an immense number of details of a character more or less to interest the watchers.[56]

For the first few months of his rule, Lowe believed that he was receiving secure and reliable background information about Napoleon's everyday thinking at Longwood – including Napoleon's abusive monologues against himself.

In October 1816, before either Lowe or Bathurst became suspicious that O'Meara was sending correspondence to another government minister, O'Meara had discussed what he might properly reveal to the Governor from his conversations at Longwood. O'Meara agreed that anything that hinted at 'any plot for his escape, or correspondence tending to it, or anything suspicious, I should conceive it my duty to give him notice of it', that he would also pass on 'anything of political importance uttered by Napoleon, or anecdote clearing up part of his history' but that he 'could not think of telling him everything, especially anything abusive or injurious … unless ordered so to do.'

Lowe, according to O'Meara, at first agreed to this but then as was his wont, changed his mind. Napoleon, he said, would use such attacks as a means of undermining his authority on the island and consequently persuading ministers to remove him from the island and back to Europe. Therefore, it was indeed necessary for O'Meara to reveal all, including the abuse, so that he, as the only official link with the government, might pass it all on to Lord Bathurst. It was at this moment that O'Meara revealed the bombshell of his own contacts with 'someone' in government. There were ministers who did not necessarily share Lowe's views:

> I replied, that it did not appear that all the members of his majesty's government were of a similar opinion, as I had received letters from official persons, with a view to communicate circumstances relative to Bonaparte, and returning thanks for my former letters, which had been shewn to some of the cabinet ministers. The governor was excessively uneasy at this, and observed that those persons had nothing to do with Bonaparte.[57]

In O'Meara's account, a somewhat shaken Lowe says that his correspondence ought to be subject to the same restrictions as any other that was intended for Europe. O'Meara, with the mere position of a Naval Surgeon to support any defiant stand against the island Governor and Commander-in Chief replied that this was unacceptable to him and that he stood ready to 'resign the situation' and 'go on board ship, as soon he liked' rather than give up his rights as a British officer. This was all so much posturing. If he was dismissed then Napoleon would have been without a doctor. O'Meara was the only British medical man on the island in whom Napoleon placed any trust.

Lowe's response, again according to O'Meara's book, was to reply that 'he would renew the subject on another day'. What O'Meara was doing was corresponding with John Finlaison, a clerk at the Admiralty. More significantly, he was secretary to the First Lord of the Admiralty, Lord Melville. With such backing O'Meara thought himself untouchable. Lowe had to bide his time.

In 1818, O'Meara had presented the two Anglican priests who had officiated over the funeral and burial of Cipriani with snuff boxes on behalf of Napoleon. On discovering that the acceptance of such gifts was contrary to the new regulations, these were returned. O'Meara asked that this incident be kept quiet. Lowe, however, had been informed of the presentation. An investigation was undertaken. O'Meara had inadvertently provided the context for his dismissal.

O'Meara wrote to the Governor pointing out that he had accepted the post of medical attendant upon Napoleon only if he were regarded as being on active service as an officer within the Royal Navy. Now that the Governor had placed restrictions upon him, he felt unable to carry on and tendered his resignation, along with a request for a passage home. O'Meara had jumped, Lowe had not pushed him. Neither Lord Melville nor the Prince Regent had any means of interfering in the matter. No amount of back pedalling by O'Meara would induce Lowe to return this letter of resignation. O'Meara wrote a letter of apology to Napoleon, through Bertrand, explaining why he had resigned:

> … however painful it is to my feelings to do so in the actual state of ill health in which he is at present, it is impossible for me to sacrifice my character, and my rights as a British subject, to the desire which I have of being useful to him, I have in consequence formed the resolution to depart and return to my native country.[58]

It was a poor explanation; in essence an apology for having been outmanoeuvred by the Governor. The next day Bertrand wrote to the Governor asking that O'Meara be reinstated; that Napoleon would accept an Italian or French doctor of note but not any British doctor other than O'Meara. Lowe had O'Meara confined to Longwood and would not issue a passage home until he had received instructions from Bathurst. Napoleon meanwhile, incensed at the apparent constructive dismissal of his favoured medical attendant refused to see him.

O'Meara cleverly raised the stakes once more, sending out a report from Longwood that Napoleon was in fact seriously ill. He then pointed out that were

Napoleon to die whilst he himself was effectively under house arrest then the governor would be held responsible. Lowe could not take that risk. O'Meara was released from confinement.

In London, Gourgard, who had just returned from St Helena, now informed Bathurst that Napoleon's liver complaint and other illness was all an illusion, which Napoleon had arranged using O'Meara as his agent. Bathurst saw that the advantages of having O'Meara corresponding with Melville were vastly outweighed by the disadvantages, now that he had been exposed as a double agent. Bathurst agreed with Lowe. O'Meara was to be sent home. Balmain and Lowe discussed Napoleon's supposed illness at this time.

> [Lowe]: 'I cannot give you a word about his health. He sees nobody, and I hardly know whether he is even living. What do you think of his illness?'
> [Balmain]: 'They tell me he is suffering in his head, liver and stomach, that Montholon spends the entire night at his bedside putting warm cloths on his stomach.'
> [Lowe]: 'Dr. O'Meara committed unpardonable mistakes. He kept those people in touch with everything that was happening in the town, in the country, on board vessels. He hunted out news for them and flattered them disgracefully. Moreover he gave to an Englishman secretly from Bonaparte, a tobacco-box.'[59]

The confusion over who was outwitting whom was neatly encapsulated in the arrival of two letters on the island. In July O'Meara received instructions from Bathurst directing him to return to England. The same day he received a letter from the Lords of the Admiralty, 'praising his zeal and his conduct and testifying to his capacity, allowing him to expect another appointment, honourable and lucrative.'[60]

He would of course, be returning to dismissal rather than reward. His revenge would be only a little time in coming with the publication of his diary. Napoleon, in cheerful mood in March, had commented:

> 'I suppose,' said he, 'that when you get back to England, you will publish your book. You certainly have a better right to publish about me than Warden, and you can say, that you have heard me say many things, and have had long conversations with me. You would gain a great deal of money, and everybody would believe you. Truly, no French physician has ever been so much about me as you have been. I saw them only for a few minutes. The world is anxious to know every little circumstance of a man that has happened to make any figure in it, such as all the little trifles about how he eats, drinks, sleeps, his general habits, and manners. People are more anxious to know those sottises that to know what good or bad qualities he may posses. *Pour moi, il suffit de dire le vérité.*'[61]

Lowe, on learning of the confirmation of his own wish, 'directed' O'Meara to leave a copy of his medical notes concerning Napoleon with Dr Baxter. This he refused, saying that the unofficial bulletins held by Bertrand would cover his medical notes.

Henry thought that O'Meara deserved to be dismissed from the service for his 'vile' conduct in insinuating that Lowe had urged him to poison Napoleon. Henry pointed out that O'Meara had kept this 'information' to himself for ten months prior to disclosing it to the Admiralty. Lowe had been appointed to the lucrative post of Governor that carried the promise of greater rewards. That he should be involved in an attempt to poison his prisoner, as Henry says, 'carries absurdity on the face of it, even putting out of sight any moral considerations of the question'. O'Meara's delayed and calculated attack on the Governor was indeed, vile. Henry again:

> I have been informed since, that Mr O'Meara had a friend in London, the pri-vate secretary Lord M—l—lle. This gentleman found it very convenient to have a correspondent in St Helena – then a highly interesting spot, who should give him all the gossip for the First Lord of the Admiralty; to be sported in a higher circle afterwards for the Prince Regent's amusement. According to my informant; a person high in rank in town – the patronage of Lord M—l—lle was thus secured; and Mr O'Meara, confident in this backing, stood out stiffly against the Governor. The latter was ignorant of this intrigue against the proper exercise of his authority; and when he discovered it afterwards, he found it a very delicate matter to meddle with, involving the conduct of a Cabinet Minister, and affecting, possibly, the har-mony of the Ministry. Even after the development of the poisoning charge against Sir Hudson Lowe, my information adds, that the influence of the First Lord was exerted to screen Mr O'Meara, but in vain; for Lord Liverpool said – as in another well known instance, and perhaps with greater truth, 'It is too bad.'[62]

In O'Meara, Napoleon had found someone who was quite prepared, for money, to inflate accounts of his illness, which were at this time arguably largely the result of Napoleon's refusal to exercise. O'Meara in an unguarded moment with Balmain admitted as much in December: 'Dr O'Meara told me confidentially that he did not give him more than two years of life. Only exercise can bring him back. But he will take none I am willing to guess, as long as Sir Hudson Lowe will be Governor of St Helena.'[63] A fortnight later he confided in Balmain again, assuring him: 'Sir Hudson Lowe does not walk straight or sincerely. One can have nothing to do with him, for one is never sure of what he says or writes.' This was from a man who proposed that Napoleon was suffering from hepatitis – a disease of the liver which, if true, should have resulted in Napoleon's removal from the island and his return to Europe. A short while later, Lowe realised that O'Meara was supplying him with very little real information about Napoleon's medical condition. In a heated exchange at Plantation House, when the Governor revealed that he believed O'Meara was playing a double game, Lowe ordered him to leave the house.

Gorrequer in his private diary records how he could hear their exchanges whilst the Governor pursued O'Meara down the corridor from one of the day rooms. Lowe's voice was loud and his words clear, O'Meara's a series of indistinct replies. The only words Gorrequer recorded were those of Lowe who repeated several times, 'Dishonourable, shameful, uncandid conduct,' as he followed O'Meara out of the room. Gorrequer remained in the library shocked by what he had heard, particularly as Lowe's raised voice could be heard through the entire house.[64]

Gorrequer paints a consistently unflattering view of Lowe as an indecisive, irascible and suspicious employer. Yet this particular explosion could well be justified as the outpouring of all his frustrations with O'Meara, Napoleon and of course the Finlaison correspondence. To have a senior member of the Cabinet using the imprisonment of Napoleon for his own amusement was an undermining of his position both as a military officer and as Governor. To whom might he complain with confidence? Bathurst probably, but even he was to prove less than even-handed in his later treatment of Lowe. Whatever Lowe's shortcomings, and they were legion, he was still the military appointee of the government, carrying out their orders based upon the laws which they had devised.

The government's response to Lowe's investigations and confrontation with O'Meara was a damage limitation exercise. Initially they held off from dismissing O'Meara until it became obvious that he had betrayed their trust. Then he was shipped home and after claiming that Lowe was contemplating Napoleon's murder, dismissed from the service.

His letters to Finlaison, most of which were burnt on O'Meara's death, were amusing. His diary, published in three volumes, was to prove even more so in London. Lowe, who had scrupulously maintained a professional silence over his arguments with the French on the island had few people to speak for him in the British press when these volumes first appeared and then went through five editions in Britain, with another translated in France. In two of the more serious journals they were received with disbelief and torn apart for inconsistencies; by John Wilson Croker in the *Quarterly Review* and by Christopher North in *Blackwood's Magazine*.

O'Meara in *Napoleon in Exile or A Voice from St. Helena*, created a sensation, with what might be called a 'kiss and tell' approach; a heady mix of truth and fiction, featuring a wounded hero in a foreign prison. In a passage dated August 1817 he has Napoleon speaking about his fears of murder on the island. Napoleon declares that it had been the policy of '★★★' to force every Frenchman to leave him and 'to induce me to commit suicide, or to have me altogether at his disposal'. The asterisks do little to hide the name of Lowe.

'Doctor, a man must be a worse blockhead who does not perceive that I was sent here to be ★★★★★★★★, either by the natural effects of ill treatment, combined with the badness of the climate, or by the probability of my being induced to commit suicide, as I have said, or by ★★★.'

'Were I in England,' added Napoleon, 'I would receive few visitors and never speak upon political subjects: here I do, because I am here and am ill treated. To live quietly, to enjoy occasionally the company of some *savants*, take a ride now and then, reading and finishing my history, and educating my son, would form my occupations. Here the want of books greatly retards *the advance of my works*.'[65]

A man who wished only for the contemplative life of the scholar was to be mur-dered. This combination of fact and fiction was made all the harder to disprove as it was published in 1822, a year after Napoleon's death.

Balmain wrote in December 1819 that Montholon had told Lowe Napoleon's health was improving and that he might decide to ride on horseback and that he had begun gardening

> … and puts his whole suite hard at work – men, women, even old Father Buonavita. Everyone, including a party of Chinese workmen were hard at work. For his imme-diate staff it was probably a relief from the ferocious pace of dictation, that had seen them writing for hours at a time with little time for recovery.[66]

Writing two days later Balmain describes the scene in the Longwood garden: 'He leads a tranquil life, seems to enjoy good health, and is extremely busy with his garden. He is having big trees placed, and flowers planted, which he waters himself, in full view of everyone.'

Balmain again had the report for Plantation House, produced by Captain Nicholls the Orderly Officer at Longwood, copied for his letter. Nicholls had seen Napoleon in his garden and described his appearance. His morning dress was a white gown, and straw hat with a very wide brim. In the afternoon he changed into his traditional cocked hat, green coat, white breeches and stockings. Nicholls also reported that he walked a good part of the afternoon in the Longwood gardens, with either Montholon or Bertrand at his side. In the evenings he often paid a visit to the Bertrands. At the end of January Balmain met the Bertrands in the open carriage and conversed with them. They assured him that the Emperor's health was good,

> … that he is devoting himself entirely to gardening, and that he is quite satisfied with the present conduct of Sir Hudson Lowe. For four or five days he has been amusing himself with shooting chickens and other animals which enter his garden. Yesterday he killed Mme. Bertrand's favourite goat, believing it to belong to the orderly officer.[67]

He may have been 'quite satisfied' with the Governor but clearly not satisfied with all governors. On 25 January Lord Charles Somerset, Governor of the Cape and therefore someone who had worked closely with Lowe, landed on the islands on his way home on leave. He straight away applied to Montholon for an audience but received no reply. 'This morning his Lordship sailed away in a very bad temper.' Somerset had been responsible for the detention of Las Cases, Piontkowski and the Archambault brothers. Whether Napoleon held this against him we cannot be sure. Perhaps Napoleon was too engrossed at the height of the summer in gardening to be bothered with a minor governor.

Bathurst was delighted at Napoleon's new hobby. Here at last was something constructive and positive, an activity that indicated that at long last Napoleon was turning his prison into a home. Lowe was to assure him that the government would derive a great deal of satisfaction

> ... from contributing by every means in their power to his gratification in this particular. I have therefore to desire that you would take a fit opportunity of communicating this to General Buonaparte, and of assuring him that, if there are any plants either at the Cape or at any other British settlement, or in this country, which he may wish to add to his present collection no effort on my part shall be wanting to procure and forward them to St Helena in the manner best calculated to insure their safe arrival.[68]

Lowe was urged to communicate with the governors of those colonies 'at once' should Napoleon express such a desire. It was probably the only period during Napoleon's incarceration when Bathurst received a set of consistently positive reports from the Governor.

The Britons who, theoretically, had the greatest opportunity to see Napoleon were the Orderly Officers stationed at Longwood. They occupied a room at the side of the main house and were responsible for liaising between the French inhabitants and the British. Their single most important daily task was to confirm the presence of Napoleon at Longwood twice in every 24 hours.

Not surprisingly, not all of them enjoyed it. The first one, Captain Thomas Poppleton of the 53rd Regiment, probably had the most positive experience of any of them. It was Poppleton who was on duty when a fire suddenly erupted in the drawing room at five in the morning. His prompt action in organising the guard to put out the fire was most fortunate as the walls in the drawing room were built of timber and the roof of tarred paper. When his regiment was ordered home he applied for permission to remain in post as orderly officer, but this was not permitted.

Poppleton had the unfortunate duty of escorting Las Cases to the Castle prior to his embarking for the Cape and then Britain. O'Meara was astonished to learn that Baron Gourgard and Count Bertrand went to Jamestown and spoke with Las Cases in the Castle 'at length', which Poppleton was unable to monitor as he understood little French, particularly when spoken quickly. The Governor had stipulated that a British officer must accompany La Cases if he were to have a last interview with Napoleon, an arrangement which the latter refused. Yet with Poppleton present anything of a controversial nature could easily be communicated between them by intermediaries. Napoleon observed Poppleton in March 1817 'as he was busily employed in digging some potatoes out of a little garden that we [O'Meara and he] had endeavoured to cultivate in front of the house'.[69]

He was the only orderly officer to be invited to dine with Napoleon. He seems to have been favourably disposed towards Napoleon and created a good impression with him, to such an extent that he was presented with a snuff box, which he accepted without reference to the Governor. Having gained the admiration of Napoleon it was inevitable that the Governor took against him for contravening the regulations which stated that no gifts were to be accepted without first referring the matter. The box was described to Thomas Creevey in 1822 as being 'beautiful' and it was observed that Poppleton was indeed 'devoted to Nap[oleon], and as averse to Lowe as O'Meara, and that all the officers of the 53rd were the same'.[70] Many years later, Poppleton's granddaughter claimed that a letter was discovered in the box which was a communication to Las Cases containing instructions concerning his son to be handed on to supporters in France.

As the orderly officers changed, so did Napoleon, who made it more and more difficult for them to see him. This was not an attempt to make life difficult for them personally but to frustrate the regulations that defined him as a prisoner. To that end he would at times suddenly rise up from his seat under the Napoleon oak or whilst in the garden and rush indoors to avoid being spotted by the prowling orderly officer.

One of the more curious stories concerning his efforts to frustrate both the regulations and Lowe was that of the holes bored in the shutters around Longwood. Using these he was able to use his glass to look out at anyone riding or walking up towards the house. At Dalmeny House near Edinburgh, the home of the Rosebery family, amidst their Napoleon collection are two sets of wooden shutters. These are reputed to come from Longwood and do have holes bored in them that would accommodate a small telescope.

Captain Blakeney was the next Orderly Officer, from July 1817 until September 1818. He too made a favourable impression at Longwood, despite the accusation levelled at him of his having examined the dirty linen from Longwood in order to detect any correspondence being smuggled out. It was Blakeney who had the unenviable task in May 1818 of assembling all British servants at Longwood and informing them of the new regulations. Napoleon, when he heard of this, ordered that these British servants who had replaced some of the French should be dismissed.[71]

Blakeney did however finally resign his post. This was most unfortunate as his replacement, Lt Colonel Lyster, was a disastrous appointment. He became the target for Napoleon's ire when he mistakenly believed that Lyster had served under Lowe in the Corsican Rangers. Lyster then added to the dispute when, having been shown Bertrand's letter of complaint against him (composed by Napoleon) he challenged Bertrand to a duel. Lowe in consequence had to send him off the island for the offence of attempting to duel. Blakeney was then reappointed. It was to be Blakeney who, along with Lt Col Wynyard, presented O'Meara with the letter telling him of his dismissal. Blakeney informed him that Wynyard was waiting for him along with a cart to move his possessions – immediately. He was to gather his possessions and leave without communicating with any of the French inhabitants at Longwood. After O'Meara had received the letter Wynyard delivered another to Bertrand. This had been written by Sir Hudson Lowe. It informed him that O'Meara was being removed from Longwood, along with a proposal to appoint Mr Baxter in O'Meara's place.

O'Meara told Finlaison that he stepped out of his room to call his servants and to organise some 'remedies' (medicines) for his Longwood patients. On returning at about a quarter past five he discovered that Wynyard had ordered O'Meara's servant to pack up whatever he thought appropriate into his luggage. His servants had managed to borrow some trunks that did not have locks on them from the house and were busy packing what they could. On his return O'Meara extracted some papers, a snuff box he had received from Napoleon and coins from his bureau and locked them into his portable writing desk. Wynyard had returned to O'Meara's room at this point and in his presence he gave Blakeney care of his money, as the borrowed trunks had no locks.

Captain Nicholls of the 66th Regiment was next and he too resigned the position, in February 1820. Napoleon still proved to be elusive. The Governor suggested Nicholls look in at the windows on an evening or at the edges of the window shutters in order to spot his quarry; poor, farcical work for a Captain.[72]

Captain Lutyens of the 20th Regiment followed and he too resigned his appointment in April 1821, after being censured for accepting, on behalf of the regiment, Coxe's *Life of the Duke of Marlborough* from Napoleon. It was a petty reaction to the generous offer by the first soldier of the age to the Regiment.[73]

The last few weeks of Napoleon's life were supervised by Captain Crokat and it was he who was given the responsibility of bringing news of Napoleon's death to Britain, despite his short period of time in the post. The man returning with such news could expect a promotion and possibly some other reward in the form of cash or an honour. Major Gorrequer did resent Crokat receiving such an opportunity when he had done little to merit it and he felt himself treated 'worse than any man on the island'.[74]

Notes

1 O'Meara, B., *Napoleon in Exile or A Voice from St. Helena*, Volume 1, Peter Eckler, New York, 1890 page 46.

2 O'Meara, B., *Napoleon in Exile or A Voice from St. Helena*, Volume 1, Jones & Company, Sixth Ed., page 69.

3 Poppleton to Lowe, 24 July 1816, Lowe 20115, folio 340, BL.

4 Mellis, G., *St Helena*, L. Reeve & Co, London, 1875, p. 396.

5 Balmain in a letter to the Russian Court, September 1816 in *Napoleon in Captivity: The reports of Count Balmain Russian Commissioner on the Island of St Helena 1816–1820*, Park, Julian, (trans) London, George Allen and Unwin, 1928, page 22.

6 Ibid., page 23.

7 Ibid., pages 27–28.

8 Ibid., page 29.

9 Barnes, op. cit., page 33.

10 O'Meara B., op. cit., page 13.

11 Marchand, L-J., *In Napoleon's Shadow*, Proctor Jones, 1998. page 364.

12 South American termites attacked many of the buildings on the island including parts of Longwood House. Today African hardwood is the preferred building timber on the island.

13 Jackson B., *Notes and Reminiscences of a Staff Officer: Chiefly Relating to the Waterloo Campaign and to St Helena Matters during the Captivity of Napoleon.* Ed R. C. Seaton MA, John Murray, 1903, pages 128 and 132.

14 Ibid., page 128.

15 Ibid., page 129.

16 Chaplin, A., *A St Helena Who's Who,* 1919. Republished by Savannah Press in 2002.

17 O'Meara, B., *Napoleon in Exile or A Voice from St. Helena,* Volume 1, Jones & Company, Sixth Ed., 1830: pages 40–42.

18 Young, N., op. cit., page 166–7 lists thirteen sets of books sent to Napoleon between 1817 and 1821, five of them being sent by either Lady Holland or both Hollands.

19 Young, N., op. cit., page 163.

20 Shorter, Clement, Ed., *Napoleon And His Fellow Travellers,* Appendix III, Sir George Bingham, Cassell, 1908, page 332.

21 Malcolm Lady C., *A Diary of St. Helena (1816, 1817) The Journal of Lady Malcolm,* A. D. Innes & Co., 1899, page 20.

22 Ibid., page 23.

23 Ibid., page 31.

24 Ibid., page 37.

25 Ibid., page 38.

26 Ibid., page 41.

27 Ibid., page 54.

28 Ibid., pages 57–58.

29 Ibid., page 59.

30 Ibid., page 62.

31 Ibid., page 64.

32 Ibid., page 76.

33 Ibid., pages 80–81.

34 Ibid., page 110.

35 Ibid., page 148

36 Ibid., page 148

37 Ibid., page 159.

38 Ibid., page 160.

39 Ibid., pages 163–164.

40 Ibid., page 166.

41 Letter addressed to Admiral Cockburn, Cheltenham, 1817, COC/8, NMM.

42 Lowe Papers 20117, folio 47, BL.

43 Examination of James Scott, in, Lowe Papers 20115, nd, folio 1, BL. There is a comment at the end of these notes that they were not taken upon oath.

44 Balmain, op. cit., letter 12, page 71, December 1816.

45 Lowe papers 20117, letter from Lowe to Bathurst, folio 97, BL.

46 Balmain, op. cit., page 78.

47 Ibid., page 111, letter 20, October, 1817.

48 Ibid., page 21, letter 5, September, 1816.

49 Balmain, op. cit., letter 2, January 28, 1817.

50 Lowe 20146, letter from O'Meara to Finlaison, folio 88, BL.

51 Ibid., folio 89.

52 Ibid., folio 91.

53 Lowe 20146, folio 94, BL.

54 Ibid., folio 95.

55 Ibid., folio 98, BL.

56 Balmain, op. cit., page 32, letter 5, September 1816.

57 O'Meara, 9 October 1816, page 145–146.

58 Letter from O'Meara to Count Bertrand, April 1818 quoted in Balmain, page 175.

59 Conversation between Lowe and Balmain quoted in Balmain, April 1818, page 177.

60 Balmain, op. cit., page 190.

61 O'Meara, op. cit., page 430.

62 Henry, W., op. cit., page 235–236, 1839, WL.

63 Balmain, op. cit., Letter 27, December 13, 1817.

64 Gorrequer, op. cit., page 29.

65 O'Meara B., *Napoleon in Exile or A Voice from St. Helena*, Volume 2, Simpkin & Marshall, Third Ed., 1822, pages 141–142.

66 Balmain, Letter no. 29 December 1, 1819.

67 Letter no. 2, January 28, 1820.

68 Bathurst to Lowe, Downing Street, June 2nd, 1820, quoted in Forsyth, Vol III, page 238.

69 O'Meara B., op. cit., page 403.

70 Maxwell, (Ed) Sir H., *The Creevey Papers: a selection from the correspondence & diaries of the late Thomas Creevey M.P.*, Volume 2, John Murray, 1903, page 47.

72 O'Meara B., op. cit., page 403.

73 Kemble, J., *St Helena During Napoleon's Exile*, Heinemann, 1969, page 94.

74 These volumes now reside at the Museum of the Lancashire Fusiliers in Bury.

75 Kemble, J., op. cit., page 228.

Chapter Eight

Keeping the Island Supplied

In St Helena as elsewhere, the first object of consideration is food. The necessary restriction on the night fishing, consequent on the custody of the State person, have exceedingly diminished the supply of that wholesome and cheap fresh animal food to both soldiers and inhabitants.[1]

There were times when the food supplies almost ran out. There were also the Cape naval squadron's needs to be met as the naval headquarters were moved from Cape Town to Jamestown. These were the responsibility of the Simonstown naval agent who was expected to purchase approximately a third of the Cape's available food supplies for the use of the naval squadron. Mr Luson the St Helena Company agent was to supply the increased garrison and civilian population of St Helena by access to the other two-thirds of the food grown at the Cape.[2] Life was made even harder for all classes when night time fishing was forbidden. Even Count Balmain, the Russian Commissioner grumbled:

No vessel after the evening gun may leave or shift its position … This state of things has deprived St Helena of an important means of livelihood – fishing. It now carries on that occupation only by day and fish is becoming as scarce as fresh meat.[3]

Shipping such foodstuffs was difficult, as legally only naval and East India Company vessels were entitled to anchor off the island. By 1816 Luson, already experiencing difficulties in supplying sufficient food, attempted to alleviate matters by hiring a private vessel. He received a stern rebuke. Such a practice was 'objectionable' and Luson was told not to repeat it.

Thereafter he had to rely on space on board both passing and patrolling naval vessels as well as those of the Company which called at the Cape at irregular times. Furthermore, these vessels were of course already full of goods for sale in Europe. The same difficulty applied with the naval vessels. What little space they possessed was divided in the ratio of two-thirds for the garrison and one for the naval squadron. However, Arkin points out that as the naval agent had precedence when loading these ships, Luson felt like the poor cousin when it came to loading his supplies. Then there were times when Luson's goods were loaded as a third priority when goods for Bonaparte took precedence over those for the garrison. This miserable situation was made worse by the bad weather of the winter months, when commercial vessels virtually ceased sailing from the Far East.[4]

This haphazard system of conveying goods to St Helena made the foodstuffs more expensive as contractors increased their prices in order to cope with times when they would have to wait for a ship and in consequence had to feed livestock or store wine or grain for long periods. Since Luson did not know which ships might appear at Simonstown or Table Bay, nor what space they had available for livestock or other food, he was unable to arrange to buy at a good price. Above all hung the terrible possibility of Napoleon being snatched from the island. Nothing was to interfere with the security of the state prisoner.

By 1816 Luson was already warning the St Helena government that the haphazard nature of the transportation arrangements would lead to problems in keeping the island fed. Finally, after several occasions when food shortages on the island became positively alarming, Luson received permission from Sir Hudson Lowe to improve the system. In November 1817 Lowe granted Luson the right to use any homeward-bound British merchant vessel, which would in future be authorised to stop at St Helena.

Some time in 1818 two particular vessels, the *Perseverance* and the *Centurion* of 460 tons, registered at Scarborough, Yorkshire, began regular voyages to St Helena. However, such was the nervousness on the island about Napoleon's security that Captain John Amber of the *Perseverance* received the following instructions prior to sailing for the island in 1819:

1. no passengers were to be taken on board nor any additional members to the usual crew
2. that a certificated list of his crew be obtained from the Cape Post Office and handed to any Officers of the naval vessels which patrolled off St Helena
3. that no one was allowed to send any goods beyond the foodstuffs supplied by the agent to St Helena
4. that sealed copies of the ship's manifest were to be delivered, unopened to the government of St Helena
5. that no one from the vessel was to communicate with the island without the express permission of the governor
6. that the master was not to accept any package for delivery to St Helena unless it came from an official government agency
7. that the master was to provide a security of £1,500, which would be forfeited should any of the regulations listed above be broken.

Examining the list above, it seems that supplies reached the island in spite of, rather than because of Sir Hudson Lowe. By 1816 Luson was hiring warehouses in both Simonstown and Cape Town. In the summer months, Luson's assistant,

Alexander Duncan, supervised the warehousing in Cape Town and in the winter months at Simonstown. The board in London, with an eye on the pennies, questioned the need for the appointment of Mr Duncan.

In an exasperated reply (to be found in the Cape of Good Hope Factory records), Luson pointed out that the matter of shipping goods to St Helena was 'comparatively trifling' compared to the issue of inspecting bags and wine casks, scrutinising the quality of hay and barley, checking the accurate weighing of the same and the general examination of the state of the shipping and the loading. In short, without Duncan he would be unable to supervise all of the tasks. If he dispensed with his assistant the Board would in all consequence pay out more than his salary in compensating for lost and damaged goods that had not been properly prepared for the voyage to St Helena. Some time later, the Board having established a more reliable service using space on board its own chartered vessels, dispensed with Duncan's services and Luson was obliged to hire a part-time assistant.

Sheep for the island were to be reared on a farm managed by an agent. Luson had to point out to the Board that some investment in farm machinery, livestock and the cultivation of fodder for the dry months was necessary for the scheme to succeed. However, once the details of the financial outlay were received at the end of 1815, Luson was told to dispose of the contract with the farm, which he did, at a loss to the Company. From then on sheep were to be bought from local farmers and not reared on a Company-leased farm. It was found that a greater proportion of Merino sheep died on the voyage out to the island compared to the more hardy African sheep. By the summer of 1817, the island hospital and garrison were consuming these sheep at a rate of 100 per month.

With the enlargement of the garrison beef cattle were as welcome as sheep. In May 1816 Cockburn was dedicating three transport vessels to importing Cape cattle.[5] Cattle farms were not to be found on the outskirts of the Cape but further inland and the quality of the beasts purchased was variable. One delivery being driven up the high street had people standing outside their houses in Jamestown complaining how miserable and lean the cattle seemed compared to those purchased for the naval squadron, which had just arrived on board the naval store ship *Camel*.

Attempts were made to purchase some cattle from Benguela on the African coast. Angola is significantly closer to St Helena than the Cape. The Island Council hoped that the shorter voyage would lead to more animals arriving in a better state. Benguela farmers, however, were not able to supply the number of cattle required. There was also the tricky matter of preparation before shipping. Cattle were to be held close to the embarkation point for a time so that they did not suffer during a long walk and they had to be used to dry fodder before boarding the vessels.[6]

Arkin quotes an 1816 investigation to ascertain why out of a load of 264 Merino sheep, 31 had died on the voyage and a further 28 within six days of landing. It was believed at first that the master of the vessel had loaded extra animals as a private venture for his own profit but it was found that this was not the case. Shipping livestock from the Cape to St Helena was a difficult business. By the middle of 1820 Luson was supplying the island with roughly 120 sheep per month. Luson's closer supervision of the cattle prior to loading led to healthier cattle arriving at the island, particularly when compared to those supplied by the naval agent.

At the end of 1816 Lowe had the operation of the Company farms on the island investigated by the Island Council. A three-man committee said of Mr Breame, who was responsible for them,

> … that he … mismanaged the Company cattle, mismanaged the growing of fodder and green corn for animal food, missed opportunities to grow crops on farm land currently full of weeds, wasted opportunities to collect manure from stables and piggeries to spread on the land.

Breame defended himself over the loss of Company timber, saying that it was due in large measure to the

> … extreme and heedless depredations by the Sailors of the *Northumberland* and the other Workmen, at the time the Buildings were carrying on at Longwood for the reception of General Buonaparte and his suite and also more recently by Chinese who were allowed to build the whole of their new huts with them.[7]

Breame was to be condemned by Lowe and later exonerated by the Company in London.

There were concerns about the quality of food being imported and its storage. In August 1817 the Master Attendant was being ordered to send on board any vessel delivering foodstuffs the Master Cooper, who was to check the state of the casks prior to their being loaded into the boats. He was then to inspect them a second time. Poor warehousing as well as poor storage on board ship had led to unnecessary waste.[8]

Other goods supplied by Luson to the island included horses for the Longwood stables, whale oil, and lime – for use either in construction or as a fertiliser – and builders' tools and materials. He was also to supply firewood as there was little timber available on the island. Napoleon disliked the smell of coal burning and insisted that timber be burnt in his fireplaces at Longwood. In October 1820 the brig *Aquatic* brought twelve wagon loads of firewood.

Home-grown crops were of course subject to the vagaries of the weather. In some wet seasons there was a greater amount of forage available than in others. Measures were brought in to force to maintain what little there was. In October 1816 the Council declared that stray goats found in Jamestown could be shot by anyone, in order to minimise crop damage.[9] Some goods were not lost to goats:

> Sir
>
> In answer to your letter wishing me to explain the nature of different articles shipped on board the *Tortoise* being short delivered.

The Cask of Beef was lost over board by accident on account of the heavy surf, by shipping out of the sling at the crane. The soap was stole out of a box after it was delivered on shore and out of my charge. The Ale must have leaked out on account of the badness of the Cask. The other articles short, must have originated from the labouring of the ship as the casks was found stove in the hold and the Coals which was laying in open lighters in the Thames nearly a week exposed to being stole or made off with by the people belonging to the Lighters.

I have the honor to be &

8th April 1817 Thomas Cook[10]

Fears over the security of Napoleon's person had eased by 1818 as the Governor then sanctioned the use of private British merchantmen from the Cape. However these had to be en route to British ports only. When Luson hired the British vessel *Mary* which was en route to Rio de Janeiro to call at the island, Mr Brooke, secretary to the Island Council, wrote of their disapproval along with a reminder that only those vessels that were bound for British ports were to be used in future.

There were smaller but more profitable contracts to be had with the French at Longwood. They after all had a style to maintain as befitted the entourage of an exiled emperor. Henry complained about the monotony of a British officer's diet when he first arrived on the island but this was not to be the case for Napoleon and his followers. The Prince Regent had declared that he was to be indulged as if he were a British General who liked to live well; and so it was. By 1816 three companies at the Cape; Marsh and Cadogan, Nourse and Christian and J. Harrington, were supplying Longwood via Balcombe. Much to the irritation of Luson they received precedence when it came to loading their goods on to naval vessels until Lowe laid out a detailed list of precedence in the matter of loading at the Cape. The overall needs of the island were to take precedence over other loading, then those of 'General Buonaparte', provided that a note signed on the Governor's authority accompanied it and thirdly the wants of the Foreign Commissioners, the island staff officers and the various regimental messes. Only then could privately ordered goods be stored on board. St Helena merchants who ordered goods from the Cape were informed that they would be at the bottom of the list when it came to loading goods for the island at the Cape.

Notes

1 Lowe 20240, memorandum on the state of food supplies on the island, folio 78, BL.
2 Much of the background to this chapter is taken from Arkin, M., 'Supplies for Napoleon's Gaolers', *Archives Year Book for South African History*, South Africa, 1964.
3 Balmain, op. cit., page 16.
4 Lowe 20115, Cockburn to Lowe, folio 165, BL.

5 Lowe 20116, Malcolm to Luson, October 1816, folio 244.

6 Correspondence in the Consultation ledger, folio 162, 9 December 1816, StHA.

7 Correspondence in the Consultation ledger, 16 December 1816, StHA.

8 Correspondence in the Consultation ledger, 29 July 1816 and 21 August 1817, StHA.

9 Correspondence in the Consultation ledger, 7 October 1816, StHA.

10 Correspondence in the Consultation ledger, 8 April 1817, StHA.

Chapter Nine

The Threat

They are Buccaneers of the most enterprising and desperate character. Men of all countries, though the greatest proportion are Americans. The Captain is named Sontag, probably a German. There are some Italians; and these live at St Salvador of an Italian who keeps the Cafe at St Salavador:– and this man's wife, it is stated, resides at St Helena; all these adventurers are full of schemes as well as wishes to effect the release of Bonaparte – and they seem to be much favoured by the American Consul at Bahia. The Italian Tavern keeper has been … trying to get a passage to St Helena to visit his wife.[1]

Bunbury to Lowe, 1816.

With the end of the War of 1812, Lord Liverpool's government had concluded a peace treaty with the United States. American vessels, like all other foreign ships, had been expressly forbidden to trade with, or anchor at, St Helena. Yet in the St Helena archives a significant part of the admittedly small amount of correspondence which deals with intelligence refers to American vessels crewed by citizens of the United States. Early in 1816 Bunbury informed Lowe about an intercepted letter to Napoleon, which Cockburn had sent on to London. Bunbury informed Lowe that

… the Ex Emperor has large sums of Money in different parts … his Agents have lodged Money on his Accounts in the Principal towns of America as well as in England, with the hope of being able to get at some one or other of their Deposits.[2]

More alarming for Lowe, in the letter from Bunbury was the news that the American Consul was shipping presents of oranges to Napoleon. Lowe must have wondered what messages arrived with those fruits, for it was also stated that 'a principal officer on the privateer lives in the Consul's house' whilst the crew 'are kept together but with no employment apart from wanting to assist Napoleon'. In London Bunbury speculated that it was perhaps Napoleon's money that was keeping these 'adventurers' together. The Americans had talked of fitting out 'a schooner or two' and it was thought that they intended to send one to Tristan da Cunha and to keep one cruising at a distance from St Helena 'as a point to which Napoleon might steer, if he could be apprised of their intentions and could contrive to push off in a boat. The whole account wears a face of probability, and deserves attention.'

Lord Melville wrote to Admiral Sir Pulteney Malcolm about this matter, instructing him to occupy Tristan da Cunha immediately. Finally Lowe was urged to 'send away the Italian wife if such a person exists on St Helena and anyone else with whom a clandestine communication might be kept up with the Brazils'.[3] We do not know if she really existed.

It was not just Americans who were under suspicion. There were still concerns in London about the loyalty of some British servicemen who worked at Longwood. In his diary Walter Henry writes of Madame Bertrand declaring shortly after Napoleon's death that there were two officers on the garrison who had been used more than once to send secret correspondence back to Europe.

In a letter to Lowe, Bathurst remarked that the Prince Regent thoroughly approved of his plans to screen all of Napoleon's mail, given all of the intelligence that pointed to a possible escape attempt. As well as the removal of the Polish officer Piontkowski and some of the French servants, Bathurst also urged the discreet removal from Longwood of 'the 12 British sailors – as they may be wrought upon by fair words & many promises to consider rescue as something generous & creditable, because it is hazardous'.[4]

In a letter from Paris, dated 27 May 1816, Lowe and Stewart at the Cape had received intelligence from Castlereagh in Paris:

> By a remarkable coincidence the Frigate appointed to carry out Count Dupois, the Governor of the Isle of Bourbon and the French Establishments in the East Indies is the *Amphitrite* commanded by a Captain Philibert and navigated by the crew who received Bonaparte at Rochefort in the month of July last, and whose good will was conciliated by the distribution of a considerable sum of money during the few days which immediately preceded his surrender to the officer commanding the British Squadron off that Port.[5]

Charles Bagot, the Ambassador in Washington wrote about information he had received from a M. Neuville. The Frenchmen Rousseau and his companion Joseph Archambault, who was brother to Achille, the coachman who had remained on St Helena, had been deported on 19 October 1816. They had landed at Spithead on 15 February 1817, then travelled to Brussels where they parted from Santini.[14] Some time later, they appeared in Philadelphia where Rousseau had passed about a fortnight in the company of Joseph Bonaparte. After that he had travelled on to Long Island, where he lived in the house of William Cobbett, the radical pamphleteer and journalist who had recently fled to America, for a second time, to avoid arrest for his seditious writings. Bagot:

Cobbet is a principal agent in the plan which is in agitation for effecting the escape of Buonaparte from St Helena ... he is the channel of communication for such of the English as are privy to the design. He says that Lord Cochrane and Sir Robert Wilson are both deeply engaged in it, and that a correspondence is carried on upon the subject with some persons in France, through the means of a female relation (he thinks a sister) of Sir Robert Wilson's, who resides at Brussels. He says that Lord Cochrane's intended voyage to South America was connected to this design, and that there was to be a general rendezvous of all the agents of the plot at the island of Fernando de Noronha, which is a small island off the coast of Penambuco, and which is used by the Portuguese as a place of banishment for criminals.

The remarkable, disgraced Cochrane, who had earned the name 'the Sea Wolf' from the French during the war, was indeed on his way to fight for Chile in their war for liberation from Spain. He had supported many radical causes whilst an MP, and such support had put him in very bad grace with Liverpool's government. Undoubtedly his radicalism was one of the contributory factors in his public disgrace and removal from the Royal Navy list. He was also a close friend of William Cobbett. Fernando de Norohna was a viable rendezvous point for any invasion group as it is directly to the west of St Helena island.[6]

Sir Robert Wilson also had a distinguished fighting record and a disdain for authority. In politics he was a radical Whig and supported the reform of Parliament. Like Cochrane, he was seen by the government as 'unreliable' and too independent, as Wellington famously remarked, 'a very slippery fellow'. Wilson probably did not take any active part in planning a raid to free Napoleon, indeed he may not even have been involved in any initial discussion, but with radicals like Cochrane and Wilson, in an age of political turmoil at home, the most unlikely plots had to be considered by the authorities.[7] With the arrival of this intelligence, Lowe probably worked even more ferociously. By 1817 the fortifications had been repaired and extended, there were new telegraph posts and batteries in various places and the guard at Longwood had been increased.

Of even greater concern than the possible arrival of 'the Sea Wolf' was the indication of a link between Lowe's most troublesome islander, Barry O'Meara, the disgraced naval surgeon and Napoleon's supporters abroad. In a letter marked 'Private and Confidential', dated December 1818, written to Lord Stewart at the Cape, Bathurst explained that a communication had been sent from a Mr Franklin to O'Meara. Clearly, O'Meara's mail was being clandestinely opened. Bathurst, having read the letter, gained the impression that a message was concealed within it and it led him to

... entertain suspicions that it has some connections with the plans which there is every reason to believe are in agitation for the escape of General Buonaparte. It is therefore most important that your Lordship should keep a watchful eye on the Correspondence and proceedings of Mr Franklin and ascertain, if possible, whether he is in actual Communication with St Helena, and if so, the nature of his Communication.[8]

It would seem that Franklin was then living at the Cape but not as a citizen of that colony, which probably gave Bathurst some cheer as it would be legally easier to remove him as an alien rather than as a resident with full rights of citizenship. Stewart was urged to investigate any possible link between Franklin and those of 'Napoleon's adherents' who had stationed themselves in Brazil. He reminded Stewart that he had previously urged him to contact Sir Hudson Lowe should Franklin attempt 'either by himself or his agents to communicate with General Buonaparte at St Helena'.[8] Finally, should the Governor discover that his 'sole purpose for residing at the Cape' was in order to maintain a secret communication with Napoleon, then Franklin he was to be deported from the colony.

One of the great worries on the island and at the Cape was the presence of foreigners who might be already working for, or be persuaded to work for, Napoleon's agents. In a letter about Piontkowski's incarceration at the Cape in 1816, Stewart had spoken of the 'needy adventurers' at the Cape, many of them foreigners. 'Half of the military force here is the 1st Bn 60th Regiment, composed exclusively of foreigners who have nearly all served under Buonaparte's Banners'.[9] It was not that they had gathered there to work for the release of Napoleon but that the Cape was still, in its population, a Dutch colony. Only in 1806, after the battle of Blaauwberg, had it passed into British hands.

Suddenly there was a new hi-tech angle to the idea of a raid on the island. Writing in January 1818, Count Balmain mentioned the despatches from the British Chargé d'affaires in Rio. Two men had arrived at Penanbuco on the Portuguese vessel *Rainha*. M. de Malet, the French Chargé d'affaires in Brazil, identified these men as former soldiers of Napoleon. They were arrested on suspicion of having arrived to take part in an impending rebellion. One was a Colonel Latapie and the other an Austrian who had been a captain in the French cavalry. They were released after confessing that they had intended after the rebellion to raise an expedition to take Napoleon off St Helena. Latapie claimed they had a number of small steam vessels to get to the coast after carrying them on large ships close to the island.[10]

The Marquis d'Osmond, the French ambassador in London, had already written on 11 September warning about Latapie. Now there was the prospect of steam vessels being used to move against the ocean swell and the wind. Operating at night they could have been used for embarking Napoleon at any of the more inaccessible landing points – and there were of course many, despite Wellington's assurances that there were not.

Stacked against them, just as Wellington had outlined, was the fact that all the valleys now had walls across them and each a small garrison. At night a general alarm would have placed the entire island at 'stand to' with the island volunteers corps also being mobilised. By 1818, every rocky shore was observed by both artillery and infantry. Jackson, having walked Gill's Point, for example, was able confidently to state that it had a descent that was

> ... extremely difficult & almost impracticable for any persons unaccustomed to it, the ravine joins the seashore a little to the westward of Shon Rock & from there, Gill's Point is reached by scrambling over the rocks at the base of overhanging cliffs. If it should be deemed necessary to cut off the communications with the sea by Dry Gut, it may be effected by Scarifying the Rocks, which are generally of a soft nature.[11]

As he had shown at Rochefort, Napoleon would not compromise his imperial dignity and risk being laughed at by his enemies. Unbeknownst to him, this was already happening on St Helena. Napoleon believed that he had the measure of almost everyone on the island; but not quite all. O'Meara, right up to his dismissal, was sending letters to Lord Melville via John Finlaison for the amusement of some government ministers and the Prince Regent.

Intelligence came to St Helena in several forms: the official government information which came via London from Brussels, Paris, Vienna, Washington, South America and the Cape, as mentioned earlier, and other local information came via British and foreign vessels. On 1 October 1816 Captain Elliott of the merchantmen *Hope* recorded in his log that at 7:00am, whilst he was several days north of St Helena, he had seen a brig which an hour later tacked 'with a view to speak to us apparently, which I endeavoured to avoid on account of delay'. An hour later she hoisted English colours and tacked again 'and stood towards us'. Shortly after this she hauled down her English colours and

> ... hoisted a Blue White & Blue Flag with a Pennant of the same colours: at the same time we hailed her & asked her from whence she came. She answered, from Buenos Ayres, & was bound to Gibraltar, & said she would send a boat on board of us. At this time she was within half Pistol Shot; she hauled up her stern ports & ran out her stern chase guns: she mounted 16 carronades and was very full of men who were apparently all at their quarters ... Her boat came alongside apparently manned with Englishmen; and one man who said he was the Captain of the privateer was an American and his name was Gardener: & another who said he was the Purser & he was a native of Devonshire.[12]

This encounter with a Patriot Argentine brig seemed plausible. In a separate letter, the intelligence content of which originated from Paris, Castlereagh was informed by the French Government that a person named 'Carpenter', an American was fitting out a fast sailing vessel in the Hudson River 'for the express purpose of facilitating the escape of Bonaparte from the Island of St Helena'. No likely date for the escape attempt was given. Was the captain of the small but powerful warship one and the same man? The names 'Carpenter' and 'Gardener' could easily have been misheard when being taken down by a clerk on the island. [42] About the same time that the Argentine cruiser had been spotted a British official in Brazil, a Mr Chamberlain, had heard from the wife of a tavern keeper that the crew of a former American privateer was proposing 'to liberate Napoleon'.[13]

In April, the British agent in Rio de Janeiro reported that a 'considerable number of Frenchmen and their families' had landed from France. They had left chiefly 'from motives of disgust at the Restoration of the Bourbons; it is by no means improbable that attempts will be made by some of them, or at any rate by their means, to open a secret correspondence with General Buonaparte'. He had already urged the master of the vessel from St Helena to refuse to take any letters for the island and mentioned that the leader of the French party was a Monsieur le Breton, who had been 'one of Buonaparte's Secret Police, which is quite sufficient to authorise my putting you upon your guard respecting all correspondence from hence'.[14]

Meanwhile in London Bathurst was apologising in a 'secret' letter to Lowe for not being able to load the mountain guns and equipment that Lowe considered essential for the defence of the island. HMS *Eurydice* simply did not have enough room. However, they would be sent out on board the next available East India man. In the meantime Lowe was urged to redouble 'the precautions which you may consider necessary to defeat any attempt at affecting his escape'.

In a letter to Castlereagh, Sir Charles Stewart, the British Ambassador in Paris reported that the French frigate which would shortly pass St Helena carrying the new Governor of the Isle de Bourbon in the Indian Ocean would be commanded by Captain Philibert. His crew would be that which had been with him in Rochefort. Stewart had also received intelligence from the Austrian Minister in Paris that the police in Vienna had intercepted a letter addressed to a General Morand in Krakow, which contained 'an obscure allusion to St Helena, Ascension and Philadelphia and a reference to future communications in cipher which General Morand is to receive from General Gilly'.[44] Philadelphia was the home of Napoleon's brother Joseph. Unlike Napoleon, Joseph had managed to cross the Atlantic on a ship from the west coast of France.

One of the strangest letters in the Lowe Papers is a copy, written in English, purporting to come from a friend of Napoleon and addressed to Marshal Bertrand. It had been sent through the British Post Office system and had been received at the St Helena Post Office. In line with Lowe's wise policy of examining all mail sent to the occupants of Longwood it was opened and read. It is amusing and could well be the work of a slightly deranged admirer of Napoleon or an agent provocateur; but as there is no correspondence referring to it in the Lowe Papers, presumably Post Office agents working in the secret department back in London were unable to unravel the mystery.

The original had no date but had a post mark from the 2nd Post office at Pall Mall and was dated 13 March 1816 and the same from the East India Letter Office. The Governor intended to send the original letter to England, to help to track down the author.

Bertrand was addressed as a 'Dear Friend' who was to work with the utmost secrecy lest the two were found out more credible if the author had sent the letter in a more discreet manner. He reminded Bertrand that a collapsible boat would drift to the 'back of the island in the shape of an old cask'. When two ropes were pulled this would then be transformed into a seaworthy craft with sails. All the Emperor then had to do was 'bear away right before the wind' until he was four miles from the island when he would observe a light showing out of one of the portholes of the ship which had come to pick him up.

Once on board the rescue vessel, circumstances would decide to which American port they would sail, there hopefully to meet both the Empress and the King of Rome, along with 'a great many … faithful subjects led by the Marshals and Ministers'. Talleyrand was already there, wherever 'there' was, with huge sums of money. The Americans were ready to honour him and 'have him for an Emperor' marching with him to secure a new Empire in South America. All these plans ended with an exhortation for the Emperor on the appointed night to slide down the concealed rope that the author had previously provided.

Given the indicators in these letters and log books, there was still a great deal for a man as troubled and driven as Lowe to do to make the island more defensible. In a letter written in August 1816 to Robert Peel from Croker, we get a good impression of how Napoleon was viewed by leading members of government. Cockburn had informed Croker that Napoleon was eating huge amounts, taking regular exercise and was 'so very careful of his carcass that he may live twenty years'. Cockburn was convinced that though Napoleon and he 'parted bad friends' Napoleon now wished he had Cockburn back again, for Sir Hudson Lowe was as strict as Cockburn without any of his 'liveliness'.

The one significant factor that all of these secret correspondents overlooked was Napoleon's attitude towards any escape plans. He would not compromise his imperial status by taking part in any scheme over which he did not exercise complete control. At Rochefort he had listened to more than one scheme to spirit him past Captain Maitland's blockading vessels and he had rejected all of them. He was as concerned as anyone to avoid detection and capture but above all he was determined not to be publicly humiliated. He was already damaging his health by remaining indoors, in his battle with the British Government to be recognised as the Emperor and not as 'General Buonaparte'. It seems inconceivable that Napoleon would risk his dignity in a headlong flight down the rocky tracks to the seashore.

When I walked down to the fortifications in Lemon Valley, in good daylight, I stumbled more than once in exactly the same manner as Lt Jackson described almost 200 years previously. The soft volcanic rock crumbles easily into oddly sized shards which then slide easily over each other as the walker moves down. A few days later, I spoke to Mrs Brenda Bizarre, a native Saint Helenian, about walking along the hill side track into Lemon Valley. She assured me that few people on the island had walked that track knowing how unstable it was and that her husband had only walked down it twice in his entire life.

Cockburn was convinced when he left the island that given 'common vigilance' Napoleon could not escape. Though he also mentioned that there were some 'mad and wild' schemes emanating from America to rescue him. Lowe continued to work to counter those schemes. Croker summed up the threat: 'His friends there have money, talents, audacity, and despair. What would you have more?'[15]

Notes

1 Lowe 20115 Bunbury to Lowe, 1 May 1816, folio 109.

2 Lowe 20115 Bunbury to Lowe, 6 March 1816, folio 26.

3 Ibid, folio 109.

4 Lowe 20115, Bathurst to Lowe, June 1816, folio 236.

5 Lowe 20115 Castlereagh to Lowe and Stewart, 27 May 1816, folio 174.

6 There has been some speculation that he did actively consider taking Napoleon from St Helena and then escorting him to rule over South America as Emperor. An amazing fighting sailor, he is probably best remembered for taking the Spanish frigate *Gamo* of 32 guns and 319 men against his brig of 54 men and fourteen 4-pounder guns. Cochrane provided the model for Patrick O'Brien's fictional Captain Jack Aubrey.

7 Vane, Marquess of Londonderry, C. W., (Ed.) letter from Bagot to Castlereagh in, *Correspondence, Despatches, and other Papers of Viscount Castlereagh*, Volume II, London, John Murray, 1853, pages 380–381.

8 Volume 1/23 Government House, General Despatches, Bathurst to Lowe, Colonial Officer, 30 December1818, folios 140–144, SAA.

9 Ibid, folios 140–144, SAA,

10 Balmain, Letter 1, 1 January 1818 page 154.

11 Lowe Papers 20225, letters of military officers, folios 30–31.

12 Lowe Papers ADD MSS 20116 Folio 160, 12 October 1816.

13 Ibid., folio 306.

14 Lowe Papers 20115, folio 57, letter dated 17 April, 1816.

15 Pool B. (Ed), *The Croker Papers, 1808–1857,* London, Batsford, 1967, Page 38.

Chapter Ten

Guarding Boney – Defence of the Island

... in consequence of events which have happened in Europe subsequent to the signature of the Convention aforesaid ... St Helena shall be the place allotted for the future residence of General Napoleon Bonaparte, under which regulations as may be necessary for the perfect serenity of his person and it has been resolved that, for that purpose, that all ships and vessels whatever, as well as British ships and vessels as others, excepting only ships belonging to the East India Company, shall be excluded, from all communication with, or approach to that island.

The *Sun* newspaper, 18 February 1816.[1]

The effective defence of the island required good command and control by the governor, professional troops, prepared defensive positions across likely landing places, good communications across the island and between the land and the sea forces and all of it capable of working effectively day and night.

In a secret letter to the then governor Colonel Mark Wilks, dated August 1815, it was made clear that although Wilks remained Governor until the arrival of Sir Hudson Lowe, in all matters relating to Bonaparte he was to defer to Admiral Cockburn. Wilks was to make available any house that the Admiral saw as a fit residence for the prisoner, 'with the exception of the Governor's Plantation House'. He was also encouraged to devise any local regulations that would assist in preventing the escape of the General or his companions.[2]

Early on, Wilks was asked to produce an initial assessment of the state of the island's defences. He proposed that there was a need for a 'good military police' and for an officer to see him periodically 'as courtesy and humanity shall admit'. It was he who initiated the ideas of excluding

... blacks and all natives of the Island, who are the best guides; and perhaps also persons who have been long resident and possess local information – of limiting his range to Longwood, including the road as far to the north west as the little building called Alarm House.[3]

Wilks provided the initial boundaries around the Longwood estate, which was south west to Miss Mason's house and on Deadwood and Longwood to the 'posts by the verge'. He raised the matter of future escape attempts. As the French became familiar with the island then there might be greater concerns about their freedom of movement.

His assessment of the current defensible state of the island must have given the government pause for thought. They had thought St Helena ideal. It was remote and apparently inaccessible and impregnable. Wilks assured them that it was not. He gave the example of Hold Fast Tom, which overlooks the eastern side of the island. A stranger, he declared,

> ... would pronounce that particular spot to be an inaccessible precipice and all access from the bay within his view to be nearly impracticable – this is the point at which a landing was made by Sir R. Munden when he recovered the island from the Dutch ... it is a popular fishing place – accessed from above.[4]

He asserted there were many places where a landing might be made and with few defences in place to impede an invader.

Admiral Cockburn's initial instructions from the Secretary of State issued at the end of July were detailed and specific. First they had dealt with the removal of Napoleon's various monies, which had led to the awkward inspection of Napoleon's luggage on board ship off the English coast. Cockburn was told to explain to the General that the British Government was not confiscating his property, but rather taking on the duty of Napoleon's accountant in order to prevent his goods 'being converted by him into an instrument of escape'. The government had probably corralled most of his ready money but not all, as Saint-Denis admitted when he went ashore at Jamestown. He and others carried large amounts of gold in money belts ashore at Jamestown. So much so that he admitted, as we have seen, that by the end of the day he was much relieved to remove it as his 'hips were flayed'.[5]

Napoleon was to be always attended by an officer appointed by the Admiral or Governor. If he were to ride beyond the boundaries where the sentries were on duty then at least one orderly was to accompany the orderly officer. When strange ships, any vessels other than those of the Royal Navy or the East India Company, were sighted the General was to be confined within the area where the sentries stood on guard. His followers would be subject to similar regulations. Were he to attempt to escape, then on capture he was to be 'subject to close custody' and this was also to apply to any of his followers who had taken part in the attempt. His correspondence out of the island was to be open and directed to the Admiral until the Governor arrived and then to him. The same was to apply to any correspondence sent by his followers. The only letters which could be handed over to Napoleon or his followers were those that had been composed on the island, though even this was to change later. If he wished to write to the British Government then he was entitled to do but again in an open letter, so that the

Admiral or Governor might also make any representations they felt were appropriate. Cockburn was told to take action 'immediately' on arrival at the island to remove

> ... to England or to the Cape or to the East Indies according to the circumstances of the case such non Commissioned Officers and Privates in the Military Forces at St Helena as the Admiral may deem appropriate to release from their military duty in the island, by reason of being Foreigners, or on account of their general character and disposition.

Any foreigner who might possibly be inveigled into aiding the escape of Napoleon was to be removed. By the end of his time on the island a small trickle of these foreign Company soldiers from both the resident infantry and artillery battalions, had been moved to the Cape.

If Napoleon fell ill then the Admiral was to organise for a medical person 'in whom they may have confidence', to be in attendance upon him. In the event of his death, Napoleon's body was to be conveyed to England. Burial in Geranium Valley was not yet an option.[6]

By July 1816, with Sir Hudson Lowe having been in place since April, Captain Barnes was able to offer an opinion of the new Governor to Admiral Cockburn. It was very complimentary to the Admiral. There was 'more bustle, noise, and fidget than enough' since his departure but a lack of organisation and energy. The Governor was everywhere:

> Sir Hudson is himself very active, he rides a great deal about, looks at everything, and everybody very minutely, but the results of his exertions and observations are, as far as I can see, enveloped in unyielding incommunicability. I have the pleasure to stand very well with him, for which my thanks are due to you.[7]

Every soldier of the 66th Regiment, the Royal Artillery and the St Helena Infantry and the St Helena artillery regiments, when not on duty, was 'incessantly employed in some task'. Barnes had met Admiral Malcolm, whom he had found to be 'very gentlemanly, polite and kind'. Of Napoleon he knew nothing:

> Bonaparte is, as if he was not – his name is scarcely ever heard – whatever there may be concerning him reaches no further than the impenetrable obscurity of Head Quarters – I believe he enjoys perfect health. The two Acts of Parliament relative to his detention have been recently promulgated, preceded by a Proclamation from the Governor, which is merely a recapitulation of those which you issued from time to time.[8]

Barnes assured Cockburn that the same keen vigilance with which he had guarded Napoleon remained in place. Every nation was to be excluded from either landing or even anchoring.

Sir Hudson had two great assets in his favour. Against a well defended shore, in an age of sail, the odds were always against any amphibious landing. Lowe also had extensive experience in wartime of commanding an island under siege in the Mediterranean.[9]

The men who supervised the infantry and Chinese workmen who laboured across the island were the tradesmen of the 7th Company of the 4th Bn The Royal Sappers and Miners. They were commanded by Major Emmott of the Royal Engineers. A company of 48 men, they spent a great deal of time on detached duty across the island working at different times at Prosperous Bay, Turk's Cap, Sandy Bay, Great Pound Ridge, Horse Pasture Point, Lemon Valley, Rupert's Hill, Rupert's Valley, Ladder Hill and so on. There was indeed a great deal to do. Some road surfaces, for example, were in a critical state. In a report presented to the council on 10 July 1817, Lt Den Taffe said that a part of the road that led from Lemon Valley out towards Sandy Bay was in such a bad state of repair that if it was 'not to become impassable' it required immediate repair. The council, not surprisingly, adopted his proposal.[10] Today the island roads follow the same course as they did on Barnes' map. They twist and turn alarmingly when driving along them in a car. But of course they were built to accommodate horses and pedestrians and not car drivers.

By 1823 all the coast had been mapped and the depth of the water off the rocky shore had been measured. The map was produced by a Captain Seale. Fresh water points were recorded and the position of Martello towers marked. Every valley had undergone building work. Walls, or lines, as the military call them, had been built across each entrance. Battery positions on these lines and on the hillsides to provide interlocking fields of fire had been constructed and above them a line of telegraph stations enabled communication around and across the island during daylight. Seale also provides notes on each landing place, commenting on the ease of landing and the degree of difficulty in marching into the interior. The letter code on the left is part of the alphabetic listing of all the valleys around the island.

Landing	Roads	Access	
ff	Manatee Bay	5	Easy
gg	Shepherds Plain	1	Very difficult
hh	Middle point	1	do
ii	New do	1	do
kk	S.W. do	1	Easy
ll	Dry Gut	1	do
mm	Thompson Valley	2	do
nn	Old Woman	2	do
oo	Bennetts Point	2	Difficult
pp	Thompsons do	2	Easy
qq	Horse Pasture do	1	do
rr	Friars Valley do	2	do

ss	Youngs do	2	do
tt	Breakneck do	2	do

The defence of the island prior to the arrival of the King's troops rested with the two resident battalions of Company troops. These two small regiments probably offered a healthier lifestyle than the India-based regiments. The climate being sub-tropical is milder than in India. There was also the prospect of service in the Pensioner Company well into old age. With a good service record it was possible for old soldiers to apply for permission to remain on the island.

These resident, professional, single battalion Honourable Company regiments were the St Helena Regiment and the St Helena Artillery. Both units were organised along British Army lines, each under a Lieutenant Colonel. Both battalions were subdivided into companies, each commanded by a Captain, who was assisted by two and occasionally three subalterns. Prospective officers were termed cadets, and served in the companies in a similar manner as the Gentleman Volunteers in the British Army.

Uniforms were almost identical to those of the British Army, with the artillery wearing a blue short tailed jacket with red facings and yellow lace and the infantry a similar red one with blue facings.[11] At one point the officers of the Royal Artillery on the island protested to the governor that the new Commanding officer of the St Helena Artillery was wearing a Royal Artillery uniform coat with Royal Artillery buttons instead of his Company regiment.

The small St Helena Regiment also had a band; in 1817 they played in the town church after the resignation of the church organist. The band got his salary divided up amongst them until another organist was appointed.[12]

The two regiments did have some experience of active service. In 1795 HMS *Sceptre* on convoy duty brought word that Holland had been taken by the French. Governor Brooke immediately decided to organise an expedition to take the Dutch Cape by a *coup de main*. Whilst he was organising his small fleet news arrived of a British expedition that was already on its way to the Cape with the same intention. This expedition landed and then found itself blocked at Muizenberg. Assistance was sought from Governor Brooke, who responded by sending a company of the St Helena Artillery with ten field pieces and three companies of the infantry.

On 16 September the Dutch surrendered the Cape. The Court of Directors was delighted with Brooke's actions. A potentially dangerous port had become a friendly one and was now able to support Company trade. Lord Mornington, the Governor-General of Bengal, (brother of the Duke of Wellington) echoed the Court, sending a dazzling Indian sword by way of a personal gift to Governor Brooke. Brooke also received letters from the naval commander, Admiral Elphinstone, later Lord Keith. Elphinstone thanked him for his speedy response to his request for assistance and praised the efforts of the men of the two regiments.

The trick had to be repeated, as the Cape was handed back to the Dutch as part of the settlement of the Peace of Amiens in 1802. After General Baird and Admiral Home Popham had reconquered the Cape early in 1806, Popham set off on what was more or less a private venture. Prior to leaving London this restless individual had met with the American patriot Miranda. Popham was convinced that the enfeebled Spanish authorities in South America were close to collapse. It was he who would help free South America and open up trade for Britain.

On calling at St Helena he managed to persuade Governor Patton to support his call for volunteers to join his small regular force that General Baird had provided to him. So it was that 200 men comprising elements of the artillery regiment and the light company of the St Helena Regiment sailed for Buenos Aires. A year later the muster roll for the Light Company of the St Helena Regiment listed the names of fifteen men 'not returned from Buenos Ayres'.[13] The Light Company was only briefly re-established a few years later.

Four years later, in 1811, elements of the infantry regiment participated in a mutiny when discontent over the withdrawal of cheap rum led to an ill-judged attempt to seize weapons in Jamestown, storm Plantation House and seize the Governor. Loyal soldiers, the majority of both units, gathered at High Knoll and Plantation House along with the Volunteer Corps. Next day, with most of the mutineers having slunk away in the night, the ringleaders were seized, tried and nine of them were hanged at High Knoll.

Service in either regiment offered men who did not have the wealth to buy a commission an opportunity to be promoted on the basis of seniority. What they gave up by not serving in India was the tantalising prospect of promotion through active service and the faint hope of making money there.[14]

If William Hickey is to be believed, signing up for commissioned service had none of the glamour associated with Wellington's army. Hickey applied to be a cadet at the end of the eighteenth century and went to be interviewed for his post at India House in Leadenhall Street, London. He recalled entering a room where three old men (Hickey was nineteen at the time) sat. It was, according to Hickey, a cursory affair. Having given his age he was asked whether he had any service with the British Army, he said he had not. He was then asked whether he knew the 'manual exercises' for handling weapons to which he replied that he did not and bowed when one of his interrogators told him that he must do so. He was then asked whether he knew the terms of service for a life in the Company's army and whether he was satisfied with them. He said that he was and the clerk told him he might withdraw. He then went to Mr Cognac's office and received the document appointing him a cadet in the Company's service. These cadets received no training prior to leaving for India and presumably it was the same for those going out to St Helena. This would change in 1816 with the establishment of the company military college at Addiscombe.

On St Helena cadet appointments were a family affair. In 1817 the following men were appointed as cadet officers and only Kennedy appears not to have had either a father or brother serving in one of the units:

Artillery
Mr Chas Sampson
Mr Wm O. Kennedy
Mr Wm Doveton

Infantry
Mr James Pritchard
Mr Wm Mason
Mr Wm Hayes[15]

The private soldiers were generally recruited in Britain, with hardly any recruited oin St Helena. A few soldiers were recruited as they sailed back from India, having previously served in an Indian-based Company regiment such as the Bengal Artillery. Having served out their time in India, they decided to specifically re-enlist in a regiment based in a healthier environment. The Company records show us soldiers serving generally for over six years before returning to Britain.

Choosing to take the snapshot on the day of the battle of Waterloo, 18 June 1815, the infantry battalion comprised five companies, which mustered a battalion of 329 effective rank and file with the artillery regiment mustering 429 rank and file. There was also the attached company of invalids and pensioners, who mustered a further 89. A fear of Napoleon's influence and power upon fellow Europeans and republican Americans would lead to their quiet removal from these musters in small numbers for detached permanent duty at the Cape. They included Americans and a few men from the West Indies, Frenchmen, Germans, a Pole, Portuguese, a Russian and Spaniards – many of whom had enlisted during the wars whilst serving on board merchantmen that had called at the island.

The artillery company of Captain John Shortis, gives a good impression of the type of men in the two regiments. The company muster book for 1 November 1820 to 31 January 1821 shows Shortis commanding a company consisting of two officers, eight sergeants, thirteen corporals, five gunners, two drummers and 33 matrosses.[16] Only three of his men came from St Helena. The rest had mostly enlisted in the United Kingdom, some for unlimited service and others for a shorter engagement of perhaps six years.

Twelve men gave their place of birth as Ireland; from Cork in the south to Dublin in the east up to Antrim in the north. Five men came from Scotland; from the expanding cities of Edinburgh and Glasgow to the hills of Perthshire and the lowlands of Dumfries. The Enlgishmen came from Yorkshire and Lancashire, the Midlands, Dorset in the south-west and Essex in the south-east. There was one Welshman, born in Glamorgan, and one man who was born in the West Indies.

Before joining the army of the Company they had been engaged in as varied a set of occupations as any of those men who entered the King's Army. Most of them, not surprisingly, had been 'labourers'. There were 22 of those and then the nearest figure was three 'sawyers' and three 'blacksmiths'. Amongst the rest there were sixteen other trades or occupations given, among them a baker, a cord-wainer, a painter, two stone hewers and a weaver. Intriguingly the Saint Helena recruits do not have trades recorded by their names. In all, 55 of them had enlisted into the Company army. Three of them had previous military service, having served with the Bengal Artillery of the Honourable Company.

Their ages ranged from 24 years of age to 49 – a generation. One of the older men had enlisted in 1795, giving him perhaps 26 years service. They had enlisted at the rate of one or two a year in most years since 1795. However, there are two clusters of enlistments for the years 1805–6 and 1811–12. The first period was the time when an invasion of Britain looked distinctly possible. Napoleon's army sat poised on the cliffs above Boulogne ready to cross the Channel. The British Army had seen little or no success in Europe and to many appeared incapable of achieving any victory against the mighty French Army. Victories in the West Indies and in India counted for little in the public imagination following the battle of Trafalgar. Though the fear of invasion now subsided, it did not disappear. Less than two months later, Napoleon having marched his army into Europe and won a brilliant victory at Austerlitz, the Third Coalition was no more, Britain was alone again. Perhaps the prospect of an exotic life on a British island near Africa was a draw for some, and for others a last resort. Or perhaps some did not like the idea of being balloted for the local militia regiment, with an obligation to serve somewhere on the coast guarding against Boney's invasion. When the second glut of recruits enlisted there were more reasons to feel confident at home; Lord Wellington had command of the Peninsular army, and was winning battles.

The island volunteers were probably clothed and armed as riflemen, for during the mutiny there is a reference to both musket and rifle ammunition being taken up to Plantation House in preparation for its defence. Later in 1817, in a letter to the Company storekeeper there is a reference to the sale of damaged goods, which included 117 green feathers, a distinction of light troops.

There is also a direct reference to rifle-armed troops during the trial of the errant storekeeper, who in his deposition for his defence commented:

> Hats. – The deficiency of Rifle caps, could not possibly have occurred in any other way than their having been issued instead of other Military Felt Caps or the indents neglected to be sent in after the Caps were delivered upon urgent demands.[17]

In 1817 new clothing had arrived for the Volunteers, which was to last three years. There was a reminder that a fine would be payable if this uniform was: 'spoilt or torn within that time through carelessness or neglect, such fine will be levied and shall be awarded by the Volunteer Committee'.

It had been nine years since the officers had been granted any clothing and they were to receive 'Cloth Trimmings and Cap gratis' providing the Court of Directors agreed. There was also a reference to the incorporation of the Artillery Volunteers into the Rifle Corps as a fourth Company, this

> ... not having occurred at the time the Indents were framed no clothing was indented for them. Resolved therefore that W. W. Doveton Esq the Commandant be authorised to draw sufficient materials from the stores to clothe the fourth Company as nearly as may in uniformity with the rest of the Corps and that caps shall be furnished from amongst the best of those now in use.[18]

This reference to the artillery volunteers is the only I found in any of the island correspondence. We do know that the men of the volunteer corps were also to receive the inducement of one piece of meat and 7½lbs of flour for each day of attendance. This largesse was probably linked to the suppression of the mutiny. Presumably the volunteers had proved their worth by being present the morning after the rebellion had petered out to help disarm the rebels and move them to high Knoll under armed guard.

There is a set of colours for the volunteers, which has remained furled and cased on the northern wall of St Paul's church above Plantation House probably since the death of the then commandant, Sir William Doveton, over whose memorial they are placed.

The Royal Navy squadron stationed at St Helena was part of a larger organisation that covered the Cape of Good Hope. The vessels at St Helena did spend some time on patrol between the island and the Cape. However, with the end of the Napoleonic wars their principal concern was the protection and detention of Napoleon and to that end most of the squadron was stationed off the island.

Even those Company vessels which were entitled to anchor for fresh water were kept under a close guard. But what should be done with 'Private Vessels', non-Company vessels that were short of water and claiming not to have any knowledge of the prohibition against them anchoring off the island? Lowe agreed that Lemon Valley was the best place for them to anchor and take on water. The military commander at Lemon Valley was not to allow any boat from a merchant-man to land on the shore.

From this time on there was invariably a warship stationed off Lemon Valley. Its sole purpose was to provide security over those merchant men who came to take on water. In June 1816 it was the HMS *Orontes* under Captain Cochrane. He was to ensure that there was never any communication between these vessels and the island. At night it was the responsibility of the warship to ensure that no boat was allowed to leave any of the merchant vessels anchored off the valley. In the day such boats were only allowed to land at Lemon Valley. Any attempt to row elsewhere was to be prevented. In 1815, Lemon Valley already had a fresh water stream running out under the extensive defensive wall. This line was strengthened by an artillery platform and a blockhouse further up the valley. The anchorage was well covered from both the land and sea. As Lowe remarked 'we shall I think be pretty secure'.[19]

Usually the flagship was based in James Bay, unless it was on patrol between the island and the Cape, with a smaller warship, a sloop of about 20 guns patrolling off the northern coast, another sloop patrolling off the southern coast.

June 1819 was a typical working month for the Royal Navy squadron. There were no great alarms in this month, nor any particular successes. All the events which follow in the next few pages are taken from the ship's log books for that month in the ADM Series held in the National Archive at Kew, London.[20]

On 1 June the flagship HMS *Conqueror* (74 guns) noted in the ship's log that both the *Bombay* and *Herefordshire*, merchantmen, had left James Bay for China. Meanwhile, the sloop HMS *Leveret* (20 guns) was at anchor off Rupert's Valley but had to send a boat off to board: the English ship *Comet* from Calcutta, bound for Liverpool.

Later that day, a Tuesday, *Leveret* sent in a boat to collect fresh rations, 'soft bread, beer and vegetables'. At sunset she took responsibility for the James Bay to Buttermilk Point half of the night guard. During this time an armed boat would be expected to row to Buttermilk Point once in both the first two watches, checking that all the boats registered on their list were either secured to their parent vessels or hoisted on board. They were also to check that all the local fishing boats were secure at their moorings and that absolutely no vessel other than their boat was moving towards the anchorage. If there were then they could summon support in minutes as naval standing orders required that each naval vessel would supply an armed boat. This would be lowered on the appearance of either the 'blue light or false fire', which the guard boat carried as a means of calling for assistance in the darkness.

On 5 July 1816, the system was partially tested when the Fourth Master of the *Sovereign*, an East India man, approached the landing place in James Bay some time before the day gun. Unfortunately, the man was drunk and although warned off repeatedly by the gate picket and fired at on two occasions by the sentry, continued to row towards the shore

> ... and was promptly arrested by two of the Sea Gate Guard ... He was then thrown into the jail where his conduct was most outrageous and abusive, particularly to the Officer of the Guard Lt Shipley 66th Regt.[21]

Reade had spoken to the ship's master, Captain Telfor, who gave a very bad account of him. Reade could see that the man would end up in jail 'presumably nursing a sore head and would remain there until the Governor decided what to do with him'.

Lieutenant Basil Jackson, on Lowe's staff, inadvertently tested the security system himself, when going from the land out to *The Marquis of Camden*, which was to take General Gourgard to England. He had not thought to obtain the password for the night, presumably intending to row out and back to the vessel in daylight. As the night fell, responsibility for security around the anchorage fell to the armed boat from the flagship, which in this case was HMS *Conqueror*.

> We had not got far from the shore, when the guard-boat of the flag-ship stopped us, and the parole was demanded. Not expecting to be so late, I had not thought to provide myself with the password, so I explained to the officer of the boat the nature of the duty I was upon, but all in vain, so I had only to return and obtain the necessary word. Again we started, only to be again stopped, and peremptorily ordered back although giving the parole, the officer saying his orders were not to allow any boat to approach a vessel after sunset without special permission.
>
> Here was an unfortunate dilemma. The ship had cleared out and was ready to sail; she would not lose precious hours by waiting for a passenger, even though he was a *ci-devant* French General. It then occurred to me to request that we should be taken

to the flag-ship, and have the business submitted to her captain. This was assented to, and on explaining the matter to him, he, as the chief authority afloat, ordered the officer in charge of the guard-boat to escort us to the vessel, when I took leave of my charge, and returned to the landing steps, but still escorted by the guard boat. Gourgard had thus an opportunity of seeing that leaving the island was attended with no little difficulty. The Governor smiled with evident satisfaction when I told him of my evening's adventures.[21]

Jackson met Gourgard in Paris in 1828 and was invited to stay on his estate, where they talked about the politics of Longwood. Gourgard spoke 'not unkindly of Sir Hudson Lowe … since an angel from Heaven as Governor would not have pleased them'.

Jackson mentioned to Gourgard that as a French-speaking officer he had been proposed as a possible orderly officer for Longwood. However, as the position was usually regarded as a captain's post he had not been offered it. Gourgard, says Jackson thought he was most fortunate as the Longwood party did not want a French-speaking orderly officer: 'In fact, we should have found means to get rid of you, and perhaps ruin you.'[22]

To return to June 1819: HMS *Tees* was anchored off Lemon Valley to the east of James Bay, where she was engaged in transporting ballast from Lemon Valley and being painted. She was probably transporting the ballast by boats along the coast to be used in building roads and defences. Lowe was in a high state of anxiety and was supervising an island-wide programme of building defensive works and improving the roads to enable troops to move swiftly to any point of likely incursion.

On 3 June *Conqueror* noted that the schooner *Hardy* from the Cape had arrived and that *The Ganges* had sailed for England. *Sophie* meanwhile had spotted at day-break the American *Samarress* bound for Rotterdam, 'laden with sugar 78 days out'. The same day *Tees*, still anchored off Lemon Valley, found herself supplying the American ship *Brilliant* with water, which was in desperate need of it. According to the ancient customs of the sea, despite the intense level of security around the island, any distressed foreign vessel was entitled to expect basic help in the form of food, fresh water or medical support.

Next day HMS *Leveret* fired a salute to mark the King's birthday and with the sudden tropical ending of the day ordered 'up boats,' and then took the night guard in James Bay. *Conqueror* meantime had supplied HM *Schooner Hardy* with provisions for two weeks. Monday 17 June was a bad day for seaman George Dixon and a number of others from *Conqueror*, a punishment day.

AM Modt Breezes & Cloudy at 4 do Scrubbed Hammocks & Wash'd Clothes at 6 punished George Dixon with 12 lashes alongside being part punishment as per sentence of Court Martial on Saturday last at 7:30 Punished Daniel Stewart (S) with 24 lashes for theft Edward Bane (S) & Michael Worth (S) with 24 lashes each for theft Wm Jones ((4) S) with 18 lashes & John Jacobs with 12 lashes for stopping on shore without leave Timothy Lynch with 0 disrated Thos Sparrow (M) with 18 lashes for Drunkenness & fighting Thos Hartley (S) with lashes for Disobedience and & Insolence Edward Hawcliff (M) with 12 lashes for uncleanness & Matthew Arnold (S) with 12 lashes for Drunkenness on shore.

The next day was punishment parade on board *Tees,* which was now 'standing on and off shore' on the northern side of the island: 'Punished William Stephens Seaman with 42 lashes for Insolence and James Spedigrew with 36 lashes for neglect of Duty.'

Over the next few days *Sophie* boarded and inspected the paper of a French ship from Calcutta bound for Baede, an American brig (which entailed opening a barrel of tobacco) and the following day boarded a Dutch ship. Two days later she 'exchanged numbers' with HMS *Eurydice*, sailing to St Helena from the Cape of Good Hope. When naval vessels or ships of the Honourable Company 'exchanged numbers' they showed a series of flags that could be looked up in a signal book, confirming the name of the vessel.

On 24 June the *Leveret, Tees* and *Sophie* received a signal for their captains to attend a court martial the next day on board the flagship. Mr McIntosh, the purser of the sloop *Sappho* was charged with dishonesty. In the meantime the *Thalia* from Bengal had arrived and anchored on the roads. On 26 June a second court martial board assembled on board the *Conqueror* at 9:00am, to try George Dixon, carpenter's mate of the *Sappho*. (Meanwhile the *Larkins* had arrived from England with stores for the island and anchored off James Bay. The *Sherburne* from Calcutta had also arrived along with the *Camden* from the Isle of France and both anchored near the flagship.)

At 1:00pm on a breezy and cloudy day, George Dixon was found guilty and was to be flogged. He would receive 54 lashes. Dixon and McIntosh were both from the *Sappho,* but they were at separate and distant rungs on the service ladder. George Dixon would be flogged until his back was a bloody mess and the attending Naval Surgeon judged that he could no longer safely be flogged. He would also lose his rating as a skilled technician and resume his career lower down the ranks. McIntosh would be financially ruined if, as seems likely from the evidence, significant mismanagement had been traced through his books. Pursers funded all the major purchases for food and clothing from their own purse before recouping costs from the Admiralty. The quality of what they supplied and the percentage profit they creamed off were linked. What was found to be missing had to be replaced; if not, then imprisonment and bankruptcy would follow. It had been a miserable day for McIntosh and Dixon.

On 28 June at 6:40am a boat 'manned and armed' was sent to attend a punishment round the fleet. This was probably the punishment of George Dixon, rowed from naval vessel to naval vessel and tied either to an improvised frame or grating to receive twelve lashes alongside each ship in the squadron.

By this time it might seem that Lowe's worries were largely at an end. He had begun a programme of defensive building works across the island. There were now seasoned King's troops to supplement the local regiments and a professional staff to execute his orders. However, looking at many of the Lowe Papers and examining some of the private letters written by officers on the island at the time, he was a man slowly collapsing under pressure.

As for communications, there was a telegraph system on St Helena before Napoleon arrived. It had been set up by Governor Patton some time after 1803. This consisted of a large frame into which were raised four wooden balls. This simple system enabled over 100 different signals to be transmitted. The NCO operators on the island were awarded 'approbation money' for being accurate and prompt in their signalling. This system was still in use at this time as Surgeon Henry makes a clear reference to 'black balls being hoisted' when he was on the island. Sir Home Popham's sophisticated system of flag signalling had been brought into use across the island. It allowed a sophisticated system for interrogating vessels at sea. This information could then be quickly circulated around the island and to the governor either at the Castle in James Town or at Plantation House.

Captain Henry Huff Pritchard seems to have been one of the more enthusiastic British officers on the island. He was an officer of the St Helena Artillery Regiment and Superintendent of Telegraph Stations. Stationed at Ladder Hill, immediately above Jamestown, he coordinated the work of all fourteen telegraphic stations. His written notes to Lowe, Reade and Gorrequer lack the formal guarded tone of much of the correspondence from the other officers. This is probably because he did not have to meet any of the French party. Consequently he never came to be regarded with the same suspicion that attached to any officer who might have conversed with members of Napoleon's suite. Pritchard seems to have had a good working relationship with Lowe, thanking him for aiding his promotion to Major and presenting the governor with a volume of signals which Pritchard himself had drawn up.[23] Of course, in the end, relations did sour. Lowe was to remove him from command of the St Helena Artillery Regiment, much to the annoyance of both Pritchard and the Board of Directors in London. Earlier, his notes expressed a pleasure in his work. In June Pritchard had written to Major Gorrequer as Lowe has suggested that they use the soldiers of the Royal Artillery as telegraph assistants – especially those who have 'small families of good repute as the Telegraph Officers have hitherto had the indulgence of rearing Poultry for the Honble The Governors Tar [Table]'. He also offered to include Gorrequer in this scheme so far as he was able. Pritchard required four men, one for the three permanent stations, which currently only had a single operator, and an assistant for the portable station. There were fourteen stations listed along with the assistants they required. Pritchard has already written to Captain Greatly, commander of the Royal Artillery detachment, asking for his assistance:

Plantation House 2

Castle James Fort 2

Ladder Hill 3

High Knoll 2

Gason Gate 2

Horse Pasture 2

Man & Horse 3

Egg Island 1
Long Range 1
Sandy Bay 2
Prosperous Bay 3
Long Wood 2
Sugar Loaf 2
Buttermilk Point 1
or Portable Telegraph
to attend his Excellency if required.

The telegraph system worked on a group of three letters which gave a word or phrase which could then be looked up in the code book. Beneath is an example taken from Pritchard's notes. Sir Hudson had sent a message to Lady Lowe from the Castle, presumably to reassure her that correspondence would arrive at Plantation House tomorrow. Unfortunately the word tomorrow was omitted from the transmission:

Ladder Hill
18 June 1816
6 am
Telegraph message sent to High Knoll:
233 Telegraph officer
50 @ High Knoll
613 + 3 Repeat
831 Signal
301 + 1 to
110 Governors
216 Lady
402 + 1 yesterday

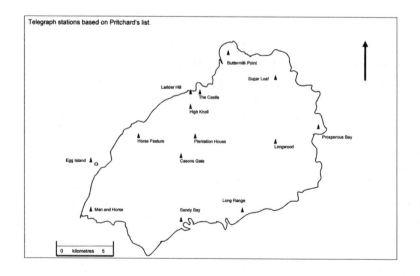

Telegraph stations based on Pritchard's list.

Answer:

233 Telegraph Officer 149 Capt Pritchard

64 Plantation House

110 Governor

216 To His Lady

161 + 1 from Adj. Genl.

520 Letters

734 will

313 be

800 in

708 time[24]

'547 + 1, tomorrow', should have completed the message. This mistake led to Corporal Watson, Telegraph Officer at High Knoll, being severely reprimanded and in having his 'approbation money', extra pay for his skill and responsibilities, withdrawn for a month. Pritchard also took the opportunity to adjust the system for recording the time when signals had been sent and their reply received by the initiating station. None of this really mattered when dealing with correspondence for Lady Lowe but were Napoleon to go missing, the consequences for everyone on the island and beyond could have been far more grave.

Pritchard proposed that fishing vessels should have a permit to fish and on leaving James Bay to do so they should hoist a large black flag. As some of the grounds were up to nine miles distant from the island they should keep within sight of a telegraph station so that in the event of danger they could be recalled. This would be signalled by the raising of a red and white quartered flag and the firing of a signal gun. This signal to recall fishing boats would then be repeated across all the telegraph stations until the danger had passed. Pritchard was ready to have the black flags and staffs made up and delivered to the harbour for handing out to the owners of the fishing boats.[25]

The time of greatest potential for an attempt to take Napoleon was at night or when the local fog descended. The south-eastern part of St Helena is frequently affected by fog which can roll onto that part of the island and cover it within minutes. It quickly creates the supposedly unhealthy miasma that Napoleon so frequently complained of. The fog covers the same portion of the island at times on a daily basis whilst the north-west part is untouched.

Late on 10 January 1817, Pritchard flashed a message to Plantation House. Owing to the impenetrable fog that had covered half the island all day, a messenger had arrived from Bolley's Hill near Manatee Bay sent by the senior signalman, J. Watson. They had spotted 'a large sail close in shore in Manatee Bay standing to Windward'. They also saw a boat from the ship coming into the Bay. 'All posts are covered in fog.'

Pritchard could do no more as the entire western half of the telegraphs were covered. At 18.50, the leeward cruiser had 'fired a gun, and hoisted her colours', apparently steering for this strange sail. Nothing came of it, though Pritchard kept Lowe fully informed of developments by written messages.

There was one minor incident when two newly arrived East Indiamen were almost fired upon as their recognition numbers, flown as pennants, had not been transmitted to the island from East India House in London. It was later discovered when they had anchored in the roads off Jamestown that this was their first voyage as Company vessels. This was also the first occasion since the arrival of Admiral Malcolm on which vessels had been allowed to pass into the bay at night – every other vessel having been requested to stand off until the morning when recognition could be confirmed prior to entry.

Vessels that approached from the north-east, as most did when approaching Jamestown, were tracked by each battery and post as they passed before them. In March 1817, several guns were fired at 10:45pm from Bank's Battery, at the north-eastern tip of the island, at a passing vessel. The vessel then 'made herself known to Bank's Battery' and at daybreak she was seen off Lemon Valley. She proved to be the *Europe*, an East India Company ship from Bengal.[26]

Another intriguing story about a possible rescue mission, is that of the 'suspicious' schooner which appears in 1818 and also in 1819. On 10 April 1819 an unknown schooner appeared to windward of the island at a distance of eight leagues and hove to south-west of Long Range. The telegraph stations were asked to examine their log books. The same vessel was thought to have been seen on several occasions years before:

> … and from that circumstance was thought suspicious, and to the best of my knowledge reported as such – the same vessel after having stood to Windward about an Hour, altered her course, and disappeared steering West. I also find that a vessel which the Signalmen took to be the Same was seen several times in various directions off the island, both to Windward and to Leeward in August 1816.[27]

Was it the vessel from the Hudson River at New York with perhaps a mixed crew commanded by Carpenter, or were they other Frenchmen from South America? Or were they perhaps South Americans fighting for independence from Spain?

On 12 January 1820 there was an investigation into why two shots were fired close to 'a strange sail under American colours', which was passing 'in Company with the Leeward Cruizer towards the anchorage' two days before. They were fired ahead of the American vessel at Bank's Half Moon Battery on the orders of an inexperienced though 'zealous' young officer. Major Hodson having investigated the matter discovered that the signal for admission had not been hoisted. Gunner Charles Young had fired both guns. The first shot being fired from the second embrasure and the gun being traversed to 'incline towards the harbour, and clear both the vessels, which were then close to each other.' The second shot was fired from the third embrasure, striking slightly ahead of the American vessel. At this point the American vessel was astern of the man of war and the ships were opposite the battery. This incident appears to have been unique.

Notes

1 Volume 1/17 Government House, General Despatches, October 1815–March 1816, folio 88, SAA.

2 COC/4, Secret letter: copy of instructions to the Governor of St Helena dated 1 August 1815, NMM.

3 Lowe Papers 20115, Remarks on the defence of the island, Jan–August 1816, folio 44.

4 Ibid., folio 45.

5 Hunter Potter, F., (Trans.) Saint Denis, L. E., *Napoleon from the Tuileries to St Helena*, Harper & Bros., New York, 1922, page 164.

6 COC/1, Instructions from the Secretary of State, 30 July 1815, NMM.

7 COC/7, Letter Major Barnes to Cockburn, dated 24 July 1816, NMM.

8 Ibid., COC/7, NMM.

9 Gregory, D., *Napoleon's Jailer*, Assoc University Presses, 1996.

10 Correspondence in the Consultation ledger at, 9 July 1817, StHA.

11 An imposing memorial to Captain Benjamin Hodson in St James' church in Jamestown clearly shows a kneeling figure of a grieving artilleryman in profile, wearing the short tailed jacket with cuffs in the Royal Artillery style.

12 Correspondence in the Consultation ledger at, 17 February 1817, St Helena Archive, page 107.

13 L/MIL/13/6, Muster Roll, 1807 July to September, Indian Office, BL. Quoted in Gosse, P., St Helena 1502–1938, Anthony Nelson, page 250.

14 Callahan, Raymond, The East India Compensate and Army Reforms 1783–1798, Harvard University Press, 1972, page xi.

15 Correspondence in the Consultation Ledger at, 29 May 1817, StHA.

16 L/MIL/13/10 muster roll in the India Office, BL.

17 Correspondence in the Consultation ledger at, 22 April 1817, page 155, StHA.

18 Ibid., 9 June 1817, page 213, StHA.

19 Lowe 20115, Lowe to Malcolm, 29 June, 1816, folio 43. Barnes Map 1811, BL.; Site survey by the author, 2004.

20 Ship's log books: ADM53/465B HMS Eurydice; ADM53/1309 HM Sloop Sophie; ADM51/2226 HMS Conqueror; ADM51/2501 HMS Leveret; ADM51/2893 HMS Tees. NA.

21 Lowe 20115, 5 July 1816, folio 266, BL.

22 Jackson, B., Seaton M. A. (Ed), *Notes and Reminiscences of a Staff Officer, Chiefly Relating to the Waterloo Campaign and the St Helena Matters during the Captivity of Napoleon*, John Murrey, reprinted 1903, pages 156–7

23 Lowe 20225, Pritchard to Lowe, folio 90. Later on the 27 Nov 1818 he will present a pocket volume to the Governor which contains all the signals required to communicate across the island and with the RN and HEIC vessels at sea.

24 Lowe 20225 signal example, folio 86 & 87, BL.

25 Ibid., Ladder Hill, 10 pm, 10 January, folio 103–10

26 Ibid., dated 19 March 1817 Folio 108–109.

27 Ibid., dated 10 April, 1819. Folio 124.

Chapter Eleven

Napoleon's Illness, Death and Funeral

The age has lost its greatest name. NAPOLEON BONAPARTE, but lately the most powerful and splendid of Monarchs, has expired on a little rock in the middle of the Atlantic Ocean. He has died of a lingering illness, the consequence of confinement and the bad climate. He has died in solitude, in the dreadful calm of his distant prison, – shut out from his family; from his friends, from the scenes of his immortal career of glory; from everything which could supply association and sensation to the dreary void of his naturally active mind.[1]

There were indications two years after his arrival on St Helena of the illness which was to kill him but these were not detected. The principal debate over his health centred around the French party's claim that he was suffering from hepatitis generated by the supposedly unhealthy climate of the island and the British, other than O'Meara, claiming that he was invariably in good health, but which was continually impaired by his refusal to take any exercise at a time when he was significantly overweight.

The disease that killed him was cancer of the stomach. Some have claimed that he was poisoned, but it was the disease which killed him and not any poison. That controversy will not be entered into here in any detail. The facts are now established. Napoleon's desire for a post-mortem was prompted by the wish that his son be assisted in understanding what Napoleon believed to be an hereditary complaint. Napoleon's father had apparently also died of cancer.

In part his history of restless nights could be explained by cystitis, since Antommarchi at the post-mortem found small calculi in the bladder and the coats of the organ diseased. Difficulty urinating was something from which he suffered all his life. His medical history at St Helena can be divided into four phases:

1. October 5 to July 1818 under O'Meara
2. July 1818 to September 1819, without medical supervision save for five visits by Stokoe

The new house, Longwood, that Napoleon never entered. The entire building was shipped out as a prefabricated structure complete with fittings and furnishings by George Bullock and Co of London. Their manager, Andrew Darling, would supervise its fitting out and would also become Napoleon's funeral director. Author's collection.

3. September 1819 to May 5 1821 under Antommarchi
4. Antommarchi being joined by Arnott during the last 35 days.

Napoleon enjoyed fairly good health on the island until June 1817, despite his sedentary lifestyle. Though in October 1816, O'Meara reported that he had suffered with toothache, slight oedema of the feet, and some enlarged glands in his right groin. These conditions soon cleared up. Up until this time he took exercise, either riding or walking and sometimes had himself driven about Longwood. This activity ceased as he began his struggle with the Governor over the restrictions placed upon him as to where he might go unaccompanied. In May and June 1817 he suffered with headaches and in July he was afflicted with a slight case of bronchial catarrh. On September 25 he was nauseous, suffered with gingivitis, the gums being 'spongy and bleeding at the slightest touch'. The oedema of the feet returned.

O'Meara had great difficulty in treating Napoleon as he had a strong aversion to taking any medicine. The inexact nature of medicine also made him uneasy and he said on several occasions – with good reason at that time – that physicians killed as many men as generals.

On September 30 1817, the first symptoms of his fatal illness appeared. He complained of a dull pain, of a feeling of heat in his right side and of pain and numbness in the right scapular region. O'Meara was either genuinely convinced that Napoleon had hepatitis or had been persuaded by the French party to promote this view. If it was the latter, then it was done in order to prompt Napoleon's removal from the island and back to Europe. As a result he recommended 'sea water baths, frictions, calomel and anti-scorbutics'.[2]

From this time on Napoleon was never entirely free from the symptoms listed above and apart from a short period of remission from October 1819 to June 1820, his health slowly deteriorated. Early in October 1817, Sir Hudson Lowe objected to the title of Emperor appearing in O'Meara's official reports, and as Napoleon would not authorise O'Meara to give out any report without that title, O'Meara was withdrawn as Napoleon's physician. Lowe then found himself in a difficult position. Having withdrawn O'Meara he now had no information at all available to him. A compromise was reached whereby Dr Baxter, Deputy Inspector of Hospitals, was to give reports to the governor based upon a verbal report delivered by O'Meara. O'Meara continued to promote the diagnosis of hepatitis, which no other doctor or surgeon agreed with. Then came the first breakdown in his medical supervision when O'Meara was dismissed by Lowe and deported to Britain in July 1818.

Next, the Governor appointed Dr Verling of the Royal Artillery to be Napoleon's physician. Napoleon refused to see him as he was the Governor's appointee. From July 1818 until September 1820 Verling lived at Longwood and never saw his patient except by lying in wait to 'ambush' him. It was a ridiculous situation.

We know little about this period except from the French diarists. Montholon claims that Napoleon was never well and that he spent many hours in his bath and took practically no exercise. On 17 January 1819, Napoleon suffered with a serious attack of vertigo followed by fainting, which so worried the French that a messenger was sent to the Governor asking for help. John Stokoe, naval surgeon of the *Conqueror*, was despatched, as Verling was not permitted to see the patient. Napoleon agreed to take a little medication from Stokoe. The future suddenly looked more positive. But then Stokoe infuriated the Governor by repeating a conversation on Ascension Island between O'Meara and two Naval officers, during which O'Meara had intimated that it was Lowe's desire to see Napoleon dead, by fair means or foul. Stokoe was withdrawn from Longwood. A note from Dr Baxter in the Lowe papers also hinted that Stokoe was simply not competent enough for such an important position.

The British Government meanwhile had accepted that a doctor chosen by Napoleon's family would be permitted to sail to St Helena. Francesco Antommarchi, a Corsican anatomist, arrived in St Helena on 20th September, 1819. Napoleon quickly saw that the man had failings as a doctor and not surprisingly, bluntly told him so.

Fortunately for Antommarchi there followed the ten months of the 'gardening period' of Napoleon's island life, which, apart from his time at the Briars was undoubtedly the happiest period that he spent there. He slept well and regained his old vigour, at least in public and the pain in his right side became more bearable. In 1820, with the relaxation in his right to roam, he resumed horse riding.

Then in July 1820 the pain took control. Constipation, sweating, vomiting of bitter bilious matter, and a slight dry cough all appeared. According to Chaplin, the treatment was enemas and frictions with liniments of different kinds. He then experienced a remission during August and until half way through September, when he was attacked with even greater pain. From now on, after any short physical activity, he was left drained of energy. Being Napoleon, he attempted to overcome these new developments by force of will, but it was not to be. On the 18th he rode round Longwood but returned exhausted after two and a half hours.

On 4 October he took his last horse ride in public, going south to Sandy Bay and the home of Sir William Doveton, where he breakfasted with the family. He still had his well rounded figure. Doveton in his report described his appearance as being 'as fat and round as a Chinese pig'. On the way back the effort of riding proved too much and he had to dismount and wait for his carriage to carry him back to Longwood.

He took to riding in his carriage and taking short walks but even this exercise proved painful. Now he began to suffer with alternate bouts of constipation and diarrhoea, with the motions consisting of mucus and undigested material. From mid-September on there would no more respite from the illness. On some days the pain and discomfort would lessen but there would never be a day when he would summon his horse or stride about the gardens playfully abusing his staff.

In March 1821, Antommarchi wrote to his colleague Colonna, reaffirming that hepatitis was the correct diagnosis, declaring that if Napoleon were not removed quickly from the 'pernicious climate' of St Helena he would soon be dead.

Chaplin credits Antommarchi for 'in the main' correctly prescribing drugs that relieved the symptoms; apart from one specific set of medicinal doses. On March the 22nd, 23rd and 24th he administered a quarter grain of tartar emetic. The vomiting was 'abundant'. With the stomach in a state of significant ulceration it was hardly surprising. Napoleon was in terrible pain. Hardly surprising then that he referred to Antommarchi as an 'assassin' and refused to take any more of his medications.

In the second half of March 1821, Antommarchi recorded fever, sweating and a marked coldness of the arms and legs. Napoleon became severely constipated and he vomited more frequently. He now complained of the pain extending across his entire abdomen. He would now only eat small pieces of undercooked meat which he chewed, extracted the juices from and then discarded.

On 25 March Napoleon was so ill that Antommarchi felt compelled to consult with Surgeon Arnott. Arnott did not see Napoleon at this time but listened to Antommarchi's description of what he believed he had seen. Arnott recommended a blister to the stomach, saline draughts and a purgative. Unlike George III, suffering from porphyria, this monarch had all his wits about him and refused to undergo any of these severely painful trials. Again, Antommarchi resorted to purgatives but Napoleon became worse. On 1 April 1821, at Antommarchi's insistence, Arnott saw his patient for the first time:

> The room was so dark that I could not see him but I felt him or some one else.
> I examined his pulse and state of skin. I perceived there was considerable debility,
> but nothing that indicated immediate danger. I certainly could not form a very
> good idea of his situation from this kind of visit I made but they have requested me
> to visit again tomorrow.[3]

In 1822 Arnott published an account of his treatment of Napoleon. What he wrote does not match what he reported to the Governor, as recorded in the Lowe Papers. Arnott told Reade on 17 April that Napoleon was a hypochondriac and that should 'a 74-gun frigate appear in the bay to set him at liberty, Napoleon would be up and on his legs directly!'[4]

Arnott was following in the footsteps of both his predecessors, Baxter and Verling, but unlike them he was actually able to examine his patient. Arnott was to be in daily attendance for the last 35 days of Napoleon's life. He was held in high regard both at Longwood and at Plantation House. So much so that he received a snuff box from Napoleon in grateful thanks for his care of and money in the will. He also received a payment from the British Government.

It is possible that he baulked at revealing the truth, that Napoleon was terminally ill, in order to assist the political aims of the Governor. On the other hand he may have leaned on O'Meara's earlier observations. But a nagging doubt remains, had he made a professional blunder?

The next day he saw Napoleon in daylight and reported to Lowe a constant gnawing pain in the stomach with more or less constant vomiting and nausea. Arnott, though acknowledging the cadaverous nature of Napoleon's appearance did not report any weight loss despite Montholon asserting that his master was as thin as he had been when he was consul. On 11 April, Arnott made a much more extensive examination of his patient and admitted that his patient's legs were much reduced.

Lowe was incredulous that Arnott still talked of hypochondria when he had described such pain and vomiting and the feeling of heat over the liver. Arnott however maintained his opinion. On 9 April Antommarchi requested permission to leave the island declaring that he could do no more for his patient. The next day he refused to visit Napoleon and it was only with the intercession of Arnott that he was persuaded to resume his duties at Longwood. Why did he wish to leave at this stage? Did he realise that Napoleon would be dead soon? Was it a desire to distance him from the unflattering reports that would follow, post-mortem?

On the 14th and 15th Napoleon summoned Montholon and Marchand and dictated his will to them. From then on Napoleon's mental condition also began to deteriorate rapidly. Two days later, Arnott found Napoleon whistling. On seeing the doctor, he stopped and stared open mouthed at him.[5]

On 25 April, two days after Arnott had declared that there was no serious danger, there was no doubt as to the outcome. Napoleon vomited continually, the prostration increased and all his other bodily functions demonstrated that his death was close.

On 1 May, singultus (reflex spasms of the diaphragm) made its appearance, and at 3 am the next day Napoleon was insensible. Arnott, who had become seriously alarmed when he saw 'coffee ground' vomit on 27 April, expressed some slight hope for his patient on 4 May, but on what grounds it is difficult to say, as Napoleon had been comatose or delirious for three days previously. On that day his pulse rose to 110, he was unconscious, incontinent, *risus sardonicis* or something like it was evident, and the eyes were fixed. Napoleon remained in this condition until eleven minutes to six on the evening of 5 May, 1821, when he expired.[6]

The post-mortem was performed by Antommarchi on 6 May at 3 pm. In attendance were Arnott, Burton, Henry, Livingstone, Mitchell, Rutledge and Shortt. The French were convinced that the autopsy would reveal that the Emperor had died of hepatitis brought on by the unhealthy conditions on the island. Arnott and the other British surgeons of course fervently wished for another conclusion. Three accounts of the post-mortem were written up, the official one signed by Arnott, Burton, Livingstone, Mitchell and Shortt, a quasi-official one written by Henry in 1823 from notes in his possession, and that of Antommarchi on behalf of the French party:

The official account is a short statement. Henry's narrative, which was apparently drawn up at Lowe's instigation to confirm and accentuate the germane observations in the official document, is a most interesting report, and is written with a sense of the importance of the occasion. Indeed he alone of all the British medical representatives appeared to possess imagination enough to know that he was witnessing and participating in an historic moment and he infused into his description some life and vividness. The others contented themselves with a dry narration of pathological facts, as if they were drawing up an official report of the post-mortem of some obscure corporal.[7]

Chaplin speaks highly of Antommarchi's account of the autopsy as it was both extensive and highly detailed. He claimed to be a skilled anatomist and Chaplin says this claim was entirely justified given his report. Henry was still an assistant military surgeon, not a qualified doctor at this time and so presumably, despite his fine prose, was relegated to a secondary role by the senior doctors present.

The face presented a remarkably placid expression, indicative of mildness and even sweetness of disposition, which afforded a most striking contract with the active life, and moral character of the deceased. The features were regular, and even might be considered beautiful ... On exposing the contents of the abdomen, the omentum was seen loaded with fat of which the quantity was very great. When the stomach was brought into view, an adhesion of great extent was perceived between its superior surface and the concave surface of the left lobe of the liver. On separating them, which was a matter of very considerable difficulty, the fatal disease at once developed its seat and extent. The whole internal superficies of the stomach exhibited the appearance of a mass of cancerous ulceration, or scirrhous thickening fast advancing to cancer. It was cut out and carefully examined. The pylorus was the focus of the disorganisation, where the disease had quite eroded the substance of the stomach, and hole was formed through which the writer put his finger. This was stopped up by the adhesions to the part of the liver immediately contiguous, otherwise death must have taken place when the stomach was first penetrated. There were no indications of any injury having been sustained by the liver from contact with the various fluids passing through the alimentary canal. A ring surrounding the cardiac extremity immediately adjoining the entrance of the oesophagus was the only portion of the organ which appeared capable of discharging its important functions. It was filled with dark-coloured fluid resembling the grounds of coffee.

A very general expectation was entertained that the liver would be found in a diseased state, the illness if the deceased having been so confidently referred to an enlargement of the liver and chronic inflammation of this viscus. In consequence when the liver was next examined, the countenances of the spectators indicated much anxiety. When M. Antommarchi made his first incision into it, he expected to see a flow of pus from the abscess which had been anticipated. In its substance, but no abscess, no hardness, no enlargement, no inflammation were observed. On the contrary, the liver was of natural size, and perfectly healthy in its internal parts. There was a small adhesion of the convex surface of the left lobe to the diaphragm, which appeared to have been a continuation and a consequence of the adjoining adhesions between the liver and the stomach.

The gall bladder was of proper size and structure, containing no gall stones, but the usual quantity of apparently healthy bile. The spleen, pancreas, and intestines were sound. The kidneys were embedded in an immense quantity of fat. The left kidney was one third larger than the right, this enlargement appeared to have been congenital.

The urinary bladder was small and contained a few gritty particles. The penis and testicles were very small, and the whole genital system seemed to exhibit a physical cause for the absence of sexual desire and the chastity which had been stated to have characterised the deceased.[9]

Antommarchi's account did not comment on a diseased liver. All three accounts agreed that Napoleon had died of gastric cancer. When the liver was removed from the body only Shortt, amongst the British surgeons thought that it appeared enlarged. He said that it was 'a good liver' and that there was nothing extraordinary about it save that it was large.

However, when the time came for all the surgeons to sign the joint document, on the orders of Count Bertrand, he refused. Though according to Forsyth he declared that the British report was correct. This was a political blunder on the part of the British as it enabled Antommarchi to publish his own report. His report closely mirrored that of the British surgeons and generally only differed in being more detailed. Antommarchi, was, after all, by reputation an excellent anatomist. There was however one glaring and clumsily inserted addition to Antommarchi's report. There was no lead up it, simply an insertion in the report that the liver was affected by chronic hepatitis.[10]

Could anyone have taken organs away after the post-mortem? This was highly unlikely as Lowe was insistent that everything be replaced before the coffin was sealed. After the body was sown up it was left in the care of the junior military surgeon, Assistant-Surgeon Rutledge, who was ordered to ensure that nothing was removed. It was Rutledge who placed the heart in the silver vase with spirits of wine, and the stomach in a silver pepper box, without any preservative – the

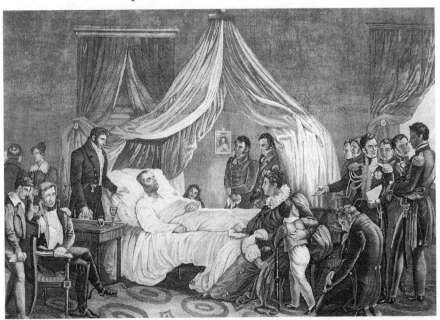

The death of Napoleon. Engraving after Steuben. Marchand, Napoleon's valet, stands by the bed whilst Bertrand sits in the chair grief stricken and his son stands near his father and weeps.

spirits having been used up. Rutledge mentions the persistence with which both Antommarchi and Madame Bertrand begged to be allowed to have the heart and stomach so that they might return to Europe with them.

On 11 May Arnott attempted to revise his history of diagnosis when he declared that prior to 25 April he had thought that there was some interference with the workings of the stomach. This was clearly an attempt to put himself in a better light as a professional surgeon. It was a poor effort, which highlighted his recent misdiagnosis all the more. After all, on 25 April, Arnott had declared that most of Napoleon's symptoms were psychological.[11]

According to Chaplin there is evidence of dysentery and inflammation of the liver amongst the troops stationed on the island and it may have been this evidence alone that led O'Meara to conclude that Napoleon's symptoms indicated the same. These symptoms did not however match those of the soldiers because the symptoms did not intensify; and O'Meara did admit to Baxter that he could not explain the cause of the vomiting and nausea. Shortly after this O'Meara left the island.

Despite the limited knowledge possessed by military and naval surgeons in 1821, by the final months it should have been plain to Antommarchi and to Arnott that Napoleon's symptoms pointed to a disease of the stomach. It would appear that Napoleon suffered initially with a chronic ulcer of the stomach and that around this developed a cancer, with the liver acting as a kind of 'cork' to the stomach. The position of the disease made it made it very unlikely that a tumour could have been felt or seen. Chaplin had an uncomfortable feeling that

> … the physicians were too often lending themselves to further the political aims of one or other of the opposing factions. No reasonable doubt can exist that Napoleon was in ill health for the greater part of his period of detention, but his indisposition was due to the slow but steady march of a mortal disease, in which climatic influences and diplomatic illnesses played no part.[12]

The doctors and surgeons were all men of limited professional competence and in Chaplin's eyes in some cases of mediocre ability. Circumstances thrust them into the epilogue of the greatest political drama of the age. 'I was thunderstruck on being abruptly told by Sir Hudson Lowe that Buonaparte was dying,' wrote Thomas Brooke, secretary to the island council on being told the news on 4 May. Like so many others Napoleon's indisposition remained just that until Arnott dramatically revised his opinion just a few days prior to the death.

Across the road was Andrew Darling, foreman for the construction of Longwood New House. He had been sent out with the prefabricated building by the furniture company George Bullock of London, who had supplied the building. He had been on site since at least 2 May, 'in case General Bonaparte should think proper to go into the new house that was built for him'. Montholon had echoed this sentiment that Darling should be on hand 'just in case' Napoleon decided on a whim to go and visit the house. Montholon's optimistic comments must have been made before everyone realised Napoleon was dying.[13]

By Tuesday 2 May, Darling was aware that all the servants 'seemed to be in an uproar' and General Montholon told him that Napoleon was very ill. Later that day he went to see a Mr Barker, who said that Montholon had admitted that Napoleon 'was all the same as dead'. That evening Darling spotted Dr Rutledge and one or two of the officers at Longwood Farm House. Next day, Darling learnt more about Napoleon's deteriorating condition from Noverraz who assured him that Napoleon could not live much longer as he was throwing up a black bile and was delirious, calling out for people who were not on the island or who were dead.

On the Friday Darling learnt that Napoleon 'was much better'. He spent most of the day on his usual duties; sending some green baize and leather skins to General Montholon to cover some cases that held his books and directing furniture for Dr Mitchell into the officer's quarters in the new house. In the evening he saw Arnott conferring with the other two doctors about Napoleon. Shortly afterwards he was approached by the orderly officer, Captain Crokat, with a request from General Montholon to collect an amount of black material to hang in Napoleon's room.

On the evening of 5 May Brooke was informed that Napoleon was dead and was requested to be at Longwood at 6 o'clock precisely the following morning to view the body. That morning he was joined on the road by the Governor and his staff, and shortly after by Montchenu, the French Commissioner, Admiral Lambert, General Coffin, the army commander, Mr Greentree, of the island council, some navy captains, the commanding officer of artillery and the six doctors and surgeons who were to be involved with the autopsy. At 6 o'clock perhaps twenty people entered Longwood to view the body.[14]

That same morning, not aware that Napoleon had died the previous evening, Darling received orders from Reade to send some plaster of Paris up to Longwood for the manufacture of a death mask. Darling already knew that there was none to be had either at the few shops in Jamestown or in the stores. Instead he had to resort to purchasing 150 small plaster figures. These he had his workmen in the town pound into powder – an idea apparently put forward by Madame Bertrand. Two Chinese workmen were then ordered to take this up to Longwood. He followed on and some time before six o'clock met Admiral Lambert, Montchenu and Major Gorrequer by the Longwood gate who informed him that Napoleon had died. As he approached Longwood House he met an orderly dragoon who had orders for him to assist in the preparation of the funeral. Darling, having acknowledged Lowe and Reade who were outside, immediately returned to Jamestown, for the third time that day, gathered his workmen together, loaded a cart with food, cloth and other materials and set off for Longwood again, arriving about midnight. All the materials were then offloaded into the dining room whilst Montholon directed him to hang the bedroom with black material as Napoleon was to lie in state there. Napoleon's body lay in the drawing room unseen by Darling or any of his workmen.

Darling directed his men and the French servants to take down the muslin from the walls and along with the furniture, move it into Napoleon's sitting room. By half past three in the morning Sgt Morley of the 20th complained of fatigue and Darling agreed that everyone could rest until daybreak, which would not be far away. In these dark hours, unable to sleep himself, Darling asked to view the body but was refused as the Governor had not yet formally identified the body. However, 'having occasion to go out of the room into the garden' he saw Napoleon lying on his campaign bed in the drawing room. He was astonished to see 'how much wasted in the body' Napoleon was and yet, he 'looked so well, so young, and with such a pleasing countenance'.

Meanwhile the Governor had met Major Emmott of the Royal Engineers on the road to Longwood and had directed him to where the tomb was to be built. The stone vault was to be constructed by two skilled workmen from the Royal Sappers and Miners, Private John Warren and Private James Andrews. It had been agreed by Lowe and the French that Napoleon's body was to be protected from any form of interference by being placed in a very secure flagged stone vault, where it would rest on stone pillars.[15]

Like Darling and Lt Darroch and so many others, Brooke was struck by the apparently slimmer face, which appeared so young and calm. Beyond the drawing room in the converted dining room stood the priest, Buonavita. On a table at the foot of the campaign bed stood a picture of his son and on another table the bust brought by Radovich on the *Baring*. A little while later, presumably after Lowe had visited, Montholon asked him to measure Napoleon for his casket, which was to be

> … first tin, lined with satin, which was to be stuffed with cotton, a small mattress and pillow of the same materials on the bottom of the ditto; and then second a wood coffin, then third a lead coffin, then one of mahogany covered with crimson velvet, if it could be procured; but I told them there was not any on the island that I could get, as I has been in search of some a few days before.[16]

Darling had the authority of the Governor to seek out whatever mahogany there was on the island. Darling allocated some of his workmen to take down the glass chandelier in the drawing room and refasten it in the bedroom. He also allocated workmen to stripping down Napoleon's carriage, which was to become his hearse and told them that they would be used to work on any task for the funeral that needed to be done.

Darling moved onto his final task. He walked into the drawing room with Montholon to measure up Napoleon for his coffin:

> Length, 5 feet 7 inches, only 18 inches barely across the shoulders, and scarcely 10 inches deep: the size of the coffin I made as follows:- Length 5 feet 11 inches, depth 12 inches, width at the head 10½ inches, shoulders 21 inches, foot 8 inches …

At about ten that morning, armed with Lowe's authority to requisition whatever men and materials he required and with a command to work speedily, Darling left Longwood once more for Jamestown.

Meanwhile, Antommarchi attempted to take a cast of the face but the plaster he used did not solidify. It was then that Dr Burton tried. The cast was then put to one side – presumably close to the body at Longwood, to minimise the possibility of damage whilst it cured. The principal part of the face and head then disappeared, leaving Burton with the minor back part of the cast. It had been taken by Madame Bertrand who smuggled it off the island and who a year later would give a copy to Antommarchi. Burton would attempt to retrieve the original cast through the courts but would be unsuccessful.

Antommarchi took several copies, one of which he sent to Lord Burghersh, the British diplomat in Florence, asking him to ensure that it was handed to the famous sculptor Canova with a view to have it turned into a bronze. Sadly, Canova died before he could begin work on the mask and it remained with Burghersh. It is from this ignominious beginning that all the current copies in both plaster and bronze have derived.

Darling arranged with Captain Cole, the town major, to have particular men sent in to Jamestown from the country and from the church, for it was now Sunday. By one o'clock next morning, with the assistance of Mr Borman the plumber, Mr Metcalfe the carpenter and Mrs Borman, who was presumably a seamstress and his workmen, all three inner coffins, with their linings, had been completed.

The coffins were then sent up to Longwood under the direction of some of the Chinese. Shortly afterwards Darling followed and saw as he approached that great crowds of people 'of all descriptions' had gathered to see the great man.

Brooke, on learning that 'any respectable persons' might view the body, returned with his wife and daughter to find that the body had been removed to another room that had been prepared for public viewing. Along with the other visitors he crossed the lawn and walked through 'Ali's Garden', to the left of the building. Having entered through the door of the dining room they walked on into the small bedroom. On entering, Napoleon was to their left, his right side towards them. Behind his head, against the wall that separated this room from the dining room, was the 'altar', draped in black with a letter 'N' on the front with a binding of yellow taken from the curtains in the drawing room. On the altar according to Darling were two silver candelabra, a book stand supporting the Bible along with a holder for a figure of Christ on the cross – which at that moment lay on Napoleon's breast. He was dressed in the iconic green Chasseur uniform including hat, boots and spurs. The Priest Vignali stood on a step in front of the altar.

On his right lay his sword and his heart and stomach in sealed containers. Those who had come to pay their respects or simply gaze at the great man in wonderment were allowed to pause in groups of six or seven, before they left by the door to 'Marchand's Garden'.

Darling was anxious to have Napoleon placed in the coffin and sealed into it while he had all the necessary workmen present. It was about this time that the cast for the bust was taken, a delay which agitated Darling. At about 4 o'clock the officers of the 20th Regiment had changed into full dress uniform and gathered, along with and many of the gentlemen of the island, in the billiard room, ready to pay their respects. Amongst them was Lt Darroch. He saw that Countess Bertrand 'looked wretchedly ill and pale' and spent some time talking to her. Now that it was all over she hoped that they would be allowed to go home. Countess Bertrand showed him and the other officers who had paused to talk with her the snuff box bequeathed to her. The lid had a miniature of Napoleon, according to Darroch, 'set around with the largest diamonds I ever saw in my life'. They were then ushered in by the orderly officer Captain Crokat and saw Bertrand, dressed in black, standing at the head of the bed, the priest kneeling at the side and an attendant who waved away the flies.

To see a man who had caused Europe and the world at large so much trouble lying in a small room, on his military cloak and camp bed, dressed in his full uniform, with only two of his General Officers near him was an awful sight. It struck me so. I could have gazed on him for hours, having taken his hand and kissed it; but I could scarce breathe. While I looked I fancied him in the different situations he has been in at Lodi, at Marengo! In fact, though I was scarcely two minutes in the room, more ideas crowded through my mind, driving one another out as quick as they formed, than I could write tonight.[17]

The next day Darroch was on guard duty at the house. Having posted his sentries he obtained permission to go in and see Napoleon and spent some time gazing at him, taking a moment to hold his hand and examine his fingers. Later in the day he arranged for his soldiers to file through the room whilst he stood at the head of the bed. During the day he went in again to observe Burton and Antommarchi moving the body whilst they took a plaster impression of the head but by this time the smell had become rather oppressive. Later he was shown both the stomach and the heart in the silver urns, commenting that the hole in Napoleon's stomach would have been large enough to allow him to place his littler finger in it. These were to be sealed up ready to be sent to Europe, 'should it hereafter be thought proper'. But this was not to happen until 1840, they would be placed in the coffin with Napoleon. Some time after 4 o'clock in the afternoon the Governor arrived with orders for Captain Crokat to take the dispatches announcing the death to England, on board the *Heron*.[18]

At midnight on 8 May, Marchand, Saint Denis, Pierron and Noverraz bathed the body for the last time. Marchand and Saint Denis then redressed him in the Chasseur a Cheval uniform.

Next morning the governor, staff, naval and medical officers and some civilians such as Brooke gathered outside Longwood House on the lawn whilst the French party celebrated mass in the chapel. At the end of this service Montholon appeared and invited the company into Longwood.

They were greeted in the drawing room by Madame Bertrand and the French party, who were all dressed in black. Only the priest was absent, who remained with the body. When everyone was present twelve grenadiers of the 20th Regiment, who had been kept in waiting, were then called in. They passed through the drawing room, and on into the improvised chapel.

The entire company then stood to either side of the room whilst the priest in his robes, with a silver censer and prayer book, walked through saying a prayer. He was followed by young Bertrand carrying a vase of holy water. Then came the grenadiers, carrying the corpse. The French party followed immediately after the corpse, and then the governor, the Admiral, and the French commissioner bringing up the rear.

The hearse was Napoleon's carriage with the body of it removed and replaced with a stage and canopy. Madame Bertrand and her daughter followed it in a phaeton covered with black cloth. Then came junior officers of the navy, the staff and medical officers, the naval captains according to rank, and finally members of the council, General Coffin, the Admiral, the Marquis de Montchenu and the Governor. The coffin moved past Longwood New House and out beyond the outer perimeter of Longwood plateau towards Geranium Valley. As the cortège approached the gate

... the left side of the road from Longwood gate, in a direction towards the burying place, was, on 9 of May lined with all the troops of the garrison; the Royal Artillery on the right of the whole, then the 20th Regiment, the Royal Marines, the 66th Regiment, the St Helena Artillery, the St Helena Regiment, and on the left the St Helena Volunteers.[19]

The soldiers were in open order with their arms reversed. Through the gate came the priest and then Bertrand carrying the censer followed by Dr Arnott and Dr Antommarchi. They were followed by the undertakers and the hearse, drawn by Napoleon's horses and managed by his coachmen in their Imperial livery. The plain mahogany coffin was draped in his cloak, on top of which lay his sword and a Bible. On either side of the hearse walked the young Napoleon Bertrand and Marchand, whilst behind them marched six grenadiers of the 20th Regiment without arms. The band of each corps lining the route played sombre music or a dead march.

When the procession had passed the left of the line the troops then fell in and followed on. At the top of the path leading down to the burial site the hearse halted and a party of soldiers, three from each corps, went down the sloping path to the graveside. Here it was connected to the block and tackle system set up by Major Emmott and the sappers and was lowered into the tomb. Three salvoes of artillery were fired from the field pieces on the road above. Finally, the priest said prayers and sprinkled the censer.

After everyone had left, a large stone slab from a gun platform, according to those who were present at the exhumation in 1840, was lowered into position. On top of this was a layer of masonry, almost a foot thick, secured by iron bands. On this was laid Roman cement and above this five feet of earth, finally three 6-inch slabs, cramped with iron bands. A sentry was put on guard whilst the cement set. Later a wooden fence circling the grave was added.

Notes

1 *The Examiner*, XIV, 8 July 1821, page 417.
2 Lowe 20156 O'Meara's observations, folio 12, BL.
3 Lowe 20157, Arnott's account of his initial examination, folio 2, BL.
4 Ibid., folio 9, BL.
5 Ibid., folio 8, BL.
6 Ibid., folio 9, BL.
7 Chaplin, A., *The Illness and Death of Napoleon Bonaparte,* Hirschfield Brothers Ltd, 1913, pages 46–47.
8 Ibid., pages 49–50.
9 Lowe 20214, Henry's account of the autopsy, folio 200, BL.
10 Chaplin, A., op. cit., page 68.
11 Lowe 20157, folio 32, BL.

12 Chaplin, A., op. cit., page 93.

13 Darling's account of his work as the undertaker, *Times Literary Supplement*, 30 September 1915.

14 Shorter, C., Letter from T.H. Brooke in *Napoleon in his own Defence*, Cassell, 1910, pages 269–271.

15 Connolly, T.W.J., *History of the Royal Sappers and Miners*, Vol 1, Longman, Brown, Green, Longman and Roberts, 1857, page 257.

16 *Times Literary Supplement*, 30 September 1915.

17 'St Helena: Past and Present' in *The Lancashire Fusiliers Annual*, 1904, page 11.

18 Ibid., page 13.

19 *North British Advertiser*, 2 August 1873, quoted in Mellis, J. C., *St Helena: A Physical, Historical and Topographical Description of the Island*, London: L. Reeve & Co., 1875, p. 27.

Watercolour of Plantation House. Courtesy of Stephen Emanuel.

Appendix A

Walter Henry's Account of the Audience between the Officers of the 20th Regiment and the Emperor Napoleon Bonaparte

On the afternoon of the 1st September 1817, the officers of our regiment ... repaired to Longwood. We called at Marshal Bertrand's house, fifty or sixty yards from the residence of Napoleon, to pick up the Marshal, who accompanied us to the billiard room, where we found Counts Montholon and Gourgard. After waiting five or six minutes, the folding doors of the ante-chamber were thrown open – we entered, formed a ring round the room, according to seniority, and in about a minute Napoleon walked into the circle.

He was dressed in a plain green uniform coat, without epaulettes or any thing equivalent, but with a large star on the breast, which had an eagle in the centre. The buttons were gold, with the device of a mounted dragoon, in high relief. He had on white breeches with silk stockings, and oval gold buckles in his shoes, with a small opera hat under his arm. Napoleon's first appearance was far from imposing – the stature was short and the thick head sunk into his shoulders – his face fat, with large folds under the chin, the limbs appeared to be stout, but well proportioned – expression sinister, and rather scowling. The features instantly reminded us of the prints of him we had seen. On the whole, his general look was more that of an obese Spanish or Portuguese Friar than the Hero of modern times.

Buonaparte walked around the room, with an attempt (as it seemed) at the old dignity, and addressed a few words to most of the officers. Colonel Nicol was first introduced by Sir George Bingham – he and Marshal Bertrand acting as interpreters. The following conversation took place; which I copy, as well as the whole proceedings on this memorable occasion, from minutes noted down immediately after the interview:

NAPOLEON 'Your regiment has lately arrived from India – coming from that rich country, you should wear gold and not silver. How many years does it take to acclimatize a regiment of Europeans?'

COLONEL NICOL 'Two or three years – a few die the first year – more the second, but the mortality is much reduced the third.'

'Did your officers save much money in India?'

'No; the expense of living is too great.'

'How many servants did you keep there?'

'I had at one time between thirty and forty – I think thirty-nine.'

'Do you think a regiment is efficient after twenty years' service in India?'

'Yes; it is fed by recruits from home.'

'What kind of troops are the Sepoys?'

'Those in the British Service are excellent troops.'

'How many battalions of Sepoys of equal strength, would you engage with the 66th?'

'Do you mean battalions with British Officers, or without them?'

'Both the one and the other.'

Sepoy regiments with British Officers, are good and steady soldiers. I should not like great dispar-ity of force with them, though I might manage to defeat four to five battalions belonging to the Native Powers, and I'm pretty sure we could.'

'Very good – you are a fine fellow. (Un brave homme.)'

'How many officers have you in your Mess?'

'We have sixteen at Deadwood.'

'You sit very late at the Mess I hear – often to midnight.'

'O yes; we have a few good fellows there, we don't stir sometimes till cock-crow.'

'But the officers get tipsy then, don't they?' (then in English – 'drunk, drunk, eh?')

'O no, no – they don't get drunk.'

'Your men, I perceive walk about very much in the sun, and without their caps. That's wrong.'

'It is, and we do all we can to prevent it.'

'Have you not a Catholic Officer in the regiment?'

'Yes, (with a nod at Lieut. McCarthy, who stood nearly opposite at the other side of the circle.)

'He has been to Rio Janeiro lately, I hear.'

'Yes, and is just returned.'

'He went there to get absolution for his peccadillos, I suppose?'

(Repeated – 'Absolution, n'est ce pas?)

(Answered by a laugh from Colonel Nicol, and a blush on the honest and naturally rubicund physi-ognomy of the officer in question.)

Napoleon then turned to Lieut. Colonel Lascelles.

'What countryman are you?'

'An Englishman.'

'From what part of England?'

'From Yorkshire.'

'Were you born in the city of York?'

'No.'

He then passed to the next Senior Officer, Lieut. Colonel Dodgin, C.B., who had several clasps and medals on his breast. He was, besides, a remarkable fine military-looking man, and when walking with me in London, had been more than once mistaken for the Duke of York. Napoleon looked at him with some complacency, and took hold with his fingers of the most glittering of the batch of distinctions, which happened to be the Vittoria medal; but as soon as he read that 'word of fear', he dropped it instantly, and rather abruptly. It was no fancy of mine, but a matter of plain fact, observed and spoken of at the time by us all, that his gesture was exactly that of a person letting fall something expectedly and disagreeably hot. He then said:

'You have decorations I see. Where did you serve?'

'In Egypt and the Peninsula.'

'Were you at Salamanca or Toulouse?'

'No.'

'Was your Regiment at Talavera?'

'Yes.'

'Were you ever wounded.'

'Yes; twice.'

'Was your name sent home as an officer who had distinguished himself?'

(When Colonel Dodgin hesitated, Captain Baird answered for him-'Yes, three times.') Buonaparte next addressed Captain Baird:

'You are a Captain of Grenadiers?'

'Yes.'

'How many years have you been in the service?'

'Nearly twenty.'

'And still only a Captain.'

'Even so.'

Next, Captain Jordan passed the ordeal. He was married to a handsome St Helena lady whom he had met in India, and whose father's house was not more than a mile from Longwood.

'You are married?'

'Yes.'

'Your wife is is pretty I hear. How many children have you?'

'Two.'

Then Captain Dunne:

'You have been in India?'

'How long have you served?'

'Fourteen years.'

Napoleon then glanced at the next officer, Captain Ellis, a Cambridgeshire man, of most uncouth and forbidding exterior and physiognomy – in fact, an evident descendant of the Colony of Barbarians that had been settled in that county by a Roman Emperor – but not being pleased with the Vandal, he passed by without addressing him, and accosted his neighbour, Captain L'Estrange, a worthy little fellow, of very dark complexion.

'Have you served in India?'

'Yes.'

'How long have you served?'

'Fourteen years – two in India.'

(There seemed to be some mistake made here by the Interpreters, in confounding the entire services of this officer with the time passed in India.)

'How is it that your complexion is so dark? Were you sick in India?'

'No.'

'Do you drink?' (and then, translating the French – '*drink? Drink?*')

(Answered by a smile.)

'Which do you think the best Town? Calcutta or Jamestown?'

(Repeated, and attempted to be translated – *Veech you tink de best town?*)

'Calcutta.'

Next in the circle stood Captain Duncan:

'How long have you served?'

'Upwards of twenty years.'

'You have been in India?'

'Yes.'

'Were you ever in action?'

'Yes.'

'And ever wounded?'

'No.'

'Then you are a lucky fellow.'

Buonaparte then addressed Mr Heir, the Surgeon:

'You are Surgeon of the Regiment?'

'Yes.'

'Do you hold any other Commission?'

(This question was answered by Sir George Bingham.)

'This gentleman is the Surgeon Major;' (not unhappily, considering that, my excellent amigo, Heir was about six feet and a half high,) and then there was some confusion, and the Interpreters, Sir G. Bingham and the Marshal, were a little at fault; confounding Surgeon Major and Sergeant-Major-Sir George not being perfect in French, and Marshal Bertrand very defective in his English. At length Napoleon said:

'Lord Wellington promoted several of his Surgeon Majors, I have heard.'

Sir George Bingham – 'Pardon, Sire, (for this Imperial recognition, which had never been sanctioned by the British Government, was evidently a lapsus of the moment.) 'Pardon, it was the Sergeant Majors, several of whom got Commissions during the Peninsular War.'

To Mr Heir:

'You had a great many sick in India?'

'Yes – it is not a healthy climate.'

'Many liver-complaints?'

'Yes.'

'Next in order was Lieutenant Moffat.

'What countryman are you?'

'An Irishman.'

'Are you a Catholic or a Protestant?'

(With marked and indignant emphasis.) 'A Protestant.'

Buonaparte now moved somewhat quicker than before, round the circle, passing by some of the officers without speaking to them, after individual introduction, and addressing merely a word as to length of service to one or two others. When he arrived at the point where I stood, Marshal Bertrand made me a bow of recognition on which the great man stopped, and the Marshal formally introduced me as the English Physician that had recently attended his eldest son, Napoleon's little favourite, and namesake. He then looked at me with a slight expression of complacency, and said:

'You have served in India?'

'Yes.'

'You had much professional duty there?'

'A good deal certainly?'

'Were diseases of the liver very common in India.'

'Yes; they occur there more frequently than in colder climates.'

'Your soldiers drink an enormous quantity of brandy in India?'

'They are much too fond of spirits – arrack is cheap there, and the climate makes them thirsty.'

'Do you bleed and give large doses of calomel there, as the English Doctors do here?'

'I believe the practice is similar.'

'Are you too, a devotee of the lancet? Ah, God defend us from it! (*Ah, Dieu m'en garde!*)

'In my opinion it is our most potent weapon.'

'To kill or cure? Eh, M. le Docteur?'

'It is our duty to cure.'

Then Ensign Wardell.

'You are a young man. How long have you served?'

'Seven years.'

'You entered the service very young then?'

'Yes; but I have served in the Navy.'

'You were a Midshipman.'

'Yes.'

One or two more were asked one question, only as to length of service, and the round was completed. He then addressed Colonel Nicol a second time

'So the Sepoys are good troops?'

'Yes; they are excellent soldiers – respectful, sober and obedient.'

'But, yet, you would fight five or six battalions of them with your own regiment?'

'Not Sepoys with British Officers – I should not like to engage two such battalions.'

A few sentences were then exchanged between Napoleon, Marshal Bertrand and Sir George Bingham; and we all bowed and retired.

As we walked home to Deadwood, and calmly reviewed what had passed; and compared the appearance, manner and conversation of Buonaparte with our preconceived ideas, prepossessions and expectations, the general feeling and result was disappointment – but this might have been reasonably anticipated. Without reference to the usual sobering effects of vicinity and contact, in dissipating the gilded halos with which a sanguine fancy invests distant and remarkable objects, the interview with Napoleon had dissolved a glory, par excellence. A fascinating prestige which we had cherished all our lives, then vanished like gossamer in the sun. The great Emperor Napoleon, the Hero of modern times, had merged in an unsightly and obese individual; and we looked in vain for that overwhelming power of eye and force of expression which we had been taught to expect by a delusive imagination.

By a Staff Surgeon, *Trifles from my Portfolio*, Quebec; S. Highley, Fleet Street, London 1839.

Appendix B

Montchenu's Pass to Move about the Island

Permit the Bearer Marquis deMontchenu Commissioner of His Majesty the King of France at the Island of St Helena and Major General in his Service, to pass Freely and uninterruptedly wherever The Officers of the British Navy and Army are usually allowed to pass Given under my hand At St Helena this 21st day of June 1816

H. Lowe

To all concerned Governor & Commander in Chief
Copy in the Lowe Papers 20115, folio 218, BL.

Appendix C

O'Meara's Letter of Application to Lord Keith for the Post of Surgeon to Napoleon

His Majesty's Ship *Bellerophon*
Torbay, 7th August, 1815
MY LORD, Application having been made to me yesterday by Count Bertrand to accompany General Bonaparte to St. Helena, in quality of surgeon (as the surgeon, who embarked with him in France, is unwilling to proceed further); I beg to inform your lordship, that I am willing to accept that situation (provided it meets with your lordship's approbation), and also on the following conditions, viz. that it should be permitted me to resign the above situation, should I find it not consonant to my wishes, on giving due notice of my intention thereof. That such time as I shall serve in that situation, shall be allowed to count as so much time served on full pay in his majesty's navy, or that I shall be indemnified in some way for such loss of time as surgeon on full pay, as it may occasion to me. That I am not to be considered in any wise depending upon, or to be subservient to, or *paid* by the aforesaid Napoleon Bonaparte; but as a *British officer* employed by the British government; and lastly, that I may be informed, as soon as circumstances will admit, of what salary I am to have, and in what manner and from whom I am to receive it.
I have the honour to remain,
My Lord
With the greatest respect,

Your Lordship's most
Obedient Humble Servant,
BARRY E. O'MEARA,
Surgeon H.M.S. Bellerophon

To the Right Honourable Viscount Keith,
Admiral of the Red, G.C.B
Commander-in-Chief.

Appendix D

Maitland's Reply to the Request for the Free Passage of Napoleon out of the Basque Roads in 1815

H B Majesty's Ship
Bellerophon off Rochefort
10th July

Sir

I have to acknowledge the Honor of your letter of yesterdays date addressed to the Admiral Commanding the English Cruisers before Rochefort, acquainting me that the Emperor having abdicated the Throne of France, and chosen the United States of America as an Asylum, is now embarked on board the frigates at Rochefort to proceed for that destination, waits a passport from the English Government, requesting to know if I have any knowledge of such passport, and if I think it is the intention of the English Government to prevent the Emperor's Voyage; In reply I have the honour to acquaint you that I cannot say what the intention of my Government maybe but the two countries at present being in a state of war, I cannot allow any Ship of War to put to sea from the Port of Rochfort; as to the proposal made by the Duc de Rovigo and Le Cte de Las Cases of allowing the Emperor to proceed in a merchant vessel it is out of my power without the sanction of my Commanding officer (Sir Henry Hotham who is at present in Quiberon Bay and to Whom I have forwarded your dispatch) to allow any vessel under whatever Flag she may be to pass with a personage of such Consequence.
I have the honor to be
Sir
Your obdt. Hble Servt
Fredk Maitland Capt
of HMS *Bellerophon*

Maitland, Frederick L., *Narrative of the Surrender of Napoleon*, Blackwood & Sons, Edinburgh & London, 1904.

Appendix E

Anonymous letter Sent from London to Bertrand In March 1816 Offering an Escape Plan for Napoleon

Dear Friend

I advised the Emperor of the critical situation and you must use the utmost secrecy and edict or all will be lost without redemption. I told you before the boat that will drift to the back of the island be in the shape of an old cask but so constructed that by pulling at both ends to be seaworthy and both boat and sails which will be found inside will be painted to correspond with the colour of the sea and when the Emperor lone more which will be requisite to transform the boat as I said above is all ready he must bear away right before the wind for the ship after drifting the boat to the island will Manoeuvre so at to get right to Leeward and display a light out of one our port holes for to shew it at the mast head would endanger it to be seen by the enemy.

You may calculate the ship distance about 4 miles at starting from the island & to prevent any mistake should an enemy ship appear in sight yours will be uncommon long and colours painted much the same as the boat and sails to admiration. It will depend on circumstances what Port in the United States His Majesty will land at but he may depend upon the most cordial reception. The Empress and King of Rome if possible will be there before him & a great many of his Faithful Subjects headed by the Marshals and Ministers. M Tallyrand is in the roads with a vast sum of Money. Men, Money & Ships his Majesty will be amply supplying with for the Americans admire him as a Deity and Swear if he don't make the Craw thumping Burbons Scamp they will have him for an Emperor & to remedy his Loss in France they will seize on all South America & never stop until the 3 coloured of the 15 Stars United Flag shall be raised on the ramparts of Bengal after that it is proposed to invade Spain and Portugal which will be done with the utmost expedition for the double purpose of striking terror & prevent-ing them from collecting their forces. For the Emperor may make sure of the French Navy when he is capable of Receiving them. They only await his Nod & when he once secures Spain, France must surrender for both soldiers & People long for him & sighs for him – there is not the least doubt but the exalted hero will have greater fleets & armies than ever. God preserve you in his holy keeping.

La M

NB I thought it best to write this in English to take off suspicion & prevent detection. I believe you before the rope I enclosed you in the last Package for the Emperor to slide down the Brow of the Cliff with when his Spy on the lookout informs him of the Arrival of the Boat is a master of Contrivance, for it is so ingeniously wrought inside (being steel) that it will render a stretch to four times the length it appears to be with a Clever Graplin at one end that will spring out with the pressure of the Thumb it cost £7 My Service Devotion to Mrs B.

Mind the least mistake might cause the greatest Disappointmen

Burn this without delay

Lowe 20115, folio 18, BL.

Appendix F

Vessels Anchoring in James Bay,
24 January 1818

Vessel	Master	From	Passengers
Minerva Transport	John Carrick	Cape of Good Hope	Major Gardiner 60th Captain Minchin 38th Lieut Daley 60th Lieut Sachs 60th Lieut Gillfillam 60th Ensign Caldwell 60th Surgeon Morle 60th Quartr Mastr Maxwell 60th
Astrea Transport	John Wilson	Cape of Good Hope	Captain Rose 89th Lieut Carmichael 60th Lieut Durnford 60th Lieut Armstrong 60th
Nearchus Transport	Chas Sinclair	Cape of Good Hope	Captain Frs Homes 60th Lieut M. Furot 60th Lieut D. L. Count 60th Lieut Jos Crow 60th Ensign Robt Andrew 60th Asst Surgeon Manay 60th
HMS *Trincomalee*	P. H. Bridges	Cape of Good Hope	Mrs Bridges Mr & Mrs Saunders & 2 children Mrs Bunt & 2 children Lieut Jas Wilson RN Lieut Geo Welchman RM Lieut Heath RE
HMS *Towey*	Hill	Cape of Good Hope	Colonel Young Artillery
Co Ship *Ly Lushington*	Thomas Dormer	Bombay	Mrs Crainger & 2 children Mr Mainwaring Lieut Michin HE Service Lieut Cochrane HM 47th Rt. Lieut Guy H Co Marine And 41 invalids 47th Foot
Lonach	Willm Driscoll	Bombay	Capt Farquarson HCo S. Lieut Mederian
Oswin Longboat		(The long boat of the Ship *Oswin* in James Bay from Calcutta bound to London; the ship foundered at Sea on the 31st January in Lat 31 18S 11.51 Longitude Captain, Crew & Passenger (Lt Nicholson of the 71st Regt) saved and arrived in the Long Boat on February 12.)	

Appendix G

General Sir Hudson Lowe's Memorial

SACRED TO THE MEMORY OF

LIEUT. GENERAL SIR HUDSON LOWE
K.C.B. G.C.M.G.
KNIGHT OF THE RED EAGLE AND MILITARY ORDER OF MERIT OF PRUSSIA
ST GEORGE OF RUSSIA, AND CRESCENT OF TURKEY.
COLONEL OF THE 50TH QUEENS OWN REGIMENT.
AFTER HAVING SERVED HIS COUNTRY UNINTERRUPTED FROM 1787 TO 1815
INCLUDING ACTIVE SERVICE IN CORSICA, EGYPT, DEFENCE OF CAPRI,
CAPTURE OF THE IONIAN ISLES, AND THE CAMPAIGNS OF 1813, 1814
WITH THE ALLIED ARMY UNDER MARSHAL BLUCHER,
HE WAS SELECTED FOR THE ONEROUS POST OF GOVERNOR OF ST. HELENA,
DURING THE CAPTIVITY OF NAPOLEON.
HIS OBEDIENCE TO THE ORDERS OF GOVERNMENT
IN THE FULFILMENT OF THIS HARASSING DUTY,
EARNED FOR HIM THE APPROBATION OF HIS SOVEREIGN,
BUT EXPOSED HIM EVER AFTERWARDS TO PERSECUTION AND CALUMNY;
AND MORE THAN ONCE CAUSED HIS LIFE TO BE ENDANGERED.
HISTORY WILL DO JUSTICE TO A BRAVE AND ZEALOUS OFFICER,
A TRUE AND GENEROUS FRIEND
AND AN UPRIGHT AND FAITHFUL SERVANT OF HIS COUNTRY.
BORN 28TH JULY 1769, DIED 10TH JANUARY, 1844

Sir Hudson Lowe. This is the only likeness generally agreed to be a true representation of the Governor.

Bibliography

Archive, Jamestown, St Helena

Council Consultation Books, Honourable East India Company, StHA.
File 31, Napoleon Bonaparte, StHA.
Photographic collection, StHA.
Parish Register of deaths 1820–31, 1839–42, StHA.

British Library

Add Mss 20115–20119 Lowe Papers, BL.
Add Mss 20146 Lowe Papers, BL.
Add Mss 20155 Lowe Papers, BL.
Add Mss 20157 Lowe Papers, BL.
Add Mss 20161 Lowe Papers, BL.
Add Mss 20224–20225 Lowe Papers, BL.
Add Mss 20240 Lowe Papers, BL.
Hansard, T. C., *The Parliamentary Debates*, VOL. XXXV, 1817.
Hansard, T. C., *The Parliamentary Debates*, VOL. XXXIII 1798.
X/3571 Captain Barnes' map of St Helena, HEIC, 1811.
X/3572/1–3 Panorama map detailing potential landing places and defences, HEIC.

Museum of the Lancashire Fusiliers, Bury

Coxe, W., *Life of Marlborough*
Gallipoli Gazette

National Archive, Cape Town, South Africa

1/17 Government House Papers, SA.
1/20 Government House Papers, SA.

National Archive, Kew, London

ADM 51 Captain's Log Books, NA
Ship's log books: ADM53/465B HMS *Eurydice*; ADM53/1309 HM *Sloop*; *Sophie*; ADM51/2226
    HMS *Conqueror*; ADM51/2501 HMS *Leveret*; ADM51/2893 HMS *Tees*. NA.

National Maritime Museum, Greenwich, London

ADM37 series Ships' log books, NMM
COC 1–9 Cockburn Papers, NMM
SIGB57 Island Signal Book, 1817, NMM
XJOD Glover letter, NMM.
The Archive, University of Hull
The Hotham Papers, UH.

Periodicals

The Century, (83) 1912: Broadly A. M., 'Napoleon in Caricature', p.824–835.
The Century, (83) 1912: Emmott A., 'New Records of Napoleon: Funeral at St Helena', p.401–8.

Printed Sources

Abell, Mrs., *Recollections of Napoleon at Saint Helena*, John Murray, London, 1844.
Abell, Mrs., *Recollections of Napoleon at Saint Helena*, John Murray, London, 1873.
Alger, J. G., *Napoleon's British Visitors and Captives, 1801–1815*, Constable, 1904.
Aubry, Octave, *St Helena*, trans., Livingston, Arthur, London: Gollancz, 1937.
Balmain, Count, (Trans: Park, Julian) *Napoleon in Captivity: The reports of the Russian Commissioner on the Island of St Helena 1816–1820*, London, George Allen and Unwin, 1928.
Barnes, John, *A tour through the Island of St Helena with some particulars respecting the arrival and detention of Napoleon Bonaparte,* J. M. Richardson, London, 1817.
Bate, Jonathan, *John Clare*, Picador, 2005.
Castell, R., *St Helena Illustrated*, National Book Printers Group, Cape Town, 1998.
Chaplin, A., *A Saint Helena Who's Who*, 1919, reprinted by Savannah Publications, 2002.
Coote S., *Napoleon and the Hundred Days*, Simon & Schuster, 2004.
Cordingly D., *Billy Ruffian*, Bloomsbury, 2003.
Fletcher I., (Ed). In the Service of the King: The Letters of William Thornton Keep, Spellmount, 1997.
Giles F., *Napoleon Bonaparte: England's Prisoner*, Constable, 2001
Glover R. G., *Britain at Bay: Defence Against Bonaparte*, Allen and Unwin, 1973
Gosse, Philip, *St Helena 1502–1938*, Anthony Nelson, 1990.
Gregory D., *Napoleon's Jailer: Lt General Sir Hudson Lowe*, Associated University Presses, 1996.
Hannay, D., *Life of Frederick Marryat*, Walter Scott, London, 1889.
Henry, P., 5th Earl Stanhope, *Notes of Conversations with the Duke of Wellington*, John Murray, London, Fourth Edition, 1889.
Hibbert C., *Napoleon: His Wives and Women*, Harper Collins, 2002.
Harris, R., Talleyrand: *Betrayer and Saviour of France*, John Murray, 2007.

Jackson, B., *Notes and Reminiscences of a Staff Officer*, John Murray, 1903.

Kauffmann, Jean-Paul, (Trans. Clancy, P.) *The Dark Room at Longwood*, The Harvill Press, 1999.

Kent, Captain B., *Signal!: History of Signalling in the Royal Navy*, 1993.

Kerry, Earl of, (Ed) *The First Napoleon: some unpublished documents from the Bowood Papers*, Constable, 1925.

Korngold, Ralph *The Last Years of Napoleon: His Captivity on St Helena*, London J. Lane, 1991

Lavery B., *Nelson's Navy*, Conway Maritime Press, 1989.

Maitland, Capt., F. L., *Narrative of the Surrender of Buonaparte*, Henry Colburn, Second Ed., 1826.

Maitland, Frederick L., *Narrative of the Surrender of Buonaparte*, Blackwood & Sons, Edinburgh & London, 1904.

Malcolm, Lady, Wilson, Sir A. (Ed), *A Diary of St Helena – The journal of Lady Malcolm (1816, 1817)*, 1899.

Mansel P., *Paris between Empires 1814-1852*, Phoenix Press, 2001.

Marchand Louis-Joseph, *In Napoleon's Shadow*, Proctor Jones Publishing, 1998.

Marryat, F., *Life and Letters of Captain Marryat*, Richard Bentley & Son, London, 1872.

Masson, F., (Trans. Frewer, L. B.) *Napoleon at St. Helena*, Oxford, 1949.

McCranie, K. D., *Admiral Lord Keith and the Naval War Against Napoleon*, University Press of Florida, 2006

Mellis, J. C., *St Helena: A Physical, Historical and Topographical Description of the Island*, London: L. Reeve & Co., 1875.

O'Meara B., *Napoleon in Exile or A Voice from St. Helena*, Vol. 1. Jones & Company, 1830.

Palmer, A., *Napoleon and Marie Louise*: The Second Empress, Constable, London, 2001.

Pickering S., Ed, *Memoirs of Anna Maria Wilhelmina Pickering. Together with extracts from the Journals of her Father John Spencer Stanhope, FRS*, Hodder and Stoughton, 1904.

Pocock, T., *Captain Marryat; Seaman, Writer and Adventurer*, Chatham Publishing, London, 2000.

Pool B. (Ed), *The Croker Papers, 1808-1857*, London, Batsford, 1967.

Roberts A., *Napoleon and Wellington*, Weidenfield & Nicholson, 2001.

Saint Denis, Louis Etienne, *Napoleon, From Tuileries to St Helena,* Harper & Bros, New York, 1922.

Sanders, Lloyd, *The Holland House Circle*, Methuen, London, 1908.

Scott, Sir Walter,

Seaton, R. C., *Napoleon's Captivity in Relation to Sir Hudson Lowe*, London, George Bell & Sons, 1903.

Shorter, Clement, (Ed.), *Napoleon And His Fellow Travellers*, Cassell, 1908.

Shorter, Clement, *Napoleon In his own Defence*, Cassell, 1910.

Thornton, M. J., *Napoleon after Waterloo*, Stanford University, 1968.

Webster, C. K., *British Diplomacy 1813 – 1815*, G. Bell & Sons, 1921.

Webster, C. K., *The Foreign policy of Castlereagh, 1812–1822*, G. Bell & Sons, 1963.

Young, N., *Napoleon in Exile at St Helena (1815–1821)* 2 Vols., London, Stanley Paul & Co., 1915.

Stroud, P. T., *The man who had been King*, Uni. of Pennsylvania Press, 2005.

Index